SPANISH LITERATURE

in the

ENGLAND OF THE TUDORS

AMS PRESS
NEW YORK

SPANISH LITERATURE

IN THE

ENGLAND OF THE TUDORS

BY

JOHN GARRETT UNDERHILL

*[Submitted in partial fulfilment of the requirements of the
degree of Doctor of Philosophy in the Faculty of Philosophy, Columbia University]*

New York

PUBLISHED FOR THE COLUMBIA UNIVERSITY PRESS BY

THE MACMILLAN COMPANY

LONDON: MACMILLAN & CO., Ltd.

1899

All rights reserved

Reprinted from the edition of 1899, New York
First AMS EDITION published 1971
Manufactured in the United States of America

International Standard Book Number: 0-404-06702-6

Library of Congress Number: 70-131496

AMS PRESS INC.
NEW YORK, N. Y. 10003

PREFACE

THIS study of the history of Spanish literature in the England of the Tudors, has been
undertaken as a thesis for the degree of Doctor
of Philosophy at Columbia University. There
are in the authorities upon the literature of
the time many references to the influence of
Spain in English letters, and many sidelights
have been cast upon the subject in several
of its aspects. No attempt, however, has been
made to present a view of it as a whole. It
consequently remains in a chaotic state, and
some of the information that has commonly
circulated in regard to it is self-destructive.
It is the aim of this study to coördinate this
material and to determine, within certain
limits, the place which the literature of Spain
and Portugal occupied in the minds and lives
of English writers previous to the death of
Elizabeth. The peninsular influence has been
considered throughout as a definite and organic
movement.

The adoption of this purpose has made it necessary that the contents of the following pages should often be political and biographical in their character. Few of the facts which have been gathered in these departments are new, although many of them are unfamiliar. The *Calendars of state papers* published under the supervision of the Master of the Rolls, with their complete indices, and the *Dictionary of national biography*, with its copious citations of authorities, have made it easy to refer at once to the original sources of political and historical scholarship. I have, therefore, generally avoided loading the pages with footnotes, which would in this case be mere pedantry. A bibliography of the principal books essential to a knowledge of the subject has been included at the close, the titles of which sufficiently indicate the scope and application of the individual works.

Upon the literary side the material has been less accessible. Some of the books which appear in the bibliography of translations exist only in unique copies, or are known solely through the entry of their names upon the

stationers' register.   Most of them are rare
and obscure.   It would therefore be too much,
perhaps, to hope that this bibliography is
complete.   Such omissions as there may be,
however, can scarcely affect the conclusions
embodied in these pages, whatever their value
as supplementary matter.   That they are not
more frequent is due to the kindness of friends
who have lent their assistance in the course of
my work.   I wish especially to thank Mr.
Frank Wadleigh Chandler, who has made tran-
scripts for me at the Bodleian Library, Oxford,
and Mr. Joel Elias Spingarn, who has freely
put at my disposal the results of his unpublished research upon John Lyly and the origins
of his style.   This study was undertaken by
the advice of Professor George Edward Wood-
berry, whose generous interest and invaluable
direction, both in matters of outline and of
detail, have been indispensable to its prosecu-
tion.   My indebtedness to him I cannot too
gratefully acknowledge.

J. G. U.

Columbia University,
    June 7, 1899.

CONTENTS

CHAPTER VIII

CHAPTER IX

CHAPTER X

BIBLIOGRAPHIES

SPANISH LITERATURE IN THE ENGLAND OF THE TUDORS

CHAPTER I

THE ALLIANCE OF ENGLAND AND SPAIN

AT the close of the twelfth century Henry II., the first of the Plantagenet kings, gave his daughter Eleanor in marriage to Alphonso VII. of Castile, and inaugurated thereby an alliance between England and Spain. The policy which King Henry formulated toward the Castilian House, embodied the principles that were well nigh uniformly adopted by his successors in the adjustment of their relations with foreign states until the death of Queen Mary. The extensive possessions of the English kings in France, so long coveted by that monarchy, and so palpably threatened by its power from the time of Philip Auguste, forced the English princes to

seek the favor of the rulers of the peninsula.
It was to protect his inheritance on the continent that King John sued for the hand of the
princess of Portugal, and it was in conformity
with an established policy of self-protection that
Edward I. married Eleanor of Castile. Whatever accommodations might be made with France,
whatever momentary reconciliation might be effected, the general drift of events toward the
end of the Middle Ages was to alienate England
from that country, and to unite it with Spain.

The campaign of the Black Prince in the
peninsula, perhaps the most brilliant episode.of
the latter part of the fourteenth century, was
designed to render the Spanish alliance more
secure. It resulted in a temporary understanding between France and Castile, but it was
fought with the purpose of preventing the understanding which its partial success failed to
avert. England supported the deposed Pedro
the Cruel of Castile at Najera, because Enrique
of Trastamara had been set upon his throne by
France. The influence of the Plantagenets in
Spain was destroyed for the moment by Pedro's
failure to take advantage of the victory which
was gained for him by the Black Prince, but

the impression which English chivalry made
in the peninsula suffered no abatement, nor was
the rehabilitation of the English alliance long
delayed. The triumph of the Black Prince at
Najera astonished the Castilians, and was followed by an exaggerated sense of the prowess
of British arms. It left its mark in literature
in the romances of chivalry, which were then
rising into popularity, and filled their pages
with a strangely distorted geography of England, thenceforth to the Spaniard the true home
of knightly courtesy. The quarrel which led
Castile to join with France and Scotland against
Edward I., on the fall of King Pedro, was purely
a dynastic one. It had no basis of international
enmity. When, therefore, the original dispu-
tants for the Castilian throne were dead, the
reigning House of Trastamara was glad to conciliate the opposition of the line of the deposed
king, by the marriage of the Crown Prince
Henry with Katherine, daughter of John of
Gaunt, to whom the right of succession had descended from her grandfather, Pedro the Cruel.
The accustomed understanding between the
countries was thus reëstablished. It persisted
through the reigns of the successors of Richard

II. in England as an offset to the coöperation of
the French and Scots, and acquired the force
of a tradition of diplomacy. It had a similar
weight in the peninsula, though its immediate
effects were more strongly marked. Spain and
Portugal were the theatre in which the chief
intercourse between the peninsula and the North
took place, they were the scene of the battles of
the Black Prince and of John of Gaunt, and
they retained in consequence an acquaintance
with the English which it was impossible that
the latter people should possess of Spain. This
acquaintance was colored by personal contact,
and its effects are to be traced, not only in the
popular romances of chivalry, but in the title
Prince of the Asturias, bestowed upon the Castilian Infante, after the year 1388, in imitation
of the custom of the English in designating the
heir apparent Prince of Wales.

The relations which existed between England
and Spain during the Middle Ages were uniformly dictated by political expediency, and
resulted in nothing of more than transient importance, except the formation of a diplomatic
tradition. The intermarriage of princes in mediæval times did not bring the subjects whom

they ruled into closer contact, although it promoted friendships between states for a time, secured neutrality, or averted war. The new life of the Renaissance, however, changed the character of the old alliances. The rapid progress of the sciences and of the æsthetic as well as the practical arts, the discovery of America and the opening of the Orient to western trade, and finally, the consolidation of the power of the European monarchs within the limits of their own dominions till it triumphed over the pretensions of the great lords at home and was free to enter upon ambitious schemes for the aggrandizement of the Crown abroad, made it inevitable that relations between nations should be determined thenceforth in their inception in some measure by commercial as well as political considerations, and should extend the consequences of their establishment quite beyond the scope of politics to intellectual and social spheres. While Henry VII. was breaking the power of the English nobility, Ferdinand and Isabella were curtailing the prerogatives of the grandees of Spain, and uniting the kingdoms of Castile and Aragon. As the interests of the nations broadened, the ability to pursue them increased. The ancient alliance between England and Castile, therefore, assumed a new aspect at the commencement of the sixteenth century, and extended its influence until it reached the social life of the English nation for the first time, and left its imprint in the literature of the people. The study of the history of Spanish letters in England begins with the appearance of the new conditions at the opening of the negotiations for the treaty which Henry VII. made with Ferdinand, when he offered the hand of his son Arthur to Katherine of Aragon.

Foreign alliances are the necessary results of the possession of dependencies whose remoteness from the mother state lays them open to danger of attack. In the twelfth century the French duchies, which were the patrimony of the Plantagenets, compelled the English to seek the alliance with Portugal and Castile, and to maintain it while territory on the south side of the channel continued to remain in their hands. When the sixteenth century had fairly begun, however, the English possessions in France had shrunk to proportions so inconsiderable that they no longer occupied other than a subordinate rôle in determining the policy of the nation. It was at this juncture that the attitude which Spain and England had maintained toward each other for over three hundred years was reversed, so that an alliance with England grew to be imperative to the interests of Spain itself. The new state created by the union of Castile and Aragon became, by spreading its sway eastward over Italy, northward over the Lowlands, and westward into America, practically the most formidable government in Europe, and commercially an unrivalled mart for the commodities of trade. This twofold preeminence of Spain as a military and colonial power, bound her to her traditional ally as it did to no other independent nation. The aggressive policy that Ferdinand adopted in Europe, which involved the invasion of Italy and Navarre in the face of the most strenuous opposition from France, compelled him and his successors to secure the neutrality of England and to seek assiduously its support. The three phases in the history of this attempt at the maintenance of friendship with the Tudors on the part of Ferdinand and the Austrian House, as they manifested themselves in the reigns of Henry VII.

and Henry VIII., of Mary, and of Elizabeth, respectively, embody quite separately the influence of Spain in England during the sixteenth century, and are distinctly differentiated from each other, not only in politics, but in the social and literary affiliations of the people as well.

Before the century was yet born, the strategy of Ferdinand was directed to strengthening the alliance that already existed, by all the ties which his cunning statecraft could suggest. The marriage of Katherine of Aragon to Prince Arthur, and to Henry VIII. after Arthur's death, was supplemented by the residence of Spanish agents as ambassadors in London, and by the distribution of pensions among the most prominent English nobles. It was the purpose of the Spaniard, indeed, to create a party of such strength at the court of the English kings that it would be unfeasible for the Crown to act in conjunction with his enemies in the face of opposition which would arise at home. This was a new feature in the history of the countries; it was the recognition in international intercourse of a power outside of the royal family, upon which the formal, dynastic alliance must depend for its efficiency in large measure. The princely stakes for which Ferdinand, and more especially Charles V., whose authority in the Lowlands would have been gravely menaced by a serious breach with England, were playing, impelled them to attempt to form a league with the Tudors, which no force that could be brought against it should be able to dissever. It was their endeavor to establish a friendly understanding with the English kings, which could, nevertheless, not be dissolved by any effort save their own.

The disaster which overtook Charles V. in Germany in his endeavor to stamp out the Reformation, effectually diverted his thoughts from the English alliance until the death of Edward VI. During the brief reign of that monarch nothing had occurred to abate the desirability of renewing the relations which had existed in the time of Henry VIII. Charles V., therefore, at once seized upon the accession of his cousin, the Catholic Mary, to further his interests in England by marrying his son to the newly crowned queen. The nation was at that crisis to be bribed and cajoled into accepting the rule of the Spaniards so gradually, that any perception of its dependence would come too late to be of avail. Philip and his courtiers planned to win the country by their mild bearing; but the dominion which they purposed, though peaceful, was designed to be final and complete. The new project was no sooner brought to trial than it was seen that its failure was inevitable. The end was hastened by the death of Mary. Philip II. then found himself with the Lowlands, to which he was an utter stranger, and a portion of Italy on his hands, both of which he was likely to lose in his quarrel with France and the Papal See. The refusal of Elizabeth to consider his offer of marriage, prevented all hope of maintaining the *status quo*. The recalcitrancy of the Low Countries only rendered the proximity of England more dangerous, so that the only course left at his disposal was to sap the strength of the English and to reduce them to dependency. In this endeavor Philip used every means that his predecessors had employed in furthering their purposes, and in addition he utilized every opportunity of promoting sedition among English subjects, both at home and abroad. He inaugurated a policy of conquest, the third and final phase in the treatment of England by sixteenth-century Spain. This policy received its death-blow in the defeat of the invincible Armada, but it was pursued feebly until Philip II. had been succeeded by his son, and the Tudor dynasty had given place to the Stuarts in the person of James VI. of Scotland. It was the collapse of this attempt to coerce England, when milder measures had been tried and proved insufficient, that sealed the doom of the supremacy of Spain.

As the possessions of the Spaniards in Europe made the alliance with England essential to the peninsular monarchy, in like manner the expansion of the dominions of both Spain and Portugal in America and India made the English commercially indispensable to those countries. The wealth of the Indies withdrew Spanish shipping from the ports of Europe and attracted it to the colonies, the trade with which was set apart to be its exclusive perquisite. The industries of the peninsula, taxed to the uttermost in the effort to supply the market opened to them in recently discovered lands, were unable either to meet the demands of the new dependencies or to satisfy longer the necessities of consumers at home. England was the nation that beyond all others was in a position to afford help in this emergency, and to profit in affording it. She had carried on a trade with the peninsula in her own bottoms since the beginning of the fifteenth century, and had long been the principal rival of its ships upon the seas. Hence when peninsular shipping was withdrawn to the colonies in the East and West, she was able not only to supply the great market for foreign goods which was suddenly called into existence in Spain, but also to succeed to the carrying trade of that country with Germany and the Lowlands. The political alliance between the peoples was thus paralleled by a commercial relationship which, although simultaneous with the alliance, had no necessary connection with it. One was artificial, the result of a determined plan, the other was the outcome of natural laws working themselves out in events whose consequences no man could have foreseen; together they sum up the relations which came to be between the nations on the practical side. This commercial intercourse, although not vitally connected in itself with the political, was nevertheless not independent of the phases of the development of the latter, nor exempt from the blight of war. It furnished the plebeian element in the relationship of the peoples, as the formal alliance furnished the aristocratic one, and ran its career of prosperity and vicissitude according to the fluctuations of the national policies.

The two nations, however, did not come in contact with each other in the sixteenth century in any but the political and commercial fields. In mediæval times, religion had sent many Englishmen on crusades and pilgrimages to the peninsula. Richard Cœur de Lion aided in the defence of Santarem against the Moors in the summer of 1190, and Lord Rivers, with three hundred followers, assisted in the assault on the Mohammedan kingdom of Granada, which effected its overthrow in the year of the first voyage of Columbus. The number of English pilgrims for whom licenses were issued to visit the shrine of San Iago, the patron saint of Spain, at Compostella in Galicia, was 814 in 1428 and 2820 in 1434.[1] Nor were these figures exceptional. Under the conditions of the Renaissance the influx of Englishmen, which, after making due allowance for exaggeration, must have been considerable, was discontinued

[1] Rymer, *Fœdera*, X. pp. 386–407 and 567–580 *passim*.

in the opening years of the sixteenth century. The subjugation of the Moors and the theological alienation of the countries brought about this result. Religion no longer attracted pilgrims from England, but became, rather, a source of discord. Catholicism was soon ranged against Protestantism as a matter of mere expediency, and religion sank to a purely subordinate place in the intercourse of the nations. It was identified with politics.

Learning was not more influential in this connection than religion. At the time of the Moorish supremacy in the peninsula, when the Arabs were instructing Europe in philosophy, mathematics, and medicine, England had sent her share of students to their schools. But as the power of the Moors declined, Italy became the intellectual leader of the West. Scholars flocked to her academies, turning their backs upon those of Spain. In common with France and England, the peninsula despatched her sons to the cradle of the new learning. A Spanish college was established by Cardinal Albornoz at Bologna in 1364, and another was founded under the patronage of the Jesuits at Rome two centuries later, when the English and German colleges

were opened in that city. In social and literary
development during the reign of Ferdinand and
Isabella, Spain was greatly inferior to Italy, but
she was superior to England and France. Yet
whatever the advantages which Spain possessed
over the western and northern peoples, her
scholarship and art, shut off from the world because of her remote geographical position, could
not compete abroad with those of the Italian
states. Nobody visited her cities for the purposes of study, scarcely anybody for curiosity
or mere love of travel. France, even, situated
on the line of communication between England
and Italy, over which students were continually
passing to and fro, was in a far more favorable
position to affect English culture directly. The
influence of Spain in her isolation, therefore,
was quite different in scope from that of the
other Latin countries. England maintained
political and commercial intercourse with all of
them, it is true; but she also entered into
other independent relations with Italy and with
France, whereby she became acquainted with
the culture of the Renaissance. Scholars visited
Italy because it was the seat of learning, and
France because of its proximity to their own

and the transalpine state.   Interchange of ideas
with these countries was not entirely subordi-
nated to the intricacies of diplomacy or the bar-
terings of trade.   Spain, however, enjoyed her
preëminence solely through the might of her
arms and the profusion of her resources.   These
alone attracted foreigners to her territory.   They
appealed above all to the Anglo-Saxons, than
whom no people was more alive to her material
greatness.   The dissemination of Spanish books
in England, therefore, was absolutely dependent
upon the course of politics and commerce.   It
followed their development closely in volume
and in kind.   The rise and power of Castilian
culture in the home of the Tudors were determined by and sensitive to the successive phases
of the political contest between the English and
Spanish nations.

CHAPTER II

THE influence of Spanish literature upon the England of Henry VIII. and Elizabeth has seldom been underestimated. The usual histories which deal with English letters in the reigns of the Tudor sovereigns, and the more detailed memoirs which are published in elucidation of the lives of the principal writers of their times, very commonly unite in assigning to the peninsula a pronounced and positive share in shaping the course of Elizabethan literature and in inspiring the productions of many of its best-remembered authors. The hand of Spain has been seen in the highest types from the beginning of the sixteenth century to its close. Wyatt and Surrey, the fathers of modern English poetry, have been, perhaps, the most unfortunate subjects of baseless conjecture. Their verse has been repeatedly referred to Castilian sources, and Surrey has even been praised for his translations from the Spanish tongue. Proficiency in that language has been attributed to Henry VIII. and all of his children, and to a long line of writers of the early days of Elizabeth. The influence of Spain at the end of the century has been traced in the dramas of Shakspere, and the plots of the *Two Gentlemen of Verona* and other plays have been referred to Castilian sources. The thoroughness of recent Shaksperian scholarship, however, has effectually dispelled this illusion, so natural amid the difficulties of imperfect information. It is recognized that the great dramatist was indebted to Spanish books for his Proteus and Julia alone, and that he was not personally affected by the peninsula any further than the least of his countrymen, in whose ears the cruelties of Alba and the terrible sweep of the invincible Armada were familiar tales. The plots over which the misapprehensions arose have been proved to be of Italian origin. The linguistic accomplishments of the royal family have suffered in the same manner. When Philip came to England, Queen Mary could not speak Spanish, though, indeed, she was able to understand it when she heard it spoken.[1] The records of the foreign office include no evidence that Henry VIII., Edward VI., or Elizabeth ever employed that language as a medium of communication even with the ambassadors of the peninsula. Unfortunately, the relations of the greater part of Elizabethan literature to that country are yet obscured in a state of precritical darkness similar to that from which Shaksperian scholarship and the history of politics have just emerged. Wyatt and Surrey have never been studied in connection with contemporary Spanish poetry. Here and there, the light of more adequate knowledge has appeared, but it has been fitful and never sufficient to illumine the whole field. In order to make it apparent that the greater part of Spanish influence in Elizabethan literature is as fictitious as that which was formerly thought to be discernible in the works of Shakspere, it is only necessary to subject the mass of translations to careful scrutiny.

The overvaluation of the influence of Spain on English letters on *a priori* grounds was

[1] Hume, *Year after the Armada,* p. 164.

inevitable. It was the result of placing im-
plicit reliance on inferences based on a supposed analogy between that country and Italy
and France. English poets and scholars had
visited the French and Italian cities from the
days of Chaucer, and brought home with them
on their return reminiscences of their stay
abroad, which were afterward incorporated into
their works. Englishmen frequented Spain
during the sixteenth century, and hence, when
a writer was found who had travelled in the
peninsula, or one whose work presented any
parallelism with its literature, the coincidence
was regarded as the proof of a necessary connection. This attitude of mind was based
upon a double misapprehension. It failed,
in the first place, to take into account the
character of Spain's golden age. This was
largely Italian in form, and though the Castilians added vigor and force at times to their
models, the imitations never reached the standard of finish and formal perfection that the
originals had attained. Parallelism with the
Spanish is not in itself evidence of connection
with it. Indeed, in the case of an English
work, the probability is always on the side of an

Italian rather than a Spanish source. Finish appealed more strongly to the English of the Renaissance than power and sincerity, which must have seemed to them very ordinary qualities. In the second place, early scholarship failed to take into account, when interpreting these coincidences, the peculiar nature of the relations between England and Spain, which did not wholly resemble those which were maintained with France and Italy. It was forgotten that these relations were exclusively political and commercial, that they were practical in nature, and that the persons who visited the peninsula were either not members of the literary class, or were else employed on business that was most matter of fact in its nature. The effect of this restriction which the intercourse of the nations imposed upon the mutual interplay of their literatures was quite ignored.

Nevertheless Spanish letters were not totally unknown to the Elizabethans. Translations from the Spanish, — and translations are eventually the basis of general literary influence, — were sent forth in goodly numbers from the English presses. The shops of the printers of the capital were stocked with an array of books, sufficiently varied and representative to afford the Londoner a glimpse of the ways of life and modes of thought which were current to the south of the passes of the Pyrenees. In bulk and in compass the translations were considerable, and in character they were so typical of the circumstances amid which they were produced, that a cursory examination of their contents reveals at once the nature and limitations of the influence of Spain.

The Spanish books which were familiar in England during the sixteenth century were either of an occasional and didactic character or purely literary in their nature. The more practical publications preponderated greatly. The achievements of Gonzalo de Córdoba and Charles V., of Cortés and Pizarro, arrested the gaze of all Europe. It was but natural that England, which was not only vitally interested in the progress of the Spanish wars in the eastern and western hemispheres, but dependent for her knowledge of the peninsula upon men of action to whom they were living topics of thought, should give her attention to a story of discovery and conquest unequalled in wonder

in the annals of the past.   The book marts of
London were consequently filled with an assort-
ment of broadsides, tracts, and pamphlets, whose
purpose was to convey information about Portugal and Spain.   They were written in verse as
well as in prose, and since they were derived
from many sources, both native and foreign,
approached their subjects from many points of
view.   It was their function to gather and
record everything in the contemporary history
of the peninsular states which possessed any
interest for the Englishman, and also to repeat
his opinions upon the great international struggle then taking place.   Their office was, therefore, that of the modern newspaper.   An
adequate account of the tracts issued by London printers to satisfy popular curiosity concerning Spain would be a history of the
foreign relations of Elizabethan England.[1]
They described the peninsula itself, the affairs
of its inhabitants and of its African neighbors, the troubles of its colonial dependencies,
its bloody wars in the Low Countries, and
the intercourse between its subjects and those

[1] A brief bibliography, intended to illustrate these paragraphs, has been appended at p. 409.

of the English monarchs. They placed the
travels of Englishmen in the Iberian country
and current news from Lisbon or from Spanish
cities before the reading public. They treated
both general and minute and curious matters.
One pamphlet was licensed in 1594, for example, which dealt with the *Present Estate of
Spayne;* another purported to be a *Tru Certificat sente from Gibralter in Spayne of a wonderfull fysshe.* The impostor who was passed off
for a time as the Portuguese king, Dom Sebastian, who was slain at Alcazar, was the hero of
several tracts, among which was one by the
prolific Anthony Munday. A *Relation of the
solemnetie wherewith K. Phillip the III. and
Quene Margaret were recyued in the Inglish colledge of Valladolid* was translated by Francis
Rivers. More momentous questions also commanded proper consideration. The *Expedycion
of Charles the V emperoure agayenst the citie of
Angiers,* and a *Dolorous Discourse of a bloudy
battel fought in Barbarie* (the battle of Alcazar) informed their purchasers of the condition
of affairs in northern Africa; the *Declaration
of the sicknes, last words and death of the
King of Spaine, Phillip the Second,* and other

tracts, acquainted them with the passing of England's relentless and inveterate enemy. Proclamations of the Spanish kings and letters and treatises of their generals and admirals that seemed likely to be of interest in London were likewise freely printed. The most important of these were the *Discourse of the battell foughte betweene the two navies of Spaine and Portugall at the Azores, 1582*, and the *Relation of the expougnable conquest of Tercera*, which were taken from the Spanish of Alvaro de Baçan, Marquis of Santa Cruz, whose death subsequently deprived the Armada of a competent commander, and perhaps indirectly caused its defeat. The floating literature which refers to the sea-fights off the coasts of the American colonies, in which the English adventurers took part against overwhelming odds, was absorbingly interesting. Henry Savile's *Libell of Spanish lies*, which was printed with alleged false statements that Admiral Bernaldino Delgadillo de Avellanado had written with the design of depreciating the bravery of British seamen, recalls by its contents Sir Walter Raleigh's more famous account of the brave but unavailing fight of the *Revenge* against a whole Spanish fleet. Other pam-

phlets which dealt with the struggles of the
Spaniards in France and the Low Countries
were no less timely. The death of Don Juan
de Austria in Flanders, where he was residing
as governor, provoked the publication of a
satirical tract. The doings of Parma on his
French campaign were noted. The conspiracy
of Philip II. with the Duke of Guise occasioned
a treatise entitled the *Spaniards monarchie and
the Leagvers oligarchie*, which was licensed to
be translated and printed by one H. O., from a
French version of the Spanish of Vasco Figueiro.
Many other events called for recognition and
comment.

The pamphlets which sprang from the immediate contact of England and Spain were, however, more numerous than these books, and not
less important. They first appeared in the days
of Henry VIII. with the *Triumphus habitus in
Anglia in adventu Caroli V.*, describing the
visit of the emperor to the English court
in 1522, and were continued by the *De Ritu
nuptiarum et dispensatione*, written in the
cause of Katherine of Aragon by Juan Ginés
de Sepúlveda, and John Bradford's *Nature
of Spaniardes*, during the reign of Mary.

The Armada stimulated the presses to their greatest activity in producing tracts of this class. It furnished a theme which the ballad-makers seized upon to be the subject of their verse. It was followed by the publication of the official orders promulgated for its guidance by the Duke of Medina-Sidonia. Then, not content with the victory which they had gained, the people began to grow impatient of the unsatisfactory accounts of the fight, as they seemed to them, which were circulated in Spain. James Lea translated from the Spanish a pamphlet bearing the title *Respuesto contra les falsedades publicadas e impresas en España . . . de la Armada.* The pamphlet was the composition of one Don F. R. de M., "a Spanish Gentleman who came hither out of the Lowe Countries from the service of the prince of Parma, with his wife and familie, since the overthrowe of the Spanish Armada, forsaking both his countrie and the Romish religion." Several songs and hymns, including some by "Christovall Bravo of Cordova, blinde of bodie and soule," were interspersed, accompanied by answers also in verse. One B. J. translated a similar work from the Spanish of a sailor

who had served aboard one of the ships of the
invincible fleet.   When the meaning of the
destruction of the sea power of the peninsula
by the British sea-dogs is considered, the appearance of these tracts cannot be deemed surprising.   It was the necessary result of the
maritime conflict, so momentous to the English
people.   Hence, as a desultory warfare continued to be waged until the opening of the
next century, there was no diminution of the
number of these pamphlets for some years.   A
*Declaration of the causes mouing the Queenes
Maiestie of England to prepare and send a
nauy to the seas for the defence of her realmes
against the King of Spaines forces* was issued
by the Earl of Essex and Admiral Howard of
Effingham, in English, French, Dutch, Italian,
and Spanish in 1596, and a *Discription . . . of the
plott of Cadiz*, also licensed in 1596, was called
for by the same expedition, in consequence of
the sack of that city.   More general treatises
also commanded a sale.   Sir Lewis Lewkenor's
*Estate of English fugitives under the King of
Spaine and his ministers*, associated likewise
with the name of Thomas Scarlett, probably
without authority, and Ralph Ashley's *Com-*

parison of the English and Spanishe nation [1] are the most notable examples of books of this class. In these the true feeling which existed against the peninsular power, which found expression in the deeds of Drake and his followers, rankled and chafed. It was augmented by the accounts of the harassing of Englishmen by the Spaniards, which set forth the details of the persecutions in the peninsula. David Gwyn, "who for the Space of elueuen Yeares and ten Moneths was in most grieuous Servitude in the Gallies, vnder the King of Spaine," composed three poems, which seem to have been acceptable to Elizabeth when presented to her, because of the experiences of the author.[2] The feeling of hatred and the exultation of triumph are discernible in this literature almost in its entirety. It indicates by its bulk and by the emotions which it expresses the seriousness of

[1] Ralph Ashley, S. J. (d. 1606), is said to have been a cook at the English college at Douay until 1590. He then became an inmate of the college at Valladolid, and, returning to England, was martyred in the spring of 1606. His translation was made through the French, and licensed in London, April 7, 1589. See Gillow, *Dict. Eng. Catholics*, I., p. 73. The treatises of Lewkenor and Scarlett belonged to the year 1595.

[2] Lowndes, *Manual*, II., p. 962.

the questions with which it deals, the diversity
of their import, and a perception by the time
of their ultimate significance to the English
nation.

The currency of such a mass of occasional
tracts and pamphlets in London could but be
accompanied with a simultaneous manifesta-
tion of literature of more dignity and permanence. The recognition of the supremacy of
Spain by the venders of news did not long
exist without awakening a desire among the
Elizabethans to obtain an insight into the reasons and manifestations of that country's prosperity. Treatises upon scientific and practical
subjects were composed or translated to meet
this demand. The methods of manufacturing
an oil called *oleum magistrale* in the peninsula,
and the state of the silk industry in that section, were described by the physicians George
Baker and Thomas Moffett. Medical science
itself, however, received but little attention.
The reputation of the Spanish physicians, which
remained very high until the rise of the Greek
school and the Hippocratic practice in the early
years of the sixteenth century, had receded to
such a low ebb in the reign of Elizabeth that

several brief treatises of Nicolas Monardes of Seville included all of Spanish medical theory that was accessible in England at first hand. In other sciences the Castilians were entitled to be heard with more respect. Their experience on the Atlantic qualified them to speak with authority about the sea, and they were listened to with some deference on the subject of seamanship. Treatises on navigation by Martin Cortés, Pedro de Medina, and Antonio de Guevara, the historiographer of Charles V., were translated. All these practical treatises yielded in interest, however, to the expositions of the art of war, in the conduct of which the Spaniards were known to excel particularly and in which they long retained their supremacy. English versions were made of the treatises of Francisco de Valdés, Sancho de Londoño, Gutierres de la Vega, a celebrated captain of Medina del Campo, and Bernardino de Mendoza, at one time ambassador of Philip II. in London. These men did not originate the military treatise. Machiavelli had preceded them with his *Arte della guerra*, translated into English in 1562; but they were the exponents of the methods of the greatest of the armed powers. The influence of Spanish tactics and that of the Spanish soldiery upon the English has, indeed, long been familiar. It did not spring from books, for it was the result of the constant contact of the men-at-arms of both the nations in the Lowlands and elsewhere on the continent. The continuity of these relations left the imprint of Spanish military science upon the English mind. The theories which the Elizabethans borrowed in their treatises were wrung from experience and not clipped from the pages of books. No writer on military topics, indeed, could fail to be influenced by Spanish tactics and methods; but this influence nevertheless was not a literary influence, nor was it transmitted through the pen. It was the result of personal association.

England was primarily concerned with contemporary happenings in Spain, and did not greatly care about the mediæval history of that country. The works of the Italian historians who had dealt with recent Spanish affairs, Guicciardini, for example, and Giovio, were sold in London, but there was a dearth of the writings of the Spaniards themselves. This neglect, perhaps, was not ill-advised, for the latter people did not excel in the historical art. Robert Beale, however, published a compilation including selections from the leading Spanish chroniclers who had written in Latin in the thirteenth, fourteenth, fifteenth, and sixteenth centuries, which also embraced writings of Italian authors having reference to the peninsula. The *Relaciones* of Antonio Perez, the fugitive minister of Philip II., who was temporarily sheltered by the Earl of Essex, had at the time a political rather than an historical value. Sundry works by Spaniards which dealt with the history of other European countries were also published, though apparently without meeting with great success. These were translations of Luis de Avila y Zúñiga's *Comentario de la guerra de Alemania*, written in compliance with the command of Charles V., and the histories of the Roman Empire, as they were called, by the imperial chroniclers Guevara and Pedro Mexía. The narration of the latter began with Julius Cæsar and ended with Maximilian, the father of Charles V., so it did not err through any deficiency in the comprehensiveness of its subject-matter.

D

The preëminence of Spain in the province of the chronicle of discovery, however, was too marked to remain unnoticed in England. It was the colonization of the new world that imparted the great impetus to this class of literature, and this was the work of the peninsular states. England, which pensioned the Cabots and sent out Hawkins and Drake to prey upon the Spanish main, did not long rest in ignorance of the exploits of its enemies in India and America. The Latin *Decades* of Peter Martyr Anglerius, descriptions of African and Asiatic territories by the Portuguese Duarte Lopes and Fernão Lopes de Castanheda, Spanish accounts of China and the East Indies by Juan Gonzalez de Mendoza and Bernardino de Escalante, and of the western colonies by Augustin de Zárate, Francisco Lopez de Gómara, Gonzalo de Oviedo y Valdés, and the benevolent Las Casas, appeared in translations in London. To these, the contemporary tracts which had reference to the peninsular colonies should be added in order to obtain an adequate conception of the popularity of the literature which described the Spanish and Portuguese conquest of regions newly explored. José de Acosta's

History of the East and West Indies was licensed
to be printed also in the year 1601 when Richard
Hakluyt made his translation of Antonio Galvão, but it was not published, apparently, until
1604. Such a mass of matter circulating in
England within the compass of fifty years
could not fail of producing an effect, and of
leaving enduring traces of its presence. Yet
it must be remembered that Spain was but the
leader in the work of exploration, — England
and France followed just behind. The Castilian chronicles, however, were antedated in the
reign of Ferdinand and Isabella, by the works
of the Italian writers, of whom Martyr, residing
in the peninsula, was an expatriated example,
and did not attain their zenith until the middle
of the century. The Spanish and Portuguese
provided the continental chroniclers with the
most valuable part of their subject-matter; but
they did not originate the type, the content for
which they were able to supply. The work of
Hakluyt, therefore, and his English co-laborers
was not an imitation of the peninsular chronicles. It was the product of similar and partially independent conditions. Undoubtedly
the English collections of voyages owe some-

thing to the stimulus of the Spanish adventurers, and something also to the literature which sprang up about them ; but their origin was quite independent, and is to be sought in the activities of the English themselves. It was purely practical, having its roots in experience, like the treatises upon the art of war. Nevertheless simultaneous movements, one of which was brought into such constant touch with the other as Spanish exploration was with the English, must be related, at least superficially. In the particular instance of the chronicles, since the influence of the Italian historians was more direct than that of the Spaniards, it is impossible to define the influence of the latter, which was not immediate and tangible, but in so far as it entered into the work of the English, was coincident with the tendency of the spirit of the times.

Spanish religious literature prospered in England in a considerable variety of forms during this epoch. Aside from the sermons preached by Spanish friars in English churches while Philip held court in the country, the Elizabethans were familiar with many of the writings of the celebrated Spanish Catholic scholars and

mystics, and to some extent with those of the
small group of Reformers, which survived the
persecution of the Inquisition for a short time.
The Reformers were men whose difficult position
forced them to take a lively interest in passing
events, against which they might be called to
struggle, and they naturally wrote often upon
occasional subjects.   Books by Antonio de
Corro, Cipriano de Valera, Perez de Pineda,
and Reginaldo Gonzalez Montano, some of
them in Latin or Spanish and others in translation, were printed and sold in London.   The
productions of Catholic scholarship, of course,
commanded much more attention.   Extracts
were made from the polyglot Bibles of Cardinal Ximenez and Arias Montano, and treatises
of the Jesuit Gaspar de Loarte, of Luis Vives,
and of the Portuguese bishop, Osorio da
Fonseca, must have circulated widely.   Vives,
who taught at Oxford for a number of years,
and Osorio, who, next to Vives, was the most
famous of the scholars whom the peninsula
produced during the sixteenth century, became generally known.   The popularity of the
homilies of the Andalusian mystic, Luis de
Granada, was quite as great.   All the more

important works of Granada, with the possible
exception of the *Símbolo de la fé*, were put
before the public. Several translations of his
Meditaciones appeared, and the *Memorial de
la vida cristiana* and *Guia de pecadores* suffered no neglect. These emotional and un-
theological treatises evidently appealed to many
classes of the people. They stood practically
alone in their kind, for the only other Spanish
mystic translated was Diego de Estella; but
this fact only emphasized their success. Of
all the publications which were drawn by the
English from a Spanish source, under the
promptings of other than literary motives,
only the writings of Vives, Osorio, and Granada
were sufficiently widely known to have any influence upon literature. Of the works of these
authors, only the homilies of Granada were
written in Castilian. Spanish didactic or occasional literature, if it influenced English literature at all, could have done so in them alone.

The Spanish pamphlets, chronicles, and
treatises that were published in London,
whether of such a transitory nature that they
were little more enduring than newspaper
paragraphs, or possessing historical or religious

worth and permanence, were valued by translators and insular readers because of their devotion to or interest in the issues of politics, the
Church, or the fortunes of trade.   These books
constituted the great bulk of the translation
from the Spanish.   The artistic literature of
the peninsula, however, made its way across the
channel, and was not without admirers in England.   The heartiness of its reception did not
always accord with its merit.   The Spanish
drama, the richest form in an entire literature,
was represented solely by the *Celestina*, a work
that is pseudo-dramatic at best.   This masterpiece of fourteenth-century Spain occupied a
pinnacle of lonely eminence in the North.
This, however, was not strange.   The splendid
maturity of the theatre of Lope de Vega and
Calderon had just begun to unfold itself before
the playgoers of Madrid at the time of Elizabeth's death.   It developed too late to affect
the writers of her reign.   The ruder plays of
Lope de Rueda, whatever their effectiveness
might have been in performance, were, of
course, too local and colloquial to pass beyond
the confines of the peninsula.   The more elaborate essays of the classical school, on the other

hand, if excellent in polish and correctness, imitated the Italians too fully and gathered too small a following, to secure success abroad. It was denied to them at home. The drama for a time comprised nothing but the opposing popular and aristocratic extremes. Similar causes prevented a wide dissemination of the lyric, which reached England only in a few random extracts from Juan Boscan and Garcilaso de la Vega, set down by Abraham Fraunce in his *Arcadian Rhetorike*. The best of the ballads were naturally so thoroughly and strictly national that they could flourish only on their own soil. The new poetry of Boscan was handicapped among foreign peoples by its close resemblance to Italian verse. Yet it can but appear remarkable, making every allowance for the fact that much that is best in Spanish poetry remained in inaccessible manuscripts for many years, that such a small quantity of verse crossed the channel. Herrera and Camoens were ignored.[1]   Other works of less important

[1] There are so many casual references to the influence of Spanish upon English lyric poetry, that it is difficult to dismiss them in a few sentences. Yet a careful comparison of the poetical works of Wyatt and Surrey, the *Paradise of dainty devices*, the *Gorgeous Gallery of gallant inven-*

types attracted more notice in England than
the lyric. The rhymed proverbs of the Marquis of Santillana, a singular physico-educa-
tional treatise by Juan Huarte, a jest-book by
Melchor de Santa Cruz, a collection of fabulous
tales which was the composition of Antonio de
Torquemada, two romances of the court style

tions, the *Phœnix nest*, *England's Helicon*, and *Davi-
son's poetical rhapsody*, the poems of Gascoigne, Turberville, and other of the earlier Elizabethan lyricists, with
those of Garcilaso, Boscan, Gutierre de Cetina, Cristóbal de
Castillejo, Diego Hurtado de Mendoza, Santillana, and other
Castilian poets of the fifteenth and sixteenth centuries, reveals no direct relationship between the English and Spanish
schools, except in the case of the songs from the *Diana* of
Montemayor, translated by Sidney and Yong. Of the Spanish writers named, Santillana was the most popular of the
poets of the pre-Italian period ; Garcilaso, Boscan, and
Cetina were the leaders in the new style, and Castillejo was
its chief opponent. Their fame, therefore, was not unlikely
to penetrate into foreign lands. The Spaniards showed
better workmanship than the English, but both were imitators of the Italian. There are, consequently, passages in
each which are strikingly similar in manner and matter. A
little patience suffices to trace these to Petrarch and other
Italian poets, or sometimes to ultimate sources so remote as
the Greek Anthology. There is no evidence whatever of
any influence of the Spanish lyric upon the English. Some
of the best poetry of this type was buried in manuscripts in
the peninsula until the next century, and other reasons,
which are explained in the text, prevented its spread to
England.

by Diego de San Pedro, and another from the pen of Juan de Flores were translated and met with success that was out of all proportion to the reception that was accorded to the drama and lyric verse. These works, indeed, which were in the original fugitive examples of Castilian prose, were in translation sufficiently representative of types not generally cultivated in the peninsula.

Had no other Spanish books been more warmly received in England, the question of the influence of Spanish literature upon the English would never have arisen. There were, besides, peninsular authors who had many English admirers throughout the sixteenth century. The writings of these favorites vied in popularity with the productions of an occasional character which were so greatly in vogue. The most highly esteemed among them were undoubtedly the moral court treatises which appealed so strongly to all Europe during the Renaissance. This class of literature, in which precepts inculcating the etiquette and proper mode of life of the courtier were mingled with the moral teachings of the ancients, must be regarded as a distinctly humanistic product. Its

Spanish development was known in England
through the *Counseller* of Bartólomé Felipe,
the *Treatise declaring howe many counsels . . .
a prince . . . ought to haue*, composed by Federico Furió Ceriol, and through the writings
of Antonio de Guevara. Eight of Guevara's
books appeared in translation in London in
the Tudor period, and they were almost all
reprinted at least once. Some were translated
twice. The *Golden Boke* of Lord Berners, the
Dispraise of the life of a courtier by Sir Francis
Bryan, and the annotated edition of that work
by Thomas Tymme, Sir Thomas North's *Diall of
princes*, Edward Hellowe's *Arte of navigation,
Familiar Epistles*, and *Chronicle of the liues of
tenne emperoures of Rome*, Geoffrey Fenton's
Golden Epistles, the anonymous *Ancient Order
of knighthoode* and *Mount of Caluarie* were all
drawn from the works of Guevara. Almost
all of them met with a favorable reception.
The fame of the Spaniard surpassed that of his
Italian predecessor Castiglione, and equalled
that of any private person of his day.

The pastoral romance and the books of chivalry also obtained an adequate hearing. The
Spanish prose pastoral possessed a claim to

recognition through its elaborate style, which
appealed certainly to a taste analogous to that
which was gratified by the writings of Guevara.
Of this type, however, only the *Diana* of Montemayor came to be known in England. This
work won much approbation. Sir Philip Sidney, Thomas Wilcox, and Edward Paston made
English versions of portions of it, and Bartholomew Yong published a translation that
was complete. The *Diana* was also current in
the original Spanish in the country. It was
unquestionably a masterpiece of its kind, but
it was read abroad without awakening any
curiosity about either its predecessors or successors. The romances of chivalry were more
truly popular than the pastoral. Unlike this
type and the court books, they may be said to
have been the especial property of the common
people. They were therefore represented by
more than one work, for, having a commercial
value in England, the success of one insured a
trial of its fellows. The *Amadis* in the versions
of Thomas Paynel and Anthony Munday, the
series of the Palmerins in the translations of
the latter author, or rather, perhaps, in those
of his assistants, and the *Knight of the sun,*

published under the name of one Margaret
Tiler, whose labors were supplemented by
those of two writers designated only by the
initials L. A. and R. P., were printed in London, and, with the exception of Paynel's *Amadis*, seem to have been extremely well received.
Don Belianis de Grecia was also Englished by
L. A.   At the close of the century the books
of chivalry apparently supplanted to a great
extent the native and Gallic Arthurian romances.   The sale of the former increased as
that of the latter declined.   The later or peninsular growth quite naturally displaced the
older and more primitive tales.

The list of Spanish books which came to be
well known in England during the Tudor
epoch ends with Mendoza's *Lazarillo de Tórmes*,
which was translated by David Rowland.   The
fantastical and anonymous second part, originally printed in Antwerp, was also done into
English by William Phiston, though it was not
added to the editions of Rowland's translation
until the next century.   *Lazarillo de Tórmes*,
aside from its own merits, enjoys the distinction
of being the first of the picaresque novels which
grew to be so popular in the peninsula and in

the England of the Stuarts. The rise of the type in Spain did not take place until the close of the century. *Guzman de Alfarache* was not published before 1599. Hence, it was not until after that date, in spite of the fact that Rowland's *Lazarillo* previously ran through four editions, that the picaresque novels began to be freely translated. Mendoza's story itself attracted much notice when it first appeared in London, and affords a suggestive parallel to the *Unfortunate Traveller* of Thomas Nash. Together with the romances of chivalry, it was the only literary work of an essentially Spanish type which made a strong impression upon the Elizabethans. The court books and the prose pastoral, which were held to excel in the matter of style, had been inspired by Italy. They appealed to the literary classes primarily, while *Amadis* and *Lazarillo* were excellently adapted to gratify the tastes of a much larger circle of readers. Among the works of æsthetic value, therefore, which were translated from Spanish into English, the books which in the original were imitative of foreign models and the books which were purely indigenous in Spain were mingled. Those which manifested the plebeian spirit most strongly were the original creations of the peninsula. But the Spanish mind had stamped its characteristics upon them all. The individuality of the peninsula was so marked, that it could not fail to impress itself upon any task it might undertake. Spanish literature, when it reached England, either in indigenous or foreign types, was national at heart.

Such, in brief, was the acquaintance of the English people in the sixteenth century with Spanish literature. It was extensive and reasonably thorough for the times. Had it been otherwise, the phenomenon would have been inexplicable. Social conditions necessitated it. With the publications which merely dealt with Spanish affairs, including national relations abroad, added to those that have been already outlined, the mass of printed matter having reference to that country and its dependencies undoubtedly exceeded that which bore upon any other foreign nation. Without those publications the number of actual translations was somewhat less than half that of the Italian books translated, which, of course, held the first place. But the Spanish works which were sold in London, were not only many in

number, they were representative in kind.
This was true, first of all, on the practical side.
The topics which were then important, and in
the discussion of which it was Spain's privilege
to take a leading part, because of her men of
action, — war, navigation, and discovery, the
Catholic religion, — could all be studied through
translations from the Spanish point of view.
Histories, chronicles, mystical and Latin prose
had their readers. Nor was this representation
notably less thorough in certain of its aspects
on the side of literature. The types which
never really flourished on Castilian soil, jest-
books, the court romances of San Pedro, and
others not more prominent were not ignored.
The didactic prose of Guevara and Mexía, the
pastoral and chivalrous romances, and the picaresque novel received their full due, and for
the most part, indeed, more than their proper
meed. In other directions the representation
was faulty. The lyric, which was not poor in
Spain, and the drama, which was exceptionally
rich, were scarcely known at all north of the
channel. The natural obstacles to the dissemination of these types abroad, however, have
already been indicated. The ballad and the

narrative poems, abortive in Castile but rival-
ling the greatest productions of the century in
Os Lusiadas of Camoens, also never made their
way into England.   The patriotism of these
poems operated against their success in other
lands, and served to make the dulness of most
of them apparent to strangers.   The subject of
Camoens did not, therefore, seem to Europeans,
generally, to be as noble, human, and inspiring
as the reactionary theme of Tasso's contemporary epic, the *Jerusalem delivered*, and its
universal significance was confounded with its
Portuguese dress.

In spite of these deficiencies, the English
possessed a good acquaintance with the contents of peninsular. literature, both in the
works of notable authors and in those of men
of lesser worth.   A body of translations so
varied, so heterogeneous in kind if not in
spirit, now popular and now aristocratic in
their appeal, might very well have moved the
English to emulation and have left a permanent impression upon their literature.   The
opportunity was not to seek.   The campaigns
of the Emperor Charles against Barbarossa,
the African pirate king, and the almost in-

E

credible exploits of a handful of warriors on the table-lands of Mexico and Peru had been placed within reach of the idlers of London. The pages which recorded the hardy deeds of the Portuguese adventurers · and the languorous complaints of Arcadian shepherds lay side by side in shops and stalls. The Spain of action and the Spain of dreams stood out against each other. The rogue Lazarillo harried the blind beggar who was his master, while Amadis pursued Arcalaus the enchanter through the black forest, and overcame by the purity of his heart the magic sprites and invisible incantations of the Firm Isle. The real mocked the ideal, and was in turn interpreted by it. In the confusion and conflict of type with type, of history with fiction, of contrary mood and spirit, that breadth and catholicity of selection is discernible in the mass of translation, which cannot be the result of curiosity or chance. The complexity was too great. It was the expression of a movement, certainly powerful and perhaps influential.

What was the contribution of Spanish literature to English literature during the sixteenth century? No publication that is merely

occasional, however important, can have any
place in determining the answer to this question.   It will appear upon reflection that there
were five classes of Spanish books whose popularity was sufficiently great in England to
enable them, perhaps, to exert an influence
upon the literature which was growing into
maturity about them.   These were the mystical treatise, which depended so largely upon
style for its effect, the treatise of the court
and court life, the pastoral and the chivalrous
romances, and the picaresque novel.   Each
was practically summed up in the work of
one man, except the books of chivalry, which
were of various authorship.   These aside, Granada, Guevara, Montemayor, and Mendoza were
the means of transmitting across the channel
whatever influence Spanish literature exercised
in England.   Their writings commanded the
requisite attention to invite imitation, and,
moreover, had their parallels in English literature.   Lyly, Sidney, and Nash have been
sometimes supposed to be indebted respectively to the *Libro áureo*, the *Diana*, and *Lazarillo de Tórmes*.   It is impossible, however, to
assert a causal relationship *a priori* upon the

mere ground of resemblance, unless conditions in England and the peninsula were so dissimilar that there was nothing in the former country which prefigured in any way the works of these Spanish writers. But this could not be during the Renaissance among two nations whose growth was so analogous as that of England and Spain. Their development was simultaneous. The false taste which was manifested by Guevara and Granada existed in both. The humanists, although they endeavored to follow the best models in prose, constantly suffered the penalty of an over-enthusiastic study of the style rather than of the thought of the classical authors. Their writings thus tended to become empty and at the same time affected. It was upon the ruins of classicism that the false taste sprang up throughout Europe. It came to be famous in Guevarism, but it was present also in England before Lyly, as the commonplace phrase of scholarship, "a euphuist before Euphues," shows. The highly rhetorical sentences of Granada must be considered as another form of the same movement. Similarly, the pastoral was not a modern type.

Italy had anticipated Spain in this branch of
literature, both in prose and verse. Mantuan
was admired in England before Montemayor.
The picaresque novel as a literary creation,
on the other hand, was undoubtedly indigenous in the peninsula; but the irresponsible
and mischievous spirit which it expressed was
not confined to any one quarter of Europe.
Boccaccio's stories of Calandrino are not without a certain resemblance to the picaresque
tales, and the German *Til Eulenspiegel* exhibits
a marked affinity with them. The latter work
appeared in English in the early part of the
reign of Elizabeth and cannot have been unknown to Nash. Finally, the romances of
chivalry, like *Lazarillo*, a Spanish birth, were
no more without precursors in England than the
other types of peninsular literature, which were
widely translated and read. Native as well as
French Arthurian romances had been popular
in the country since the days of Caxton, and the
Spanish books of chivalry proved to be most
acceptable to the very audience to which the
older romances had appealed. It was only
when the decline of this class of literature had
become perceptible in the North, indeed only

when it was far advanced, that the tardy introduction of *Amadis* and *Palmerin* was effected.

The impossibility of estimating the influence of Spanish literature upon English literature by the criterion of the resemblances of books is therefore perfectly apparent. The influence cannot be defined by bibliography and criticism alone. It must be arrived at by determining the actual contact of English writers with Spanish thought. The problem is not general, but personal and specific. A solution of the difficulties which it presents cannot be offered until data of two kinds have been collected and classified. In the first place, passages that occur in English books that are direct translations from the Spanish must be identified ; and, secondly, the exact relations of English authors to Spain, the books of peninsular origin which they read, if it may be, and the place which these occupied in their minds and in those of their friends, must be ascertained. The first desideratum is a mere matter of comparison, and is in reality comprised in the second. It is the relation of authors to the peninsula that is the basis which is indispensable to the formation of a true conception of the Spanish influence.

What were the avenues through which Spanish books came into England, and through the agency of what classes of persons were they disseminated? whom did they reach? what was the strength and durability of the impression that they made, in what groups of writers was it deep and permanent? — these are the essential questions. The movement of translation from the Spanish in the sixteenth century must be reconstructed and its status in England fixed in order that the influence which it exerted may be properly estimated. It is necessary to trace the movement of translation in its connection with the political and commercial intercourse of England and Spain, from its origin in that intercourse at the beginning of the century, to the height of its almost independent development at its close; and to inquire into the evolution of this movement as it revealed itself under the successive phases which the political relations of Spain and England presented during the Renaissance, at the court of Henry VIII., in the London of Philip and Mary, and in the ebullient and unconquerable England of Elizabeth. The elucidation of these facts is, of course, an historical and not a critical task.

CHAPTER III

I

ENGLAND obtained its first knowledge of Spanish literature through the coming of Katherine of Aragon. The retinue of grandees which accompanied the princess on her voyage to the court of Henry VIII. became, after the death of that monarch, the household of the queen. Residing in England, yet never compromising their nationality nor forgetting their home, the Spaniards introduced a new power into the life of the nation. Reënforcements came out of the peninsula to augment their numbers and influence; foreigners were preferred to offices of dignity; racial intermarriages began to be celebrated in the highest stations. After the lapse of a few years Luis Vives, the famous Valencian scholar, was brought to England by Wolsey and installed

56

as a reader at Oxford, Jorge de Ateca, the queen's confessor, was appointed to the see of Llandaff in Wales, and the English houses of Mountjoy and Brandon were allied with the Spanish families represented among the ladies of the court. Through the favor of the king and the good-will of the nobles all distinctions of nationality bade fair to be ignored, if not to be obliterated, at least among the aristocracy.

The Spanish embassy in London was also growing in importance. Ferdinand's ambassadors had been maintained in England since the closing years of the fifteenth century from considerations of a somewhat unfriendly policy, and the old monarch must have taken peculiar pleasure in strengthening his influence by a match so well calculated to aid his design of building up a party among the subjects of his ally. He failed in the execution of his plan because the Reformation had not yet divided the people into factions and embittered the thoughts of some and fed the enthusiasms of others, till they hardened into treason and ripened into overt crime. Katherine's friends and dependants were uniformly held in great esteem and affectionately regarded; there was

no attempt to keep them at a distance. These
warm feelings were not in the least unnatural.
The connection which had existed between
England and Castile by marriage and by treaty
since mediæval times, had been insisted upon in
a spectacular way as recently as 1506 by the
three months' entertainment which Henry VII.
proffered to the Archduke Philip and Juana of
Castile, on their way to Spain after Isabella's
death, and also in 1522 by a fête lasting for six
weeks, during which the English acclaimed the
Emperor Charles V., as a guest of Henry VIII.,
with similar pomp and splendor.

These ceremonies must have seemed to be
formal reaffirmations of the traditions of English diplomacy, and could not have escaped
the observation of the common people. The
nobility, the inner circle of the friends and acquaintances of the Spaniards, were most appre-
ciative of Castilian ideals, because of superior
opportunities of intercourse. The people, as a
body, had never been without jealousy of foreigners; but partiality for the countrymen of
Katherine extended even to those in the humble walks of life. The treaty of 1505, which
concluded the betrothal, guaranteed to the ships

of both nations the same rights in the seaports of the two kingdoms, — a provision that made their flags identical for commercial purposes. This free trade was too Utopian to mean much in that age; but the English did not forget the spirit which purposed giving it a trial. It was not even then a mere dream. This was plainly understood by the colony of Spanish merchants settled in London. Undoubtedly their position was far from ideal, although certainly much better than the customs of that age would generally have warranted. They were directly favored by the Crown, instead of being utterly dependent on the intercession of their ambassador; they were honored now and then by friendly intercourse with the well disposed among the aristocracy; and in some sense they were made to feel at home amidst the insular environment. One of the members of the colony, stirred by the hospitable treatment by which he had benefited, expressed doubtless the feeling of his fellows when, in the *Crónica del Rey Enrico Octavo*, he exclaimed, "Oh! good King! how liberal thou wert to every one, and particularly to Spaniards!" [1]

[1] *Crónica*, ed. Hume, p. 127.

The Spaniards at the court, or trading in London, or teaching at Oxford, were materially aided in the work of disseminating their national culture by the Englishmen who visited the peninsula. These emissaries of Henry VIII. numbered among them distinguished names. During his reign, Lord Berners, Sir Thomas Boleyn, Dr. Sampson, Cuthbert Tunstall, Sir Richard Wingfield, Dr. Edward Lee, afterward archbishop of York, Wyatt the poet, Heynes, Edmund Boner, Dr. Thomas Thirlby, and Sir Henry Knyvet bore his credentials into Spain. But as Henry VIII. never pursued the plan of building up a party by means of these men, most of them were sent on brief missions; and all of them came to realize that they were strangers in a strange country. The little that they brought back with them went of course to satisfy curiosity about foreign lands, and to second the influence of the Castilians at court; yet even such knowledge of Spain as the ambassadors themselves possessed was largely derived from their countrymen who resided in the towns of the peninsula.

Next to the formal alliance, thus so important, the expedition of Thomas Grey, Marquis of Dorset, to Guipuzcoa, was more potent than any other one force that tended to open communication between England and Spain before the death of Edward VI. No mere event in that time of the crumbling of national barriers and the sudden development of commercial empires on the ruins of the feudal state could have affected the main course of history; but the enterprise of Dorset came at a critical moment, and, following immediately upon the marriage of Katherine, did much to consolidate and give form to tendencies whose ultimate triumph was inevitable. Dorset's army of ten thousand men sailed from England in May 1512, with the intention of coöperating with the Spaniards against the French and Navarrese, and of regaining the lost province of Guienne. From a military point of view the expedition was a total failure. The troops were used only as a menace to hold France in check while Ferdinand was annexing Navarre. Idleness and indecision kept them in camp on the brink of demoralization until fall, when, Ferdinand having made good use of their presence, they were led ingloriously home.

Dorset and his companions could not well

have acquainted themselves with Spain, even superficially. Such were the conditions and the brevity of their stay that they gathered as little idea of its institutions as the captains of the Black Prince or of John of Gaunt had done. Numbers of the soldiers and artisans, however, who served under Dorset, remained behind at his departure and by keeping in contact with their countrymen, which would not have been possible before the sixteenth century, preserved the measure of their patriotism and helped also to strengthen the growing English trade with the Biscayan seaport towns. The commanders, whose home ties were not so easily severed, returned, and in some cases entered into a trade, the promise of which they had been able to observe when in the field. The men whom they had led in the ranks were commissioned to be their factors in the more peaceful activity of importing merchandise and books. Sir William Sandys, treasurer of Dorset's army and subsequently of Calais, became one of the many none too honorable English pensioners of Charles V., perhaps through embarking so extensively in this trade. Cromwell kept up a correspondence with the merchants in Spain, who by reason of their numbers and familiarity with the local customs, grew to be quite indispensable to the official representatives of Henry VIII. Sir Philip Hoby, for example, in his mission in search of skilled labor for the new fortifications at Dover, relied on the good offices of one Thomas Batcock of Renteria, an expert in ordnance who had served under Sandys at Guipuzcoa, and a person well known to Cromwell. Nor was Batcock alone valuable to most of the men sent to the northern provinces. The merchants resident in the peninsula constantly increased, and grew in importance; special legislation had to be enacted for them in Andalusia in 1530; they became active agents in furthering across the sea ideas which had been first inculcated at the court or in learned circles by the queen. The rough organization they possessed rendered them effective in seconding the work that the Spaniards themselves were carrying on in England, through which what the merchants wrote home found a public prepared for its reception.

The alliance which Ferdinand had deemed it essential to seek, and which Henry VIII. considered it wise to enter into, thus tended to

draw the two nations closer together. The
marriage in the royal household, the diplomatic
negotiations which ensued upon it, and joint
action in military and commercial enterprises,
were all links in one great chain. The political results of this union involved the ultimate
ruin of Spain; but there was yet cast no prophetic shadow of the outcome of what seemed
not only an expedient but a mutually beneficial
policy. Social and commercial intercourse, in
their developments, however, dignified the
shortsighted opportunism of the sovereigns
and transformed its measures into expressions
of the irresistible course of national destinies.
The meaning of the alliance to literature,
which was much less evident and infinitely
less important to those times and to history,
received, of course, no consideration. Nevertheless, international communication could but
affect the progress of letters. When the
English visited the peninsula, and when the
Spaniards visited London, an exchange of ideas
was inevitable between them. Hence an interest in Spanish literature sprang up in England.
It was derived from association with Castilians who were at least temporarily domiciled in

the North; it was widened by a peaceful invasion of their country for the commodities of trade; and it was expressed by the translations from Guevara at the time the Reformation was defining itself, though too early to feel that influence.

II

The first movement toward the translation of Spanish books into English began at the court of Henry VIII. It manifested itself primarily in a spontaneous admiration for Antonio de Guevara, whose affectations had made him the cynosure of Europe. The fame of this author, his elaborate mannerisms, and the pervadingly moral tone of his writings recommended him at once to the attention of English men of letters. One work of Spanish origin, indeed, received an earlier hearing in London than Guevara's *Golden Boke*, but attracted no support and won no reputation. This was the *Enterlude on the bewte and good propertes of women*, an adaptation of the first four acts of the *Celestina*, which has been attributed to John Rastell. The account of the lands found by the Portuguese, a lone fore-

F

runner of the chronicles of discovery to follow
in the reign of Elizabeth, though printed in
1512 or 1513, was an anonymous Dutch production based upon the Italian of Amerigo
Vespucci. The adaptation of the *Celestina* is
an isolated expression of tendencies then operating in the country, of which the English editions of the court books of Guevara and the
theological treatises of Luis Vives are the distinctive memorials.

John Bourchier, second Lord Berners, stands
at the head of the court group of admirers of
Guevara, which began the study of Spanish
literature in England. He was born in the
year 1467, of a noble family, and succeeded
to the title of Lord Berners upon the death
of his grandfather. He afterward formed an
alliance with the Howards by wedding Katherine, daughter of the Duke of Norfolk, in
the vicinity of whose home Berners was well
known. There is no part of his career that
was brilliant, but his youth afforded many
instances of bravery that did not remain
unrecognized. At the age of eighteen, or
thereabout, Berners was left with Dorset as a
hostage for Richmond at Paris, when Rich-

mond left that city to open the campaign
that ended at Bosworth Field. It was due
quite as much to Berners' serviceableness
as to the gratitude of Henry VII. and
Henry VIII. that he always received their
approbation. In 1518 Henry VIII. sent him
with John Kite, archbishop of Armagh, to
join Sir Thomas Spinelly in Spain, where
a more competent representative than John
Stile, Henry VII.'s old ambassador, was
deemed necessary. Berners did absolutely
nothing in his new capacity, and received his
recall at the end of the twelvemonth. An
appointment to the governorship of Calais,
which was regarded as one of the sinecures
of the day, succeeded immediately, and must
have been peculiarly acceptable to a man
fast approaching sixty, who was besides a
victim of the gout. The duties of this office,
though they were sufficient to embarrass the
utter incompetence of the next incumbent,
Lord Lisle, were extremely light, including
little more than the superintendence of the
town and the preservation of discipline in the
garrison, or, on special occasions, the welcom-
ing of diplomats or royal guests.

The thirteen years of ample leisure of which
he was master there afforded Berners his opportunity to write; they cover all of his literary activity, for he had given small thought to
books previously.   His was an unpractised
hand.   The sedentary character of the latter
part of his life led him to take up literature as
a pastime.   Berners' friends understood his
position, as Henry VIII. had done when he
sent him to Calais, and they did for him what
they could by corresponding about their reading, and suggesting translations that might be
made, thinking this would help to pass away
the time.   In this spirit Henry VIII. himself
requested the translation of Froissart, and the
Earl of Huntington that of *Huon of Bourdeaux*,
while the Spanish books which complete the
quartet of his writings were undertaken under
similar auspices.   Lady Elizabeth Carew, the
sister of Bryan, urged him to begin Diego de
San Pedro's *Cárcel de amor*, which was seemingly not published until 1540.   The famous
Golden Boke of Marcus Aurelius, the last of
the four, so much admired by Bryan, though
it was completed somewhat tardily only six
days before Lord Berners' death, was done into

English in deference to Bryan's wishes, well
known to Berners through their frequent con-
ferences on literary topics. The latter went to
the French for the *Golden Boke*, as he had gone
to it for all of his other translations, except possibly the *Castell of love*. He used the version
entitled the *Livre dore de Marc Aurele*, made
by René Bertaut, the first edition of which is
dated at Paris in 1531. It is difficult to believe
that the *Castell of love* would not have been also
much more conveniently accessible to him in
that language, in which it appeared as early as
1526, than it was in the original tongue; and
if he in fact translated in this instance from
the Spanish directly, other considerations must
have determined his choice. The success of
these two books was emphatic within the
circle of his friends, and continued into the
Elizabethan era. A tide of reprints and
imitations of them soon set in, but unhappily
for Berners it came only after his death in
1536. The putative father of euphuism, who in
his lifetime struggled on, enmeshed in debts,
left at the end his four pictures and eighty
books with the rest of his private property to
be sold to satisfy the demands of his creditors.

Sir Francis Bryan, the second prominent member of the group, was the son of Margaret Bourchier and nephew of Lord Berners. For some time his mother served as governess to the Princesses Mary and Elizabeth, and Bryan was thus naturally placed at the court in which he became so notable a figure. Young, brilliant, the favorite of King Henry, his position was made more secure for a time by his cousin, Anne Boleyn, but it required all his address to extricate himself from the ignominy of her fall. His relationship with the Boleyns was also a relationship with Wyatt, and by virtue of this, as by his office in the privy council, he was the friend of Surrey, Vaux, Erasmus, and other commanding figures of the day. About 1517 he married Philippa, the widow of Sir John Fortescue, and some time after that lady's death, Joan Fitzgerald, one of a powerful Italian house at whose head was the Earl of Desmond, settled in Ireland since the twelfth century, and more latterly become malcontents in the interest of Charles V. In the year of his marriage with Joan Fitzgerald, Bryan was selected to be Lord Marshal of Ireland. The strength of the Desmonds had

already been effectually crippled by the efforts
of Skeffington and Lord Leonard Grey, whose
drastic measures put an end to the domination
of the house, and secured a truce from turbu-
lence during Bryan's administration. It was in
the year of his match with the Desmonds, and
of his removal to Ireland, that his *Dispraise of
the life of a courtier*, translated from the Spanish, was published at London.

In the original, this work was one of a collection of treatises by Guevara, published at Valladolid in 1539, and much resorted to for the
delectation of the English public. The particular tract in question, the *Menosprecio de la
corte y alabanza de la aldea*, Bryan translated
through the French version of Antoine
Alaigre, which had been printed at Paris in
1544. The book, despite of its being of a
piece with the works of Berners, met with less
success than they. Bryan only survived its
appearance a short time, dying in 1550, two
years after going to Ireland, and before a second edition had been called for. A reprint was
made, however, with some corrections, in 1575,
by T. Tymme, minister, under the title of *A
Looking-glasse for the courte*.

The environment in which both Berners and
Bryan moved was not only one of great distinction, but the Spanish element flourished throughout it; certainly in no other surroundings was
that element more pervasive. Their friends
were the men and women who had felt most
strongly the influence which the dynastic alliance of England and Spain had introduced into
their country. Though the interests which
they had in one way or another in peninsular
affairs were various, and often insignificant in
themselves, yet in the aggregate, when considered
in their proper juxtaposition and interplay, they
made of this particular court group an agency
for the dissemination of Spanish culture. In
this social circle there was sufficient organization
to make it a positive force. Sir Francis Bryan,
especially, dwelt amid its influence, as his active
career placed him so that he was able to keep in
touch with the court much more closely than
Berners in his voluntary exile at Calais. Bryan
came in contact with the Spanish current at
almost every turn. His sister Margaret married
Sir Henry Guildford, knighted with Wistan
Browne at Burgos by Ferdinand the Catholic
in 1512, whither he had repaired after the

return of Lord Darcy's expedition against the
Moors. Guildford was frequently officially
associated with Sir Thomas Wyatt and Sir
Nicholas Carew, as indeed with Bryan and
Charles Brandon, duke of Suffolk, and he befriended Wolsey to the end, when the sly policy
the Cardinal had played so long with Charles V.
failed to answer with Henry VIII. in the intri-
cate involutions of the divorce. Wyatt and his
son, the champion of Lady Jane Grey, have
both commonly been reported to have been great
Spanish scholars. The poet was for two years
a none too popular ambassador in Spain. Sir
Thomas Boleyn, like Wyatt, a relative of Bryan,
had also been employed in that country in 1522;
while Carew, the husband of the latter's sister
Elizabeth, was an ambassador to Charles V.,
although accredited to that monarch's court in
his possessions in the north. Acquaintance with
Richard Sampson and joint service on embas-
sies with him, afforded both Boleyn and Carew
rare opportunities of informing themselves of
peninsular affairs and of profiting by the glean-
ings of the three years which Dr. Sampson spent
as Henry VIII.'s minister in Castile.

Analogous connections bound together the

friends of Lord Berners, bringing them under identical influences. They belonged to the circle of the friends of Bryan, which came into contact with Spain at so many points that it might be distinguished without great injustice from the rest of the nobility by that circumstance. Some of the set of Berners had a knowledge of the peninsula at first hand quite as extensive as his own. Walter Devereux, his cousin though not in the first degree, was one of those who accompanied Dorset in his scandalous campaign at Guipuzcoa, and both Devereux and his former commander moved in this atmosphere so widely diffused at court; their sons married daughters, one of the Earl of Huntington, Berners' friend, and the other of the Duke of Suffolk, notable as one of the noblemen who chose a wife of Spanish parentage. Lord Willoughby d'Eresby had married María de Sarmiento, the favorite and confidant of Queen Katherine, and it was their daughter who accepted the hand of Suffolk after the death of Mary Tudor, his wife. This lady subsequently wedded Richard Bertie, with whom she resided in Germany during the reign of Mary. The society of the persons who had

been most profoundly affected by the coming of
Katherine, as well as many intimacies with those
who proved most industrious in furthering its
consequences, fell to the lot of both the translators. By blood or by an affinity of occupations
the friends of one were the friends of the other.
They pushed beyond the local horizon of their
literature. For them the fog-laden air of London
was thinned at times by a warmth that was not
native to the north, giving glimpses of bits of
a southern sky.

The famous poet and diplomatist, Don Diego
Hurtado de Mendoza, the author of the much-
discussed picaresque novel *Lazarillo de Tórmes*,
visited England in 1537, and was hospitably
welcomed, largely through the efforts of this
set. He seems to have made small impression
as a literary figure at London, where he spent
three months in an attempt to arrange a double
marriage between Henry VIII. and the Infanta
of Portugal, and the Princess Mary and Dom
Luiz, brother of the Infanta. Mendoza, nevertheless, was the recipient of much attention,
took part in the ceremonies attendant upon the
christening of Prince Edward, played the host
generously, and on the whole appreciated what

the Englishmen strove to do for him; for he
had the grace to acknowledge the kindness
of Suffolk, Carew, Dorset, Dr. Tunstall, and
others of this circle, saying that he thought
the living undoubtedly very good in England,
for one who was used to it.[1]   No other Spanish
writers of note set foot in the country before
the advent of Philip, unless we except the
Canciller Ayala, who had been a prisoner of
the Black Prince nearly two centuries before;
but nevertheless peninsular authors were perhaps brought to the notice of the English by
their countrymen in London, without having
to trouble themselves to conform to a foreign
climate and table.   Guevara indubitably owed
something of his vogue to such means.   Doña
Catalina de Guevara, who has been identified
with the mother of the Bishop of Guadix,
passed at least nine years in England waiting
upon the queen.[2]   To have been chosen as a
companion of Katherine, her rank must have
been high, and as Antonio de Guevara was

[1] The official correspondence relating to the English embassy of Don Diego Hurtado de Mendoza is contained in the
Calendar of letters and papers, for. & dom., Hen. VIII.,
vols. XII. and XIII.

[2] *State papers, Sp. ser., Hen. VIII.*, IV., pt. 2, p. 407.

frequenting the court of Ferdinand during her sojourn abroad, their family at least must have been the same. The effect of the attendance of a relative of this writer upon the queen, even though personal contact with her ceased on her return at some time previous to 1532, may have done much to hasten the ripening of the influences steadily maturing in the English mind through the agency of a foreign race. It may have been the chance occasion of introducing Berners and Bryan to their author, though it could scarcely have been more.

The presence of such a number of persons of rank at court, all bound together by family ties or by the closest official relations, all in constant association with Spaniards of noble birth attached to their queen, furnishes the solution of the problem how Berners and Bryan came to undertake translation from the Spanish. From this society came the first English version of the books of Diego de San Pedro and Guevara, written for the gentlemen of Castile, and by them communicated to the English nobility. Given in England a body of courtiers sufficiently acquainted with the peninsula to care to know anything of its literature, then

these authors were those most likely to attract
notice. San Pedro and Guevara were especially
fitted to appeal to the patrician class, and when
that class demanded translations, it had recourse
at once to their works. San Pedro, the only
writer save Guevara touched by the English
Guevara group, achieved a reputation at the
court of the Catholic sovereigns as a principal
contributor to the *cancioneros* of his time, in
addition to leaving behind a name as a successful prose romancer. His romance, the *Cárcel de
amor*, combined both allegorical and chivalrous
elements, and, written in the writer's youth,
antedated the prosperity of the romances of
chivalry and the popular prose literature. It is
quite different from tales of that order because
of the different class of readers for whom it was
composed, as is illustrated by the allegorical
method it employs in its first part, which is
that of the school of Santillana and the fourteenth-century poets who amused themselves
with contriving variations of the machinery of
Dante. San Pedro did not write for the people, he aimed to obtain his elevation by subtle
artificiality rather than by the plebeian method
of fabulous exaggeration. Guevara must be

regarded in the same light. Bishop by royal
favor both of Mondoñedo and Guadix, he was
not a plain man; he had neither the fervid
piety nor the decisive authority of simplicity.
Looked at critically, his works are monotonous
moral homilies, the production of one in whom
the preacher was overshadowed, not to say
dulled, by the courtier. The *Golden Boke* is
nothing but a series of worthy reflections on
virtue and good deeds, expressed by means of
heaping up adjectives on nearly synonymous
nouns; the *Menosprecio de la corte* is a briefer
collection of meditations in Guevara's own
name upon a similar subject. Obviously, the
scope of these books made them the concern of
relatively few persons; they were set in the
court key, and designed for court approbation;
but therefore they appealed to men of birth and
of some education, those who commanded in
their day the widest influence and who by
their situation and their friends, at home and
abroad, were able to secure for them, before
all others, foreign reading and foreign fame.

The residence of Berners as ambassador in
Spain from the spring of 1518 to January of
the next year, seems at first sight to give

some warrant for assuming a more personal standpoint in considering this movement, than tracing the origin of the Guevara group to Spanish influences domesticated in England has permitted. It is indeed conceivable that he obtained the books that he translated while he was in Spain, and that he made the translations after his return. But the examination of the facts upon which such an hypothesis must rest, which have much more authority in Berners' case than in Bryan's, — for Bryan never went south of the Pyrenees, — only emphasizes the initiative power of the circle in which these men moved at home. On his embassy, Berners really saw very little of Spain. At the time of his arrival Charles V. had been in his new dominions only six months, and was already entertaining at the court a Florentine, Spinelly, as representative of Henry. This man conducted all the state correspondence in conjunction with Kite, as idleness was forced upon Berners by a severe attack of gout, which bothered him a great deal during his stay, and in the summer took on such a malignant form that it kept him almost constantly in bed. Testimony unites

upon his miserable condition, and the course of
Charles V. in presenting Kite with a thousand
ducats and Berners with a bare six hundred
on their return, is an official recognition of
his inaction. Under such disadvantages he
could have done little to neutralize the ill
will with which the Spaniards uniformly
treated the English ambassadors during that
epoch. Wyatt suffered from this attitude,
and unlike Berners, a man of letters when he
visited the country, bore away no traces of
any contact with its literature.

When he settled in Calais after his failure
in Spain, the health of Berners took a turn
for the better; he was able to be about, to exchange courtesies with the various diplomats
resorting to his town, or with royalty itself.
Yet Berners did not draw his knowledge of
Castilian authors from his friends at Calais,
among whom they were esteemed, although
he lived in France, and spent much of his
time reading French books and transferring
them to his own tongue. While it is true
that all the books which this group dealt
with were previously familiar on the southern coast of the channel, Berners cannot have

G

derived his interest in them from France. He decided on his translations because of requests from England, — those of Lady Carew and Sir Francis Bryan. It cannot be seriously believed that Bryan and his sister got their incentive to study these books through any French source, though indeed they might have done so, since Bryan was in that country somewhat, and besides was much thrown with Sir Thomas Elyot, Wyatt, and other members of the thoughtful travelling class.[1] Whether or not the *Castell of love* was done directly from the Spanish, that language had an independent standing in England, where current Spanish literature had already been criticised by Luis Vives.

The French were not the masters of the English in this matter; they were merely the means of communication. Travel between Lon-

[1] Sir Thomas Elyot (1490 ?–1546), the scholar, was the friend of Cromwell, Anne Boleyn, and Sir Thomas More. In 1531 he was ambassador to Charles V. in Germany, and in 1535 followed the emperor from Barcelona to Tunis and Naples. Elyot's *Image of gouernance compiled of the actes and sentences of the most noble emperour Alexander Seuerus*, London, 1540, resembles Guevara's *Libro áureo*, and purports, like that work, to be a translation from an obscure Greek manuscript.

don and Valladolid or Madrid was mostly over
their roads; couriers preferred crossing the
Pyrenees to trusting their lives to the storm-
swept Bay of Biscay; ambassadors and their
trains manifested the same aversion to the sea.
Not till 1543 was this uncertain overland route
traversing the territory of a third power abandoned. In that year Henry VIII. and Philip,
then regent of Castile, arranged to buy two
zabras apiece for a sea service, and state papers
were thenceforth carried between the countries
largely by ships, subject only to natural delays.
The laws to which national interests had long
conformed determined the avenues for the con-
veyance of ideas. France always outstripped
the English in the knowledge of the Spanish
people and its literature, for it was coerced
into a certain regard for their affairs by proximity, and bound to respect them outwardly
at times by an enforced alliance through marriage; but it had not yet become that reservoir
for redistribution of peninsular culture that it
was in the seventeenth century. England in
the sixteenth was something of a centre as well.
Books were imported in the original or they
were bought in translation with more facility,

but the French invariably acted in a commercial capacity. Berners was not ignorant of Spain when he set out on his mission with Kite, nor were Bryan and Elyot when they visited the continent. The society surrounding Katherine needed no stimulus to Spanish studies from without; it did not turn to the subjects of Francis I. for information concerning her countrymen; far too powerful to require reënforcement, it pursued another end, and amid the difficulties of a pre-mechanical age, its desire was only a means of contact with the object of its attention. This means it found in the French tongue.

III

The influence of the Spaniards upon the English people during the first half of the sixteenth century resulted in the formation of a second group of translators, as clearly distinguishable as that which centred around the writings of Guevara. The new conditions fostered in Britain by the influx of Castilians with the Princess Katherine, were far too comprehensive in their scope to have affected lit-

erature at one point only. Though Spanish
literature passed into English literature solely
in translations from Guevara and San Pedro,
and in the few isolated works which were
adumbrations or foreshadowings of the forces
which produced the Guevara group, there were
in English other books indicative of the presence of the Spaniards, — the translations from
the Latin writings of the Valencian scholar, Luis
Vives.

Unlike Guevara, Vives lived for a time in
actual contact with the society through which
he was spreading a knowledge of his country.
His sojourn at Oxford afforded him unsurpassed
opportunities for such a work. He gathered
a following by his learning and reputation; a
well-defined set became interested in his books.
Since Vives wrote exclusively in Latin, the
translations which were made by this group do
not represent the direct influence of Spanish
upon English letters, but they are noteworthy
as the only productions of a Spaniard resident
in England before the reign of Mary which
passed into the vernacular. With the publications of the Guevara group they are the sole
direct illustrations in English literature of the

impression which the train of Katherine made
in the land of its adoption. The work of Vives
is a commentary upon the course of the Spanish movement, and it is significant in history
because of the general light that it sheds upon
the times, quite apart from all consideration of
the events in subsequent reigns which it antici-
pates.

Juan Luis Vives was born in Valencia in the
year 1492. He received instruction in grammar in his native city and then repaired to
Paris, where he pursued the study of logic.
At Louvain he perfected himself in Latin and
Greek, and he afterward gave much attention
to civil law and to the Church fathers. It was
while he was still engaged in mastering legal
subjects on the continent that Sir Thomas More
brought Vives to the notice of Erasmus, who
grew to admire him so greatly that he sub-
mitted his own works to him for correction.
Thenceforth the fame of the young scholar
made rapid progress, and in the year 1517 the
founder of Corpus Christi College, Oxford,
created him fellow of that institution. Erasmus' indorsement of Vives must have done
much to spread his name among Erasmus' fol-

lowers in England. Recognizing the talents of
the man, Henry VIII. invited him to cross the
channel, and placed him as a reader of rhetoric
at Corpus Christi in 1523. Vives presently
commanded the highest esteem throughout the
university. He lectured on the humanities in
his own college, and, at the same time, expounded
the civil law before the whole university. Long
before he accepted the invitation to settle at
Oxford he had been regarded with great favor
by Katherine. His success was commensurate
with the reputation which had preceded him.
In the year of his arrival the king and queen
travelled all the way from London for the
express purpose of hearing him lecture. The
academicians revived in his honor the degrees
of grammar, rhetoric, and poetry, which had
been somewhat neglected before his coming,
and he received an appointment as tutor in
Latin to the Princess Mary. The injustice
which dealt so harshly with the queen was, of
course, not sparing of those who were attached
to her. Vives was banished at the time of the
trial of the divorce before the papal legate in
1528; but the ignominy of arbitrary imprisonment and exile could not have been wholly

unanticipated by the scholar whose two great patrons had both been removed from his side. Vives does not seem to have become greatly attached to persons or to places. The abode of his friends who shared his pursuits was the home of his heart. Though he made friends in the country in which he was employed, he took a wife in Bruges. Almost without exception, his works were published or written in the Low Countries, and he retired to them permanently, and not to Spain, after the fall of Wolsey and Katherine.

It was while Vives was lecturing at Corpus Christi that Richard Morison and Thomas Paynel enrolled their names as students at Oxford. At the university ample opportunity for communication between the scholar and the men who popularized him was offered. The presence of Vives, though fitful, for he spent much of his leisure on the continent at Paris, Bruges, and Louvain, was too notable an event to be overlooked in the town. Vives made his mark in England. He corresponded with Linacer; he had relations with More and his friend John Longland, bishop of Lincoln; he had sought to meet Cuthbert Tunstall at Bruges as early as 1521, and this meeting of the foremost English and Spanish scholars could not long have been delayed. The fame of the acquirements of the Spaniard was bruited far beyond the precincts of the university; the courtiers manifested an enthusiasm for the Spaniard which was properly proportioned to that expressed publicly by the king and queen. Vives, however, always remained a scholar. His influence was not that of a fine gentleman pursuing literature as an amusement or as a means of procuring the patronage of royalty; on the contrary, it disseminated the atmosphere of the university. It appealed to men of education primarily, not to men of family.

The social position of Sir Richard Morison, Richard Hyrde, and Thomas Paynel contrasts with the station of Lord Berners and Sir Francis Bryan. There is scarcely one name common to the circles in which the two groups of translators moved side by side. While the members of the Guevara group were gentlemen of birth, whose friends belonged to the highest rank, the extraction of the translators of Vives was humble. Morison and Paynel owed their elevation to industry and to a judicious im-

provement of their opportunities for advancement.   Literature was not the light matter to
them that it was to Berners and Bryan.   One
feels as if a sense of effort was always present
in their lives ; it is plain that what they obtained, they literally achieved, not indeed by
greater deeds than those of the nobility, but by
striving consciously.

The translators of Vives did not come by
their interest in the peninsula chiefly from intimacies or marriages with the Spaniards at
court, as the contemporary group had done.
They drew their information about Spain from
many sources, most of them, if not plebeian,
at least diffusing influences quite general and
widespread.   The range of acquaintanceship
with public men possessed by Morison and
Paynel was great, and it opened to them
more than one channel for the acquisition
of Spanish culture.   Men of the rank of
Sir Philip Hoby, the half-brother of Sir
Thomas Hoby, the translator of the *Courtier* of Castiglione, were closely associated
with Morison throughout his career.   When
fulfilling a mission in Spain and Portugal in
1535, Sir Philip was already among Morison's

correspondents, and at the time they had
friends who were curious about the peninsula.
Hoby wrote Morison of an acquaintance, travelled in that section; another friend sent word
that he was reading a history in Spanish, that
Richard Pate, the ambassador, had given him.
The set also included Sir John Mason, secretary
to Wyatt in Castile during Hoby's mission
there, and a man frequently sent thither as an
agent of the king. Mason was identified with
the Protestant party in the Reformation as
Morison was, and shared with him the friendship of Sir John Cheke and Dr. Thomas Starkey,
as well as a high place in the esteem of the
Duke of Northumberland, through his marriage
with the sister of Sir Henry Guildford, the
Spanish Knight, a cousin of the wife of the
duke. But Mason's origin was very different
from that of Hoby, for though an Oxford graduate and privy councillor of Edward VI., Mason
was the son of a cowherd of Abingdon. Dr.
Starkey was another of the social circle of
Morison who was not sprung from a noble
house, and rose steadily by his own endeavors
in the service of Wolsey, until he became chaplain of Henry VIII. In that office he preceded

Thomas Paynel, the translator, and as its incumbent he enjoyed a prosperity like that which fell to the lot of his fellows.

Almost all of these men were of a younger generation than Berners, and, in so far as they busied themselves with literature, belonged rather to a scholarly than to the court type. Many of the associates of Morison and Paynel were clerics, like Bishop Tunstall, the scholar, at one time ambassador in Spain and author of a Latin prayer book which Paynel put into English ; or like Dr. Thirlby, who had served Henry VIII. in the same country with Edmund Boner in 1542. Paynel himself was a priest. But the group was not essentially religious. It felt the influences that were generally abroad in England drawing attention to Spain, — those operative at court, or among ambassadors and diplomatic agents, and those which went out from the University of Oxford. Morison, Paynel, and many of their friends had been students at Oxford during the term of Vives' professorship. There was an element in their character to render them susceptible to the influence radiating from the university. The seriousness, if not consistency, of spirit that they possessed in common with Sir Thomas More is proof of qualities of mind far more akin to the earnestness of the scholar Vives than to the platitudes of Guevara, who in his own country was first hailed as a great historian, and then openly exposed as a mere impostor.

Sir Richard Morison was the most prominent of the English translators of Luis Vives. He was sent to Oxford University, where he took the degree of B.A. in 1528. He then entered the household of Wolsey, who at that time had already begun to totter to his fall, but the disgrace and death of the Cardinal soon threw his dependants out of service, and left them free to follow their own inclinations. Morison had always shown a fondness for study, and after some minor work at court with the pen, in 1535 he proceeded to Italy, where he wished to make himself master of Greek. It was during his sojourn in Italy that, like Dr. Starkey, he was befriended by Reginald Pole and Michael Throckmorton, a double traitor, who with Pole was the most offensive of the enemies of Henry VIII. But by the beginning of his residence abroad, Morison had become known to Crom-

well as well as to others enjoying the favor of
the king. Association with persons in such
good standing more than counterbalanced the
seditious teachings of Pole, and the purely literary labor that he undertook after his return
from Italy was paralleled by the composition of
tracts by which he supported the royal cause.
It was in 1540 that Morison's *Introduction to
wysdome*, translated from the Latin of Vives,
was published. This book, the only one for
which he had recourse to that author, he dedicated to Gregory Cromwell, and reissued in
1544.

The rest of Morison's career is chiefly of interest to the political historian. His brief season of prosperity was now at hand, and he
promptly surrendered literature for more remunerative employments. As a pronounced Calvinist and zealous supporter of the Duke of
Northumberland, Morison rapidly advanced his
fortunes until he was appointed ambassador to
Charles V. in Germany. He at once went into
retirement on the continent upon the death of
Edward VI., in company with Cheke and
Peter Martyr Vermilius, who had been his
protégé, and died at Strasburg in 1556.

Because of the public character of the occupations of Morison's later years, the main facts of his life are better known than those of the lives of the other translators of Luis Vives. Richard Hyrde, whose *Instructiō of a Christen womā* was published in 1540, and again in 1541, 1557, and 1592, is only a name. Hyrde dedicated his book to Queen Katherine, and as Vives' original Latin was printed in 1523, it was possible that Hyrde was a person connected in some way with the retinue of the queen. It is plain from the dedication, of course, that the *Instructiō of a Christen womā* was completed before the year of Katherine's death at Kimbolton; but as the loyalty of the queen's adherents to the king did not always master their affection for her, nor prevent them from inviting her patronage after the crown had been transferred to the head of Anne Boleyn, no precise date anterior to 1536 can be fixed for the translation. Only one Richard Hyrde, whose station is commensurate with that attributable to the translator, appears in history. This person was a physician in the train of Stephen Gardiner and Edward Foxe on their embassy to the Papal See in 1528. He was a young man, learned in

Greek and Latin as well as medicine, and highly
prized by the ambassadors. When he fell sick
with a cold after fording a river near Orvieto,
they wrote of him to Sir Brian Tuke briefly
as follows : " We suppose ye know him well.
His name is Richard Herde. He was wont
to resort much to me, Steven Gardiner, there,
and sometime dwelled with Master Chancellor of the Duchy [More]." [1] The classical
scholarship of Hyrde, the confidence that Gardiner feels in his being widely known, and
his residence with More, leave little doubt of
the identity of the physician and the translator.
A protégé of More and a scholar, he must
have been familiar with the works of Vives.
The manuscript of the *Instructiō of a Christen
womā* is to be placed about 1528, when the
reputation of the Spaniard was at its height ;
for the cold contracted at Orvieto was fatal,
and Hyrde died on the Lady Day succeeding
the letter of Gardiner.[2]

Thomas Paynel was educated as an Austin
friar at Merton Abbey in Surrey, whence he
graduated to the College of St. Mary the Vir-

[1] *Letters and papers, f. & d., Hen. VIII.*, IV., pt. 2., p. 1809.
[2] *Ibid.*, p. 1812.

gin at Oxford. Wood thinks that he sprang
from a Lincolnshire family. Leaving Oxford,
apparently without a degree, Paynel returned
to Merton, and gave himself up to medical
studies and to literature. A Thomas Paynel
was admitted to Gray's Inn in 1530, but there
is no reason for identifying this person with
the translator. In 1538 Paynel received a
commission to go to the Protestant princes of
Germany, and by 1541 he had been for some
time chaplain to Henry VIII., an office which
Dr. Starkey had previously held. Alexander
Barclay· was his intimate friend, and Sir
Anthony Browne, the lord chamberlain, Lord
Mountjoy, and John de Vere, the father of
Sidney's Oxford, were among those to whom
Paynel dedicated his translations. The nine-
teen books which he published, and which have
been recovered, are not of any one style.
Paynel depended principally upon the Latin for
his material, but men of such different times
and types as Erasmus, St. Bernard, and Dares
Phrygius were englished by his pen. Paynel's
first work appeared in 1528, and in 1550 or
1553 he first touched a Spanish author. At
one of the latter dates he published the *Office*

H

and duetie of an husband, the original of which
he found in the Latin of Vives. By the *Office
and duetie of an husband*, and by his station and
the general character of his other works, Paynel
falls into the group with Morison and Hyrde.
Though sometimes antithetic in individual
traits, there is an affinity between the three
men who belonged, in a broad sense, to the same
walk in life, and who stood in analogous relations with the one scholar who was studied by
them all.

Paynel outlived his colleagues and crossed
the threshold of a new era. In his later years,
under another sovereign, he introduced into
England the Spanish romance of chivalry.
His *Treasurie of Amadis of Fraunce*, printed in
1568, was the first translation of any of the
Amadis family into the English language.
In substance, the *Treasurie of Amadis of
Fraunce* was an essentially Elizabethan publication. The *Amadis* was a popular as well
as a court book, and its freedom from didacti-
cism not improbably made it seem trivial and
unworthy of serious attention to the older
generation of translators. It is, therefore,
best considered with the literature of another

day, for the unabated favor that Paynel enjoyed at court after the decease of Henry VIII.
affected the character of his writings consider-
ably.   He conformed to the changed conditions, although the greater part of his work
was already behind him. It was the *Amadis*
and not the man that was the development
of the new and more fruitful era.   Paynel remained, like the associates of his prime, a
writer of the time of Henry VIII.

It is because Vives did not divest himself
of all traces of his race and country, that his
books and personal history have a meaning
in the study of the influence of Spanish
literature in England. They are records of
the progress of that influence during Vives'
own time, and they were intimations of the
broader stream of Spanish letters which flowed
into the country in the Elizabethan age.   The
principal comment which Vives made upon a
Spanish book, and the most notable exemplification of the fact that he kept in touch with
the readers of the peninsula, was his condemnation of the *Celestina*.   It was in his *De Institutione feminæ christianæ*, published in 1523,
that he inserted one of those chapters which

have since become so common, showing what
books ought to be read and what really ought
not.   Among those books that ought not to be
read, he uncompromisingly named the *Celestina*.
In his later years Vives is said to have re-
tracted his condemnation of the novel; but the
discussion of it at this time indicates that it
was tolerably well known in England at the
beginning of the third decade of the sixteenth
century.   Since denunciation of books on moral
grounds has so usually been followed by an
increase in their vogue, it is not impossible
that Rastell's attention was drawn to the
Celestina through Vives.   If the interlude that
Rastell printed and the criticism of Vives have
no direct connection, they both still retain
a value as indications of a general interest in
the book.

The works of Vives facilitated and prepared
the way for the labors of the Elizabethan translators at large.   Vives' career has an extra-
personal import.   He was the pioneer of the
Spanish teachers, Catholic and Protestant, who
appeared after the alliance of Philip and Mary
at the English universities, either in the interest of their country and its faith, or to mature

in safety plans for their subversion ; he taught
the Anglo-Saxon to respect Spanish scholarship. This was the distinctive service of Vives
and his translators. They established beyond
cavil the position of the peninsular scholars in
sixteenth-century England. Ascham and Haddon subsequently paid to Osorio da Fonseca
the deference Morison and Paynel had paid to
the friend of Erasmus and Budæus. Oxford
and Cambridge received his countrymen in
later years much as they had received him.
Vives paved the way for his successors. Some
of the scholars who came after him were less
cosmopolitan than he, and by the books they
wrote and the influence they exerted encouraged the study of their language openly and
efficiently under the sceptre of Elizabeth, as he
in his time had not cared to do. The popularity of Vives, indeed, lasted into the day of
Mary, through the reign of Edward VI., when
translation of Spanish books had almost totally
ceased. During this period Spain seemed to
have been blotted from the map and forgotten.
When Charles V. sailed from Barcelona on the
first of May 1543, to begin his long campaign
against German heresy, the country was reduced

to the position of a province, and became a cipher in politics. The English ambassadors were commissioned to the emperor in Germany or Flanders. The imperial representatives at London were with one exception either Flemings or Burgundians, and the chief among them, Eustace Chapuis, was not unprobably unfamiliar with Spanish.[1] The presence of companies of Spanish mercenaries in London from the peace of Crespi until the death of Edward VI. was of no significance to literature. Despite of the bravery that they showed in Scotland and in suppressing Kett's rebellion, the soldiers were rude, and not the class to read. The England of Edward VI. knew the peninsula only through the Spaniards whom its ambassadors met in Germany, following the court of Charles V., and through the translators of the reign of Henry VIII. The books which had pleased continued to be liked, but there was no step in advance.[2] The *Golden Boke* was often re-

[1] *State papers*, *Sp.*, *Hen. VIII.*, IV., pt. 2, p. xxvii.

[2] "Notwithstanding the Spanish blood in Mary's veins, the higher circles of Spain and England had personally almost as little intercourse with one another at that period, as England and Japan have at the present." Prescott, *Philip II.*, I., p. 120.

printed after the death of Berners, Bryan's work appeared, Vives was in demand, but the activity which found expression in them proceeded no further. It was that of the press, not that of the authors themselves.

CHAPTER IV

FROM MARY TO ELIZABETH

I

SPAIN resumed her accustomed importance in the eyes of the English people when Prince Philip landed at Southampton in July 1554. Immediately upon the ratification of the marriage treaty the Earl of Bedford and Lord Fitzwalter had been despatched to Coruña with twenty gentlemen to meet their future king; Lord Dudley and the Earl of Worcester also had set out for Laredo, and shortly afterward Sir Thomas Gresham had been commissioned to raise a loan in Spain, where the new alliance was extremely popular. In England the flower of the nobility frequented the court. Pembroke, Arundel, Derby, Cobham, North, Bedford, Worcester, Surrey, Darcy, Winchester, Willoughby, Fitzwalter, Talbot, were constantly at Philip's side. They mingled daily with Alba, the fa-

vorite Ruy Gomez, the Conde Feria, Olivares,
Padilla, Egmont, Horn, Medina-Celi, the Marquis of Pescara, and many of the most famous
grandees of Castile and Aragon.   The higher
circles of the two nations came into immediate
and constant contact.   The polite bearing of
the strangers, and the considerate behavior of
the prince, made a firm and lasting impression.
Philip, in spite of his nationality, seems to have
aroused no aversions, thanks partly to his good
qualities, no doubt, partly perhaps to the liber-
ality he displayed toward the royal household
and persons in authority in the distribution of
bounties and pensions.

The marriage of Philip and Mary was a preliminary step in the attempt to denationalize the
English nobility.   The common people were
ignored by the Spaniards.   Commercially, the
relations of the states remained unaltered; the
new movement confined itself to the court.   The
effect of the alliance on the populace was violent alarm and deep disgust.   When Egmont
arrived in London to proffer the hand of Philip,
he was snowballed by the boys in the streets.
Within a few months after the ceremony at
Winchester, relatively a very small number of

Spaniards remained in England; yet át that time it was reported that "ther was so many Spanyerds in London that a man should have mett in the streets for one Inglishman above iiii Spanyerds to the great discomfort of the Inglishe nation."[1]   There was also "talke of XII. thousand Spanyerds coming more into this realm, they said to fetch the crowne."[2]   The people were on the verge of a panic.   Undazzled by favors and unsuborned by bribes, they perceived acutely the danger that threatened them.   The effect of the invasion was to draw their attention to the peninsula.   Spain, after having been swallowed up in the sea of imperial interests for so many years, had become again to Englishmen a very present reality.

The universities were not neglected by the Spaniards in the peaceful invasion of England. They were too important factors in moulding the opinions of the governing class to be ignored or forgotten.   Pedro de Soto, confessor of the Emperor Charles V., and Juan de Villa García were installed at Oxford to counteract the heretical

---

[1] Hume, *Year after the Armada*, p. 171, quoting *Chronicle of Queen Mary*, Harleian Ms.

[2] *Ibid.*, p. 172.

teachings of Peter Martyr and other Protestant scholars who had been invited to the university by Cranmer during the preceding reign.[1] Other friars frequented London. The court listened to Bartólomé de Miranda, at Kingston-on-Thames, and to Alfonso á Castro, Philip's confessor at Westminster. Tolerance and moderation were politicly enjoined upon all these prelates and teachers, and these qualities were conspicuous in the demeanor of Philip himself. Hence, intercourse between the Spaniards and the English became comparatively easy. The Conde Feria secretly wedded Jane Dormer, a maid of honor to the queen, and Pembroke, Sir Henry Sidney, and other nobles were closely drawn to the king. The division of the nation on religious grounds tended to strengthen these ties when they were once formed. The antipathy of Philip to the Reformed doctrines, however gracious and lenient he might appear for a time, was well understood. In the prospect of his regency, or the apprehended contingency of the succession of Elizabeth, the position of Philip as the most powerful monarch in the world, and as a good Catholic, procured him a party in Eng-

[1] Wood, *Athenæ*, I., p. 332.

land much more readily than the pretensions that he advanced as the heir of John of Gaunt. He became a factor in English politics, and his influence was perpetuated at court.

Upon the accession of Elizabeth the social relations of England and Spain underwent a radical change. While Mary lived, Philip and a few followers essayed to obtain peaceful control of the machinery of government through personal contact with the rulers of the state. Under her successor he retained his party, but he was obliged to use every means in his power, patrician or plebeian, in the endeavor to establish his supremacy. These Elizabeth and Burghley were constrained to combat by measures which contributed incidentally to increase the familiarity of the country with the peninsula. Ambassadors resided at London and Madrid, commercial agents of both sovereigns watched the progress of affairs at the rival courts; political and religious refugees were welcomed and harbored in England, Spain, and the Low Countries. Peninsular influences, instead of being fostered as before at London by the presence of Philip only, were stimulated and accentuated by direct, frequent, and varied communication with Lisbon and the principal cities of Castile.

The Spanish embassy in London was a centre of sedition from its reorganization in 1559 until the summary expulsion of Bernardino de Mendoza and the closing of its doors in 1584. Throughout the reign the joint plotting of the Catholics and the ambassadors was so ardent and unremitting that it attracted the attention of the government, though it was not always considered prudent to take cognizance of its progress. During the residence of Alvaro de la Quadra, bishop of Aquila in London, Durham Place, the house of the ambassador, became a hive of conspiracy. Special correspondents all over England, and even in Scotland, kept the Spaniards informed of the affairs of the realm; secret negotiations were carried on with the disaffected Catholics throughout the kingdoms; and many of the nobility found their way to the ambassador on errands of dark and questionable import. Lord Paget joined the Spanish faction in the retirement of Durham Place, accessible with little risk of detection by a water-gate opening upon the

Thames; Arundel, Lumley, Montague, and
Winchester, with Arthur Pole, Lethington,
Shan O'Neil, the Irish malcontent, Sir Henry
and Lady Sidney and others, conspired against
the state. Time and again Bishop Ross,
Maitland, and Lord Montague interceded with
De Silva and De Spes in the behalf of Mary
Stuart after her imprisonment, plotting now
for her marriage with Don Cárlos, the mad
son of Philip, or counting, as events proved
without their host, upon uniting her with
the brilliant and rash Don Juan de Austria.
Through Don Guerau de Spes the promoters
of the Earls' Rebellion received encouragement if not open support. Montague and
Southampton, Northumberland, Westmoreland, Dacres, and Norfolk inclined toward
Spain to secure aid for their arms; and some
of them, made bold by the hope of succor,
opened direct communication with the Duke
of Alba in Flanders. Henry Howard and Sir
James Crofts were bought by bribes and pensions to become spies in the service of Philip,
and thus the information which could no
longer be had otherwise by an enemy, was carried by treason from court.

Portugal, although she had never established a permanent embassy at London, was forced by the development of her colonial trade to despatch frequently agents and special emissaries to the court of Elizabeth. The intimate relations which the Portuguese maintained with Spain often led to the partial dependence of their emissaries upon those of the sister state. Thus it came about that at times the agents of Portugal were secretly drawn into the pay of Philip, and induced to become instruments for furthering his purposes, reënforcing the Spanish residents in extending the propaganda of Spain. These men grew to know persons in a lower walk of life than that in which the ambassadors moved. They worked in commercial pursuits among the people. Antonio de Guaras and Antonio de Fogaza, officially or unofficially, during the intervals of the activity of the regular ambassadors, rendered valuable assistance to the plans of the king. The principal members of the Spanish colony in England, such as Dr. Rodrigo Lopez, the Portuguese physician, sometime agent of Dom Antonio, the rival claimant of Philip to the Portuguese throne, or such as the Jorges, gained much in

influence because of the power for mischief
which they possessed. Socially, but not politically, their work was strengthened by their
countrymen who found their way to England
as refugees from Spanish tribunals. Heretical
and rebellious exiles were welcomed in both
commercial and court circles and at the universities. A Spanish Protestant church flourished in spite of the remonstrances of De
Quadra in London; chairs at Oxford were
offered to and accepted by Castilian Reformers.
Dom Antonio, the Portuguese pretender, and
Antonio Perez, the fugitive diplomat, received
encouragement at court. Spanish influences,
being embodied so variously, penetrated the
different strata of society.

The number of foreigners in England was
small and inconsequential when compared to
that of the Englishmen who dwelt on the continent. The English had long gone to Italy to
learn her ways, but hitherto Spain had come to
them. In the reign of Elizabeth for the first
time there was reciprocal exchange with the
latter country, and for the first time also the
intercourse was followed by other than political
effects. Court and country were permeated

with its influence.   Fugitive Catholics filled the
towns of Holland and Flanders, where they
lived on pensions from Philip, plotting against
the queen.   To the Lowlands the northern earls
fled after the collapse of their rebellion in 1569,
and there the vast majority of political and
religious exiles found an asylum.   The Jesuitical college at Douay was established by Dr.
William Allen in 1568, and the education of
priests for the English mission begun.   The
English refugees in Spain, the particular care
of the Duchess of Feria, were not less seditious,
and maintained unbroken communications with
friends at home.   Their influence both at London and Madrid was by far more considerable
than that of the embassy which Elizabeth supported at the Spanish capital, and which was only
maintained for eight years, while the presence
of the refugees in the city was continued.   Their
abundant energy sometimes impelled them to
act with the official representatives of the queen,
or to join with the English merchants resident
in the peninsula for the pursuit of certain ends.
It made them in these ways a vital force at
home.   The ambassadors, in frequent intercourse
with Burghley but isolated in an inimical land,

I

the refugees, welcomed at the court of Philip though alienated from the friends at home, and the English merchants, committed now to the support of the country of their birth, and now to that of their adoption, allied by business and by family ties to both, and indispensable to their countrymen in Spain whatever their station, formed a combination of great power and efficiency for the transmission and dissemination of knowledge. This organization was the distinctive creation of the England of Elizabeth, and brought into the country the first extensive information of the peninsula that was gathered by the English themselves.

II

The coming of Philip to England immediately affected the production of books. There was a general anxiety to form an estimate of the invaders, and pamphlets like the *Nature of Spaniardes*, containing an exposure of the perfidy of the race, were published in response to this demand. At the court, too, curiosity about the newcomers was aroused, though in a more polite and dignified way. What was this nation that had allied itself with England ? what were its interests ? and what had it accomplished ? A disposition to explore the history of the country manifested itself, and the story of Spanish America appeared in English for the first time. The literature which was fashionable among the Castilian nobles attracted attention. *Amadis of Gaul* was translated and the cult of Guevara revived. The new alliance between the kingdoms increased the credit of peninsular learning in London. The bonds, however feeble, that had existed between English and Spanish scholars in the cities of Germany were again strengthened and drawn close. The popularity of the *Golden Boke*, which had continued without begetting any concern for other works of similar origin, received a fresh impetus, and the readers of Vives became familiar with his successors.

Translation in the Marian period, therefore, is the result of the study of the best-known Spanish works, under the influence or through the suggestion of the train of the royal consort. In politics the period terminated abruptly with the refusal of Elizabeth to accept the hand of the King of Spain, but in literature it was of much longer duration, and loses itself insensibly in the on-coming Elizabethan age. The transition was accomplished when the ambassadors and travellers, returning home, substituted their impressions of Spain, the topics that they cared about and the books that they read, for those that had previously commanded attention in London, from whatever sources they were derived. This was a process involving a lapse of time, but it was necessary to an adequate knowledge of Spain. It implied thenceforth a predominance of translation of Spanish books from the original tongue, and sealed the doom of French as the principal medium of translation.

The first English rendering of the *Amadis* by Thomas Paynel, and the translations by Richard Eden and Sir Thomas North, are the obvious products of the early or Marian influences. The work of Paynel and North was purely literary in its character. It was stimulated and in some measure inspired by the Spanish alliance. This is beyond question because the most popular Spanish books of the time were not only translated by these men, but no Spanish book of any sort had been done

into English in the interval between the death
of Sir Francis Bryan and the landing of Philip
at Southampton.   Paynel, in bestowing his
attention upon the *Amadis*, was acting under
the influence of the latter event.   His patron,
Sir Anthony Browne, served Philip as equerry.
The seemingly frivolous nature of the romance
was forgotten under the spell of the presence of
the Spaniards.   The *Amadis* was at the height of
its fame just before the abdication of Charles V.
Since its appearance at Salamanca in 1508, it
had been imitated at home and in France and
Italy, and the popularity which it had achieved,
and that of its successors, was so great that
Charles V. had, in the interest of industry, pro-
hibited the introduction of romances into the
colonies.   It was the favorite reading both of
the people and the court.   The nobles who followed Philip into England amused themselves
with attempting to identify the scenes of the
various exploits of Amadis through the country.
They visited Windsor, one of the haunts of
Amadis, and London, where King Lisuarte had
held his court.   At Winchester they inspected
Arthur's round table, and in their infatuation
with the novel they forgot themselves and drew

impolite comparisons everywhere between the
English ladies and the damsels of the romance.

Paynel's *Treasurie of Amadis of Fraunce* was
published at London in 1568, some years after
the activity of the translator had ceased.   The
book was taken from the *Thresor de tous les livres
d'Amadis de Gaule*, which appeared at Antwerp in 1560.   The date of the English translation is probably not much later; it is unlikely
that the work was undertaken so long after the
retirement, or according to some authorities
the death, of Paynel, as the year 1568, when
the incentive to translation was less powerful
than at the accession of Elizabeth.   Paynel's
version made little impression, and was not
reissued.   The reason lies in the fact that, as
the romances were already beginning to lose
prestige in Spain, and to be replaced by a more
artificial style of writing, it was too late to
attempt to transport them in full vigor to
foreign soil.   Paynel, apart from his translation of *Amadis*, must be thought of as belonging to the pre-Elizabethan epoch.

Sir Thomas North, though too young to be a
contemporary of the earlier writers, continued
the Guevara tradition which they had estab-

lished.   North was born but a short time
previous to the death of Lord Berners in 1533,
and is believed to have completed his education
as late as 1557 at Peterhouse, Cambridge, for
in that year, at the age of twenty-two or three,
he enrolled himself as a student at Lincoln's
Inn.   It was in 1557 also that he published
the *Diall of princes*, an English rendering of
the French version of Guevara's amplification
of the *Libro áureo*, called the *Relox de príncipes*.
In this work North made his first appearance
in literature, and not long after he determined
to devote himself entirely to letters.   In his
retirement in Cambridgeshire, where he passed
the greater part of his life, far removed from
the ostentatious rivalries of courtiers and poli-
ticians, he produced the works that made him
famous.   There he revised the *Diall of princes*,
and there he soon achieved at least a local
reputation.   The freedom of the town of Cambridge was proffered him in 1568.   Six years
later, when he was at the height of his career,
he came out of his rural home temporarily, and
accompanied his elder brother Roger, Lord
North, to France, but without remitting his literary labors.   The *Morall Philosophie of Doni*,

translated from the Italian, was published in 1570, and during the last year of the decade his celebrated *Plutarch* was issued, with a dedication to Queen Elizabeth. The *Morall Philosophie* is noteworthy since it is the first collection of the cycle of Bidpai fables in English; his *Plutarch* is still held in repute, though now superseded by more modern renderings. The success of these books did not, however, coax North from his retirement into the competition of public life. At the time of the appearance of the *Plutarch*, the Earl of Leicester recommended him to Lord Burghley; but the outcome of Leicester's endeavors on North's behalf is not known. The connection of the translator with the favorite of the queen was not close enough to be of great moment, for he continued to reside with his family in Cambridgeshire as before. North took no further active part in literature, and he seldom diversified the monotony of his occupations by the performance of any public duties. With the exception of the crucial year of Elizabeth's reign, when he assumed command of a local detachment raised to resist the Armada, he remained in seclusion until his death, which occurred, it is believed, in 1601.

North continued the tradition of Lord Berners and Sir Francis Bryan in the *Diall of princes*. This enlargement of the *Libro áureo*, the parent of the *Golden Boke*, was taken from the French as Berners' work had been. It appeared at the zenith of the fame of the latter, when several editions of the *Golden Boke* were issued from the press within a short time. One appeared in the year of the publication of the *Diall of princes*, another but three years previously. The class of readers to which the earlier and the later versions appealed was, of course, the same, but it was no longer such a restricted one as it had been when Berners wrote. Bryan, the Carews, and a few families connected with Spain had given impetus to the interest in the Guevara literature, which now circulated about the country instead of being confined to a clique. The presence of the Spaniards at court reproduced on a larger scale the incidents of the coming of Katherine, and renewed the popularity of the authors who had been exploited by the admirers of Guevara. North was still at college at the time of the marriage of Philip and Mary, and he undoubtedly was not oblivious of the political and social significance of that event, for he

dedicated the *Diall* to the queen. His father,
Edward, Lord North, waited upon Philip at
Winchester. The current in which the translator was moving was that which had descended
from Berners and Bryan, reënforced and in a
new environment. The fact that the *Diall* was
borrowed from the French is a sign that North's
task was suggested by the presence of the Spaniards rather than performed under their eyes.
When a second edition of his work was demanded in 1568, North showed that he had been
sensible of the forces which had begun to act
since the printing of the first edition. The first
edition had been made from the French, although
it is said to have been corrected from the original; but in 1568 North added a translation of
Guevara's *Aviso de privados y doctrina de cor-
tesanos* to the *Diall*, as a fourth book, taking the
new part directly from the Spanish, in conformity with the general practice of the Elizabethan
translators. More than one reason indubitably
led North to make this change, — convenience,
for example, or a greater facility in Spanish than
he had formerly possessed; but the significant
fact is that the original Spanish was to be had.
A new era had been inaugurated. The *Diall of*

princes accordingly illustrates the persistence of the tradition of the earliest translators from Castilian, but, through the circumstances attending upon its publication, it discloses the phenomena of another epoch.

Richard Eden was, during his lifetime, one of the most celebrated translators from the Spanish, and won great esteem for his scholarship and knowledge of science. His pen was among the first affected by the alliance of Mary's reign. Eden was born about the year 1521, and received his education at Cambridge under Sir Thomas Smith. He subsequently was employed in the treasury and by Burghley, then Sir William Cecil, and when Philip came to England was appointed to a position in the English treasury of the Prince of Spain. In the next year he published his *Decades of the newe worlde*,[1] a compilation from the works of Peter Martyr Anglerius, Oviedo y Valdés, Lopez de Gómara, and several of the Italian chroniclers of Ameri-

[1] Richard Willes reprinted portions of this work in the volume entitled the *History of Trauayle in the West and East Indies*, London, 1577. This book, which appeared in the year after Eden's death, comprised several works by Eden, "Newly set in order, augmented, and finished by Richarde Willes."

can discovery, the idea of which came to him
during the ceremonies attendant upon the
entrance of the royal pair into London. It is
upon this book, the first in which he drew upon
Spanish sources, that his reputation now rests.
It is still one of the principal authorities on the
settlement of the new world. The publication
of the *Decades*, however, involved Eden in
trouble with Bishop Gardiner, and he was deprived of the office which he had obtained
through the favor of Spaniards, among them,
perhaps, the historian Augustin de Zárate,[1] on
the charge of heresy. He entered the service
of Jean de Ferrières in 1562, and travelled in
his train to France and Germany. Three years
later he was at Lafferta in Spain, and spent the
greater part of the rest of his life in Paris and
London. He does not seem to have been very
highly thought of at court, for his efforts to
obtain recognition from Elizabeth were futile.
It was said of him in France that he was more
celestial than terrestrial.

In 1561 Eden translated Martin Cortés' *Arte
de navigar*. This was the first treatise by
a Spanish author upon a nautical subject to

[1] Arber, *First three English Books on America*, p. xxxix.

appear in England, and in spite of rivalry it
held the first place through the century. The
treatises of Guevara and Pedro de Medina
upon the art of navigation increased rather than
diminished the demand for it when they were
issued in English. Third and fourth editions
appeared in 1596 and 1609, with corrections
by John Tapp. Eden was the true predecessor
of Hakluyt and the ambitious traders with
Spain. Writing at an earlier period and amid
more scholarly surroundings than many of
his successors, he nevertheless shared some of
their acquaintances. The nature of his works,
nearly all of which related to travel, recommended Eden to the London merchants and
sea captains. He dedicated books to Sir William Garrard and Sir Thomas Lodge, the father
of the poet, both prominent ship-owners, and
to Sir William Winter, a man of much experience upon the sea, and a master of the
Spanish tongue. His death occurred in 1576,
just as the tide of translation by the merchants
from Spanish chronicles was about to set in;
but he had nevertheless travelled extensively
and come to feel, if not to express by his
translations from Castilian, the conditions of

the Elizabethan age. He was more familiar
with foreign countries than many of his successors of that epoch. He obtained the incentive
for his *Decades* and his *Arte of nauigation* before the beginning of his travels, and not from
Spain directly, but from the Spanish invasion of
England. In this respect Eden differed from
the Elizabethan writers on these subjects, who
most of them gathered their material in the
peninsula. With Wilkinson[1] he summed up the
historical side of the Marian epoch in essaying
to inform Philip's new subjects of the achievements of the old. The period in letters, however, as in politics, was merely one of prepara-
tion for that which was to ensue.

III

The presence of the Spaniards in England
practically recreated the interest in the peninsular vernacular literature. The study of

[1] John Wilkinson translated the *Comentario de la guerra
de Alemania* of Luis de Avila y Zúñiga, the chronicler of
Charles V. The book, which describes the campaigns of the
emperor during 1546–1547, appeared in Antwerp in 1548. It
was published in Italian by the author in the same year, in
French in 1550, and in English in 1555.

Spanish authors who wrote in the Latin tongue, however, had never been interrupted, and stood in need of no rehabilitation. In Germany at the court of Charles V., English scholars, Walter Haddon most notably, and Roger Ascham, had kept in touch with the productions of the Latin religious writers of Spain and Portugal. The esteem in which Vives was held suffered no abatement until after Elizabeth had ascended the throne. As his reputation began to wane, his place was insensibly filled by his compatriots, and the continuity of the study of peninsular scholarship remained unbroken. The Spanish marriage strengthened and amplified relations that already existed. The sermons which were preached by the friars in the train of the king during his sojourn in the country attracted some attention of an ephemeral nature. The treatises of Osorio da Fonseca, however, which attained a name in the latter half of the sixteenth century as great as that of those of Vives in the earlier half, were read with much deference in England. The facility of Osorio's style blinded his contemporaries to the inferior quality of his thought, and made him the leading representative of peninsular scholarship in

the eyes of Europe.   It was chiefly as such that
he was known in London.

Radically new elements did not appear in the
province of theology, therefore, in the reign of
Mary as a result of the alliance with Prince
Philip.   Former conditions continued to exist.
It was the breach of the alliance and the relapse
of England into heresy that stimulated theological writers and threw them into contention.
Forces that had been in seeming harmony then
engaged in acrimonious debate and ranged on
opposing sides Catholics and Protestants drawn
from many ranks of society, and known to each
other only through their doctrinal differences.
But the controversy was slow in assuming its
final form.   The tradition which had been inaugurated in the time of Henry VIII. persisted
and long ·retained first place in the religious
field through the influence of Vives and Osorio,
which, unlike that of their successors, was based
upon non-partisan grounds.   In religion, as
in literature, the movement that was distinctive
in the Elizabethan age scarcely appeared until
the last quarter of the century.

In 1563 Jeronymo Osorio da Fonseca published at Paris and Louvain his *Epistolæ ad*

Elizabetham Angliæ reginam de religione, in which he urged the queen to abjure her heresies and return to the fold of the Catholic Church. The reputation of Osorio, who was then at the height of his powers, led the English government to deem the epistles worthy of an answer. Accordingly Dr. Walter Haddon was selected to draw up a refutation of the arguments of the Portuguese. Haddon set about his task with such expedition that before the expiration of the year, the *Epistola apologetica ad Hier. Osorium* was printed and sold at Paris. From this city the book found its way more speedily into continental book marts than it could have done from London. The controversy soon attracted wide notice. Two years later translations of the epistles of Osorio and the refutation by Haddon were made public by Richard Shacklock and Abraham Hartwell, respectively. In 1567 Osorio, who had been recently created bishop of Silves, replied to Dr. Haddon in a treatise entitled *In Gualterum Haddonum libellorum supplicum apud Helizabetham Angliæ reginam, de religione libri tres;* this was translated by John Fenne, and appeared in English during the next year. Haddon again took up the dis-

K

pute, and commenced a rejoinder which was still unfinished at his death, which occurred in 1572; but John Foxe, the martyrologist, continued the work, building upon the foundations which had already been laid, and published it complete in 1577. A version in the vernacular was printed from the manuscript of James Bell in 1581. The contention was finally closed after the lapse of two additional years by the publication of Foxe's *De Christo gratia iustificanti, contra Osoriam iustitiam*, of which there is an English translation bearing the date 1598. At Antwerp, evidently in the preliminary stages of the controversy, a satire had been printed in Latin verse, representing Osorio seated in triumph upon a car drawn by Haddon, Martin Bucer, and Peter Martyr Vermilius, and a reply to Haddon had been composed by Manoel d'Almada, a Portuguese in the train of Margaret of Parma; but at the end Foxe had everything his own way, besides the decided advantage of the last word, as Osorio had already been dead three years at the time of the appearance of the *De Christo*.

The great respect with which Osorio was regarded in England before usage had cheapened his name, is amply shown by the duration of the controversy precipitated by his epistles. Thirty-five years elapsed before the discussion that they raised fully subsided. They excited the curiosity of nations which they did not properly concern, and penetrated not only the confines of religious circles, but those of the upper sphere of society generally. The name of Osorio was known in England both because of his classical attainments, in which he surpassed his fellow-countrymen, and because of his interference in statecraft. The esteem which King Sebastian of Portugal cherished for the bishop would not permit him to pass his life in exclusive devotion to the duties of his see. The talents and learning which had procured Osorio fame abroad in letters, made him valuable to the court at Lisbon. Employed in its service, his style grew to be familiar to the English diplomats and also to the queen. Elizabeth professed an acquaintance with it at the presentation of Dom Francisco Pereira, the Portuguese ambassador, by Guzman de Silva, on April 14, 1568. "After the ambassador had waited for about an hour," De Silva wrote to Philip II., describing incidentally the queen's attitude toward the bishop, "he was introduced to the queen's chamber, where she received him, and after a few words from him in the king's name, the queen, with an angry look, complained greatly of the Cardinal [afterward King Henry of Portugal], who, she said, had written her a letter by an ambassador sent by her to the king containing discourteous expressions which were unfit to be addressed to her. She turned to me and said she wished I could see the letter and I should agree with her that it had been written by the Bishop of Osorio, whose style she recognized from having read certain writings of his about religion, which had been answered by a servant of hers, named Dr. Haddon, to whom the Bishop had again replied."[1]

Osorio, moreover, was personally acquainted in England. He carried on a correspondence with a warm friend of Haddon, Roger Ascham, who was at that time acting in the capacity of secretary to Elizabeth. Ascham's official connection with Morison during that gentleman's embassy to Charles V. in Germany had pre-

---

[1] De Silva to Philip II., April 19, 1568, *State papers*, *Sp.*, *Eliz.*, II., p. 24. Bacon condemned Osorio's style as "weak and waterish." See *Retrospective Rev.*, I., 322 *et seq.*

sented him with abundant opportunities for intercourse with the Spaniards who composed the train of that monarch, and these were supplemented during Philip's stay in England by others not less plentiful which fell to the lot of the secretary of the queen. Consequently, Ascham formed a friendship with Gonzalo Perez,[1] the secretary of Philip, and translator of Homer's Odyssey into Castilian; and through these or similar channels he became known to the Portuguese scholar.[2] In a letter assigned to October 1561, Osorio addresses Ascham in a purely personal vein, from which it is evident that an exchange of letters had been for some time taking place between them. After assuring his friend of the pain which the news of his illness, brought by Dr. Thomas Wilson, the queen's special ambassador and a friend of Parker and Haddon, had caused him, the Bishop of Silves

[1] Ascham, *Works*, II., p. 108. Gonzalo was the father of Antonio Perez, subsequently a fugitive in England and France.

[2] Where, if at all, Ascham and Osorio met, is uncertain. The latter spent all his life in his native country, after having completed his education at Salamanca, Paris, and Bologna, for the duties of a professor at Coimbra or an ecclesiastic of Evora or Silves, were purely of a domestic character.

concludes with the words: "Wilsonus tibi librum dabit, quo Gualteri Haddoni laudes persequor, ut possum. Gratissimum mihi feceris, si librum diligenter evolveris."[1] This is proof of the mutual interest which was manifested by the English Reformers and the Portuguese scholar in each other's works. Ascham and Osorio were in the habit of exchanging their writings, and sometimes of comparing their plans for the future. In a letter dated in December 1561, Osorio actually broached his scheme of writing the epistles which caused so much annoyance to Elizabeth. Manoel d'Aranjo, the ambassador, who was a relative of the bishop's, had just brought assurances from London of the good-will of Ascham. Having acknowledged, in an elaborate periphrase, the compliments paid to him, Osorio said: "In quo autem principes vestræ ingenium et eruditionem extulisti animum mihi addidisti, ut eam, quod jam antea facere cogitabam, libentius per literas salutarem, et quam essem studio illius incensus, multis verbis ostenderem. Nec enim dubito quum illa ex natura et studio humanitatis et clementiæ laudem assequuta sit, quin literas

[1] Osorio to Ascham ; Ascham, *Works*, II., p. 50.

meas benigne et clementer excipiat." [1] It is
clear, therefore, that as early as 1561 the bishop
had resolved to write an epistle to Elizabeth,
and that Ascham had, perhaps unwittingly,
encouraged him in his resolution.

The preëminence of Dr. Haddon as a classical
scholar, together with the high regard in which
he was held by Queen Elizabeth, led to his
being selected as the champion of the cause
of the Anglican Church against the advocates
of Rome. Haddon's training and accomplishments marked him as the legitimate successor
of Cuthbert Tunstall and the scholars of the
preceding generation. He had received his
preliminary education at Eton, where Richard
Cox was his master, and graduated thence into
King's College, Cambridge. Here he attended
the Greek lectures of Sir Thomas Smith, who
afterward supervised for him the publication of
the answer to Osorio at Paris. Having taken
his M.A. in 1541, Haddon read lectures on civil
law for two or three years at Cambridge with
approval, and during the reign of Edward VI.
he rose to a doctorate, becoming vice-chancellor
of the university. Matthew Parker, subse-

[1] Osorio to Ascham; Ascham, *Works*, II., p. 54.

quently archbishop of Canterbury, but then
master of Benet College, Martin Bucer, Sir
John Cheke, and Peter Martyr, were all numbered among his university friends. To the
list of his familiars, Roger Ascham, Sir Thomas
Challoner, and Edmund Grindal, bishop of London, must also be added. For Haddon was one
of the elect of learning. In 1552 his acquirements had won for him at Oxford the presi-
dency of Magdalen College. The Latin ora-
tions, epistles, and poems which flowed from
his pen were held in great repute, although the
reactionary measures of the council of Mary
halted his career and recommended the temporary observation of discreet silence as his
best policy. With the restoration of Protestantism under Elizabeth, Haddon's credit immediately revived. He rapidly acquired favor
at court, where he remained a noteworthy
figure until his death; he served several times
as member of parliament, and acted as master
of requests to the queen. He also accompanied
Dr. Nicholas Wotton and Lord Montacute to
Flanders, assisting in their mission, the object
of which was to revive commerce between England and the Low Countries. On occasion,

these honors were confirmed and emphasized by the express approbation of the queen. Once, when a comparison between him and the scholar George Buchanan had been suggested in her presence, Elizabeth spoke of Haddon in superlative terms, saying, " Buchananum omnibus antepono, Haddonum nemini postpono," — a gracious compliment to them both.[1]

The task of finishing the rather violent apology directed to Osorio, which was left incomplete upon Haddon's death, fell to John Foxe. The martyrologist had shared many of the friendships of Haddon, and had attached himself even more firmly to the Protestant faith. Latimer and Tindal, Cox, Cheke, Martyr, and Grindal were among those whose society he had been privileged to share either in England, or during the exile of the Protestants in the continental cities. Already his vast compilation, the *Acts and monuments*, had made him famous; it had established beyond doubt his position as one of the foremost supporters of the Reformed Church, in spite of the strange inappropriateness of its dedication addressed to Thomas Howard, the rebellious duke of Nor-

[1] Lowndes, *Manual*, II., p. 967.

folk, and a pronounced Catholic. Foxe, however, in inscribing his book to Norfolk, acted merely in remembrance and acknowledgment of the long-continued patronage which had been extended to him. He had been the much respected teacher of the duke, and, in after years, putting aside all differences of creed, Foxe always maintained sympathetic relations with his former pupil. Like all the persons who ranged themselves with Haddon in the controversy against Osorio, Foxe felt an antipathy in every fibre of his being to everything for which it was the policy of Spain to stand. Politically this was true; nothing could have been more distasteful to the spirit of the man than the plotting and caballing by which Norfolk, enmeshed in his ambitious designs, so closely bound himself to Philip II. It was also true in literature; for Foxe was far from disseminating any ideas that were distinctively Spanish. He could not abide them; it was his purpose to antagonize them. He therefore illustrates the weight which was in his time and country imputed to the writings of peninsular authors, and exemplifies the deference which they were accorded by those who differed from them most passionately.

Abraham Hartwell and James Bell, who turned the replies to the arguments of the Portuguese into the vernacular, were satellites of Haddon and Foxe. Both were younger men of very secondary importance, quite lacking the distinction of the scholars who shouldered the burden of the controversy. Their interest in the discussion sprang from the principles that it involved, from the bearing these had on the Reformed religion, and were unmixed with any personal considerations. James Bell, especially, was guiltless of the broad outlook of the men of position. The earlier part of his career was spent at Oxford, where he was admitted as a fellow of Corpus Christi College in 1547 (?), two years after Foxe had withdrawn from the university. Remaining nine years at Oxford, Bell finally rose to be lecturer on rhetoric, but at the expiration of that period he gave up his fellowship, as Foxe had done, and joined the ranks of the Reformers, becoming most zealous in their cause. He translated from Luther in the intervals of other employments, and before his death was rewarded for his services by the prebendary of Holcombe, in Wells. But by far the most lasting of his works

were his English renderings of the writings of
Foxe.   He published four of the works of Foxe
in the vernacular, including the *Answer apolo-
getical to Hierome Osorius*, which Foxe had concluded after the demise of Haddon.   Through
this connection with the martyrologist, Bell's
name has been rescued from an obscurity that
would otherwise have been well-nigh complete.

Abraham Hartwell, called the elder in distinction from the antiquarian of the same name,
was a man of greater accomplishments than
those that Bell possessed.   Like Haddon, whom
he presently came to know, Hartwell was a
scholar of King's College, Cambridge, though
he was not admitted until post-Marian times.
At that institution he remained eight years,
and there engaged in literary pursuits.   It was
while he was yet a student that his translation
from Haddon, entitled a *Sight of the Portugall
pearle*, appeared.   At Cambridge, also, he
acquired considerable renown as a Latin poet.
His verses on Elizabeth's visit to the university
in 1564 were sufficiently well thought of to be
partially reprinted in Gabriel Harvey's *Gratula-
tionum valdinensium libri quatuor*.   Such were
his attainments that they won him recognition

from many prominent persons of the day, besides Harvey and Haddon. With Foxe he was on sufficiently good terms to prefix verses to the second edition of the *Acts and monuments*, and shortly after his death he was commended by Thomas Newton, one of the best known of the English Latinists, in some Latin lines addressed to the younger Hartwell. The names of both of the Hartwells appear frequently upon the register of the Stationers' Company in connection with books of various authors, licensed during the latter years of the century, and it is evident that the elder, though his reputation proved to be ephemeral, was in his day regarded as a man of parts, and his company sought after to an extent which the records which survive but faintly suggest.

Richard Shacklock and John Fenne, the other Englishmen who took part in the controversy between Haddon and the Portuguese bishop, were members of the Catholic faction. It was their object to secure a hearing for Osorio among the rank and file of their countrymen, and to forestall thereby the arguments of the Protestants, which were at first to be procured only in Latin. Haddon's answer of 1563 was

not translated by Abraham Hartwell until Shacklock's *Pearl for a prince*, the original epistle of
Osorio, had been published at Antwerp. When,
however, an appeal was taken by the Romanists
to the people, who were then of course informed
by them of but one side of the dispute, the
Reformers immediately adopted a similar policy,
and restated their position in the vernacular.
From that moment the contention was carried
on with undiminished vigor in Latin and English by both parties indifferently.

Shacklock and Fenne were alike persons of
comparative obscurity, who owe whatever place
they have in history to the fact that they were
among the earliest of the Catholic refugees to
assume the rôle of translators. As exiles dwell-
ing in the Spanish dependencies, they belong in
a political classification to the Elizabethan epoch,
but their position in literature was defined by
the scholarly tradition of Vives and Osorio.
Shacklock had received degrees from Cambridge
in 1555–56 and 1559, but soon after the latter
date he became an ardent Romanist. His sympathies were so pronounced that he found it
advisable to retire to Louvain, where he lived
amid more congenial surroundings. In this city,

which was the asylum of so many of the English exiles, Shacklock occupied himself chiefly with the study of civil law and with his books. Besides the *Pearl for a prince*, he published religious works from the German and Latin. He had resigned his fellowship at Cambridge in the year that Hartwell entered the university, and the two men may have met in that town. Hartwell added an epistle to " Mayster Shacklock " to his translation of the answer of Haddon. But for religious reasons both were never members of one group. By leaving the country, Shacklock permanently affiliated himself with a set which was in harmony with his tenets and pursuits.

Among the Englishmen in retirement at Louvain, John Fenne was at that time a translator of considerable celebrity. Fenne came of a Catholic family of Somersetshire, and with his two brothers had entered New College while James Bell was in residence at Oxford. He applied himself at the university to the study of civil law. The far-reaching changes made by the council of Mary soon enabled him to better his circumstances by accepting an appointment as master of the school of St. Edmundsbury in Suffolk. His deprivation on the accession of Elizabeth was much regretted, as, according to Wood, "he had advanced the boys very much in grammatical learning." Fenne at once determined to leave England. Having the same inclinations as Shacklock, he crossed to Flanders, but desiring further travel, pushed on to Italy. There he remained four years, at the expiration of which he returned to Louvain, and was installed as confessor to the Bridgettin convent of English nuns then established in that city. He published the reply of Osorio to Haddon in 1568, and among other writings on religion, the *Misteries of the rosarie*, from an Italian version of the Latin of Gaspar de Loarte, a Spanish Jesuit, who had been president of two of the colleges at Rome. This work bears no place nor date, but is thought by Miss Scott [1] to have been printed about the year 1600, and by Wood [2] not later than 1603. It was issued from a continental press, and with the writings of Osorio, was the only important Catholic Latin treatise translated from a peninsular author.[3]

[1] Scott, *Mod. Language Pubs.*, XIII., p. 61.

[2] Wood, *Athenæ*, II., p. 112.

[3] An exception must be made to this statement in favor of Loarte's *Exercitium vitæ christianæ*, published without place in 1584 as the *Exercise of a Christian life*.

There were, however, persons among the group of Reformers who opposed Osorio, who busied themselves with other peninsular authors, although incidentally. One man did not absorb the attention of an entire group. This was but natural in an age when the activity of the Spanish priesthood was so great that it was scarcely possible for the religiously inclined, whatever their special predilections, to ignore it. Therefore it is not surprising that when John Day and John Bradford compiled their prayer books, they included prayers of Spanish origin. The plan of Day's collection committed him to such a course, for it professed to be drawn from all the principal languages, as its title, *Christian Prayers and meditations in English, French, Italian, Spanish, Greeke, and Latine*, sets forth; but Bradford, having no such comprehensive design, borrowed what pleased him best, and, radical Protestant that he was, proved to be not overscrupulous as to the source from which he obtained his material.

John Day, printer, was an ardent supporter of the new doctrines, and suffered imprisonment for their sake under the Marian persecution.

L

Fleeing abroad to escape the rigors of the Catholic bishops, he formed a close and lasting friendship with Foxe, and on returning to London to reopen his shop, he became the printer, both of Foxe and of Archbishop Parker, to whose bounty he was subsequently indebted. It was while Day was associated with these men, — and Foxe had lodged with him for a time, — that Day brought out the polyglot compilation just mentioned, usually known as *Queen Elizabeth's prayer book*, and so frequently reprinted by his son, Richard Day. Among the contents of this volume, passing by the prayers in Spanish, were a number of English ones, translated from the Latin of Vives by John Bradford, the martyr.[1] This unfortunate preacher was approximately of the same age as Dr. Haddon, and spent several years as a student at Cambridge while Haddon was still in residence there. But his zeal urged him to abandon

[1] *Writings of Bradford*, I., p. 223. The John Bradford who lived in the household of one of the Spanish grandees in Philip's service, must not be confounded with the martyr. The former is now known only through his letter on the *Nature of Spaniardes*, published at London in 1555, and addressed to the Earls of Arundel, Derby, Shrewsbury, and Pembroke.

scholarship for the pulpit, in which he appeared during the reign of Edward VI. His untractability and seditious teaching necessitated his confinement in the Tower when the Catholic reaction set in and the disturbances arose which also resulted in the imprisonment of Day. Bradford was of too bold and unyielding a temper to finesse or to escape from the toils when they had once closed around him. He received the advances of the bishops and the Spanish friars who came to illumine his understanding, with a firmness which showed his contempt of opportunism, but drew upon himself the penalty of death.[1] Bradford was thus debarred from sharing in the triumph of his party which was so soon to ensue, except through the success of Archbishop Whitgift, who had been his pupil, and through the popularity of his own works, many of which were published posthumously.

[1] An account of the proceedings against Bradford was printed by William Griffith at London in 1561. It was entitled *All the Examinations of the constante martir of God, M. John Bradforde, before the Lord Chauncellor . . . Alphonsus and King Philip's confessour, two Spanish friers, and sundry others.* See also the *Writings of Bradford* in the edition of the Parker Society.

Immediately upon the accession of Elizabeth, Bradford's *Private Prayers and meditations* were printed and made accessible to the public. The volume comprised eighteen prayers, all but two of which had been taken from Vives' *Preces et meditationes diurnæ*, which constituted a section of a larger work, the *Excitationes animi in Deum*. These were translated, for the most part, literally. The *Excitationes* also furnished Bradford with a brief passage for his *Godly Meditations*, which appeared in 1562. The passage was entitled a *Meditation of death*. It was afterward retranslated from the original Latin, together with the *Preces et meditationes diurnæ*, both somewhat modified and reprinted by Richard Day in all of his editions of *Queen Elizabeth's prayer book*.[1] Such was the success of the *Private Prayers* that a constant demand existed for them well into the days of the Stuarts. In 1570 they were incorporated into the *Christian Prayers*, collected by Henry Bull, Powell, and Middleton, and during the next eighty years they ran by themselves through seven editions, the last of which bears the date 1633. Thus the prayers of Day and Bradford,

[1] *Writings of Bradford*, I., 223.

translated from a scholar of a past generation, survived the more celebrated and conspicuous treatises undertaken by other Reformers, in Latin and in English, in response to the arguments and persuasions of Osorio da Fonseca.

CHAPTER V

THE HISTORIANS OF THE INDIES

I𝚃 was not until the second decade of the rule of Elizabeth that the full tide of translation from the Spanish set in. The actual contact of refugees, travellers, ambassadors, and merchants with the people among whom they were obliged to reside, fostered a movement similar to that which had in its incipiency reached England from Italy many years previously. In bulk and kind the translation of the last quarter of the sixteenth century was unprecedented. Every species of the literature of Spain, if the drama be excepted, became an object of attention. The tentative character of the period of Philip and Mary vanished in the light of superior knowledge. Travellers began to frequent the peninsula and to bring back with them peninsular books. Other books were translated from the Italian or French on the wave of the movement that is chiefly remembered by Painter's *Palace of pleasure*. Meanwhile the ambassadors and the floating English population in Spain were becoming acquainted with the resident refugees and merchants. From these they derived their power. When the organization of these classes became effective, all other influences sank to a subordinate position. The mediation of foreign countries, of Italy and France, and that of the agents or the enemies of Philip in London, had small significance. The Spanish influence, like every other literary influence of the time, came to be a movement among the English themselves, among those who had visited the land whence it sprung, and in their hands it reached for the first time its due proportion.

The translations of the promoters of the peninsular trade marked the termination of this transition from the Marian to the Elizabethan epoch less ambiguously than those of any other class. They were not the first to appear, but the surroundings and equipment of those who essayed them were unmistakable because the range of the capabilities of their authors was so limited that there is no margin of doubt. Commercial intercourse had been com-

mon between England and the peninsula during
the fourteenth century. At that time immuni-
ties were offered to the Catalans to induce
them to frequent English ports, but scarcely
before 1530 was English trade in the peninsula
organized upon the basis upon which it was
maintained steadily until it was cut off by royal
edict in 1585. The English merchants frequented Spanish ports in great numbers. The
dependence of Spain and her American and
Indian colonies upon the North endowed the
traders with great importance. A memorandum of Burghley, belonging to the year 1561,
states that Suffolk cloths in "western reds and
blues" were almost exclusively consumed in
Spain. Besides these fabrics white cloths of
the better sort, Bristol friezes, Welsh and Man-
chester cottons, lead and tin, and white kerseys
commanded a ready market.[1]   To these wheat
must be added, for an adequate supply of which
Spain was forced to rely upon England inter-
mittently throughout the whole period. Fine
silks, gold cloths, wines, trinkets of elaborate
workmanship, and lastly wool were exported
in return. According to Burghley's estimate,

[1] *State papers, for., Eliz.*, III., p. 524.

there was in 1569 property to the amount of
£59,783 in the possession of English merchants
in Spain, while the aggregate value of the
goods of all the strangers in London at that
time was only £37,486.[1] Three months later
Spanish merchandise, the value of which was
computed at £49,930, was arrested in England.[2]
The aggregate value of English goods in Spain
was about half the sum similarly disposed in
the Low Countries. When impending hostilities closed the peninsular ports to British ships,
the greater part of British commerce was with
Spain and Portugal, and goods were exchanged
between these countries and Germany almost
exclusively in English bottoms, for the English
were already becoming the carriers of the world.

The exigencies of this trade required the
presence of large numbers of Englishmen in the
peninsula, either in the capacity of factors or
independently. In January 1564, thirty ships
and one thousand English seamen were arrested
in Spain as a retaliatory measure against English
piracy. The English dwelt chiefly in the principal seaports, — Cadiz, San Sebastian, Lisbon,

[1] *State papers, for., Eliz.*, IX., p. 67.
[2] *Ibid.*, IX., p. 105.

Bilbao, and San Lucar de Barrameda,—or in
the capital cities of Madrid or Valladolid,
which were much resorted to by those seeking
redress of wrongs at court. Cordoba, Barcelona, Coruña, and Vigo, and the Canaries were
also marts of Elizabethan trade. Seville, however, and the adjacent ports near the mouth of
the Guadalquivir were, by virtue of the monop-
oly of the American trade which they enjoyed,
the principal goal of English ships. An English church was built in 1517, by the merchants, on land donated by the Duke of Medina
Sidonia, and a new chapel was erected to St.
George the Martyr in 1530, with the sanction
of Henry VIII., on the site of the original
building. The society at San Lucar flourished
uninterruptedly for over seventy years, until
hostilities destroyed the commerce which was
its means of livelihood.

Residing in these various localities, the merchants adopted in some measure the customs
of the country. They intermarried in their
adopted home, became in many cases Catholics,
or if they did not, wisely concealed all traces of
heterodoxy. Consequently they usually escaped
the persecutions which pursued the more defiant

seamen, whose contempt for the observances of
the Inquisition was untempered by politic re-
straint.   Familiarity with Spanish methods
made the resident merchants the protectors of
those whose stay was only transient, and rendered them invaluable to travellers and to the
ambassadors themselves.   As early as 1538
Hugh Tipton was regularly appointed English
consul at Seville, with the imperial sanction.
In the same year John Ratcliffe applied to
Cromwell for the post of solicitor of English
interests at the court at Valladolid.   The head
of the society which supported the church of
St. George the Martyr was styled the Governor of the English nation in Andalusia.   In
the reign of Philip II. the same methods prevailed.   Burghley and Gresham retained one
Robert Hogan as their agent in Spain, and Sir
Thomas Challoner, while ambassador at Madrid,
employed William Phayer because of his knowledge of the ways of the court.   Phayer, indeed, occupied very much the position in Spain
that Antonio de Guaras did in England.   Con-
sular credentials of a similar sort were requested
by residents at Lisbon.   Other merchants carried
on a correspondence with Cromwell or Burgh-

ley and supplemented by their advices the despatches of the ambassadors. Though some of these were devoted to the Inquisition, like John Cuerton, or so thoroughly Spanish like Thomas Batcock that not one of their children could write English, they did not forget their birth. Bartolph Holder wrote Sir Francis Walsingham and Leicester from Lisbon ; Cuerton claimed acquaintance with Sir Henry Sidney. Not only did these men communicate with influential persons at home, but they were connected in some way with all of the royal emissaries in Spain and Portugal during the course of their missions. For the merchants were agents for forwarding the letters of the ambassadors. They not infrequently furnished them with funds or cultivated their friendship by presents. Some were also on amicable terms with the Ferias. On one occasion Tipton sent Challoner and the Duchess of Feria each a barrel of salmon and one of red herrings, and Cuerton, desiring to ingratiate himself with the duchess, made her a gift of two fine cheeses. These kindnesses were reciprocated by the duchess during the trouble at Seville in 1570, when, in response to the solicitations of Tipton, then

consul at Cordoba, she awarded a *real* apiece a
day to thirty-one Englishmen then imprisoned
in the dungeons of the town. In these ways
the resident merchants came into contact with
all classes of their compatriots who visited the
peninsula.   They facilitated the progress of
strangers and helped to make their sojourn in
the country tolerable. Nor were they wholly
uninformed of affairs at court.   It was their
unrivalled opportunities of observation which
induced Burghley to rely entirely upon their
advices for information of Spanish domestic
politics, after Philip II.'s summary dismissal of
ambassador Man.

The merchants who were detained abroad for
comparatively brief periods only, were those
who engaged in the task of providing Spanish
books with an English dress.   Translations of
chronicles of discovery and of treatises of medical and military science gave expression to
the inquiring spirit of the merchants, to the
taste for the unknown, the marvellous, and the
adventurous which characterized so uniformly
the countrymen of Hawkins and Drake.   The
chronicle of discovery captivated the imagination at the same time that it appealed to the

business instinct of a rapidly developing people. The abundance of histories of the new world and of the newly opened East furnished material ready to hand for translation which was generally more easily accessible than literature of a higher class.

John Frampton, a person whose experiences were typical of those of his associates, was the most active of their number with the pen. Retaining a personal connection with England, he was one of that class which was able to make the results of the experiences of the expatriated Englishmen available in London.[1] Frampton first comes into view in 1562 when he was in Spain in the unpleasant rôle of a prisoner of the Inquisition at Seville. But he had more than common good fortune. In February of that year the intervention of Sir Thomas Chamberlain, then the queen's ambassador at the court of Philip II., procured his release, and Frampton

[1] For merchants of this description, John Browne, a Bristol trader, published the *Marchants avizo*, London, 1589. The book was intended for inexperienced persons who were sent to Spain or Portugal on business, and contained information relative to the drawing of bills, and the equivalent values of weights and measures of different countries, together with other similar matter.

was set at liberty. He was, however, commanded to leave the country immediately.
For some reason he disobeyed this command,
and at the close of the next year was living
unmolested at Cadiz. After an uncertain interval, though assuredly before 1577, he returned
to England and began the publication of various
works dealing with travel and exploration.
With the exception of an original treatise on
the discovery of Tartary and Scythia by the
northeast, these were all translations from
Spanish authors. The first to appear was the
Joyfull Newes ovt of the newe founde worlde,
printed in 1577 after the original Castilian of
Nicolas Monardes, a physician of Seville. This
book was reissued three years later with three
additional tracts by Monardes on the bezaar
stone, the herb *escuerçonera*, the medicinal
properties of iron and steel, and the singular
benefits of the use of snow. Frampton's residence in Seville, when Monardes was publishing
his treatises there, afforded the Englishman
ample opportunity of becoming acquainted with
the writings of the physician. They enjoyed a
wide vogue. Versions were current in Latin,
Italian, and French, for Monardes had acquired

in his time a considerable reputation. It was
one of his tracts that Roger Bodenham, an
English Catholic and a Sevillian by adoption,
wishing to conciliate the prime minister,
promised to bring Burghley in the winter of
1574–1575, in the conviction that it propounded
the best remedy for the gout from which he
was suffering.[1]

Frampton followed up these fantastically
named medical treatises, by Bernardino de Escalante's *Discourse of the navigation which the
Portugales doe make to the realmes and provinces of the east partes of the worlde*. This
book, the production of a Galician priest, was
dedicated to Sir Edward Dyer. Like the version of Monardes, it was the legitimate prey
of the merchant translator. As a chronicle
of discovery, it was one of a type in which
the adventurers took delight. The list of
translations was further augmented by the
publication of a treatise of another stamp,
though also dealing with the sea. This was
Pedro de Medina's extremely popular *Arte de
nauegar*, which had been published at Cor-

[1] Bodenham to Burghley, *State papers, for.*, *Eliz.*, XI.,
p. 2.

doba in 1545, and was at that time current
in Italian, French, and German, as well as in
the Castilian.   The *Arte of nauigation* seems
to have been printed at a time when there
was an exceptional sale for works of that
sort.   Martin Cortés' *Arte de navigar* had been
translated in 1561, but the general demand
arose when Edward Hellowes' version of Guevara's treatise on that subject appeared in
1578.   During the next two years Cortés'
Arte was reprinted twice, and in 1581 that of
Frampton was issued.   Robert Norman's *Rules
for the art of navigating* of 1585 and other
publications belong to the same movement.

The most notable of Frampton's works, however, was his *Trauels of Marcus Paulus*, which
appeared simultaneously with the rendering of
Escalante in 1579.   The story of the famous
Venetian reached Frampton through the Spanish of Rodrigo de Santaella.   It thus came about
that one of the best-known and most fascinat-
ing works of the Renaissance found its way into
English through the Spanish instead of the
more widely affected Italian.   This was an in-
version of the usual proceeding, which was to
go, indeed, to the Italian for Spanish litera-

M

ture.   The departure from the rule in the case of the travels of Marco Polo was due to the appeal which they made to the adventurous spirit.   It recommended the book at once to the seafaring men of England.   Works which had a mainly æsthetic interest were likely to be appropriated by the English and Italian scholars, the men of letters; but those whose adventurous side was strong could obtain no readier or more eager interpreters than the merchants of education, who above all other countries, frequented Spain.

Thomas Nicholas and Thomas Nichols assisted Frampton in disseminating knowledge of strange lands.   Both resided in the Canary Islands during the latter part of the reign of Mary and the first few years of that of Elizabeth, as factors of Thomas Lok, Anthony Hickman, and Edward Castelin, then among the most prominent merchants who engaged in the peninsular trade.   Both fell victims to the rigors of the Inquisition in the crusade against the English, in which Frampton was imprisoned at Seville.   Nicholas had pursued his business in several of the Canaries, more particularly Palma and Teneriffe, without molestation un-

til 1560. In that year the jealousy of the
Spaniards being no longer restrained by political necessities, he was charged with heresy and
thrown into prison with his companion, Edward Kingsmill. Having warned Sir Thomas
Chamberlain of his position, he was released
through the intercession of the ambassador
after two years spent in irons; but on the
representation of one Francisco de Coronado,
a Jewish confessor, orders were given for his
reincarceration. After two more years had
elapsed, Nicholas was brought to Seville and
publicly tried and acquitted in May 1564,
after a process which extended over seven
months. The judgment of the court was accompanied by the command never to leave the
city. As Frampton· had disregarded a most
peremptory order of precisely the opposite
import, so Nicholas disregarded this. He returned to London, where he doubtless considered his person more secure, and made his
appearance as a translator in 1577, contempo-
raneously with Frampton.

Nicholas occupied himself solely with the
history of Spanish America. His first publication was a little tract of six leaves, entitled

the *Strange and marueilous Newes lately come from the great kingdome of Chyna*, and was taken, he explains, from a letter sent by a merchant from Mexico to Spain.[1] As the original was forwarded to King Philip, Nicholas was able to give only an abstract of its contents, but he completed a more elaborate undertaking in the next year. This was the *Pleasant Historie of the conquest of the Weast India*, a version of the second part of Francisco Lopez de Gómara's *Historia de las Indias*. The book, the original of which has been erroneously attributed to Bernal Diaz del Castillo, was dedicated to Sir Francis Walsingham, and prefaced by flattering verses from the pen of the virulent Stephen Gosson. Gómara's history, the most incisive of the chronicles of sixteenth-century Spain, had previously been partially introduced to the English by Richard Eden in his *Decades of the newe worlde*, which was somewhat indebted to *Historia de las Indias*. It is indeed surprising that Gómara, a courtier, and for a time chaplain to Hernando Cortés, should not have been more eagerly read in London. His

[1] An analysis of this pamphlet is contained in Brydge's *Censura*, VI., p. 55. Purchas reprinted Nicholas' second work.

official position, his attendance upon the con-
queror of Mexico, and the early publication of
his history in so accessible a city as Antwerp,
should have caused him to become as promptly
known across the channel as he was upon the
continent, in Italy and France. Yet, as with
the work of many another less polished writer,
the first reasonably complete translation of his
history was from the pen of a London merchant.

In the dedication of this book Nicholas tells
of an interesting incident which happened to
him while he was in the employ of Thomas
Lok.[1] Travelling on affairs of business from
Toledo toward "high Castile," he met with a
gentleman of the country on the road, with
whose conversation he was more than ordi-
narily pleased. Nicholas might well have been
delighted, for this gentleman was no other than
Augustin de Zárate, the historian of Peru. For
fifteen years Zárate had been *contador de mer-
cedes* for Castile, and for upward of seven he
had administered the finances of the province
conquered by Pizarro. It was this meeting
that led to the. translation of the *Conquista del
Perú*. Zárate composed this chronicle upon

[1] See Collier, *Bibl. Acct.*, under Nicholas.

his return from America, and it was published at Antwerp in 1555, about five years afterward, with the encouragement of Charles V. Of this chronicle Nicholas printed but the first four books, but he included in addition an account of the *Mynes of Potosi, and how Captaine Carauajall took it into his power*. The description of the opening of these mines by Carbajal, mines so rich in silver that in their vicinity an iron horseshoe soon came to be worth its weight in the more precious metal, formed a part of the sixth book of Zárate. Nicholas' translation of the work appeared in 1581, but was not reprinted as his version of Gómara had been. This was doubtless due to the inferiority of the original, the fair-mindedness of which is its chief merit. The *Conquest of the prouinces of Peru* is, however, one of the best examples of the literary activity of the merchant class.[1]

---

[1] The most notable arraignment of the conduct of the Spaniards in the new world, the *Brevísima Relacion de la destruicion de las Indias* of Bartólomé de las Casas, was published at London in 1583. The translator is known only by his initials, M. M. S. He entitled his work the *Spanish Colonie*. No other writings of Las Casas appeared in England until the latter half of the seventeenth century.

Thomas Nichols, whose employers and whose occupation in the Canaries were the same as those of Nicholas, exhibited a less prolific vein. Though not himself a translator from the Spanish, he has an affinity to the merchants who were translators because of his labors to lay the wonders of unfamiliar lands bare to the gaze of the public, as well as because of his business environment.   Nicholas had gone to the Canaries about 1554, and remained in residence among them for seven years.   A disagreement with the Inquisition finally forced him to leave the islands.   After returning to England he came upon André Thevet's *New founde Worlde*, published from a French original in 1568. Nichols' experience abroad had fitted him to be a severe critic of authors who dealt with localities which he had traversed.   He did not find Thevet's second-hand accounts at all to his liking.   With the purpose of correcting the errors that they contained, he wrote his *Description of the fortunate ilandes of Canaria*. In this work he embodied the results of personal observation in various settlements in that group.

Robert Baker, a pensioner of the Earl of

Oxford, pursued a somewhat similar course. Baker is remembered chiefly for his first voyage, which was to Guinea. In a second expedition, on which he set out in 1563, a great storm overtook the vessel in which he had sailed and threw her upon the coast. The ensuing adventures in Portugal and France, together with the events of the venture in Guinea, Baker afterward treated briefly in both prose and verse in a volume licensed by the Stationers' Company in July 1567. The unpretentious writings of Baker and those of Nichols are quite typical of numerous other treatises and tracts published by the English adventurers, relating their achievements and hardships upon the seacoast of the peninsula or in the Spanish colonial possessions. Necessarily devoid of the breadth of horizon of the Castilian chronicles dealing with the new world, dependent upon a personal or melodramatic interest, and with less of the geographical element than their foreign competitors, they are expressions of the spirit that fostered the translations of a higher value made by Frampton and Nicholas, and of the enthusiasm which assured them readers.

The master figure among the historians of travel, whether original writers or translators from the Castilian or other tongues, was Richard Hakluyt.   It is in him that the literature which occupied the leisure of the merchants culminated and found its most enduring expression.   Though not himself following a life of wandering and hardship, Hakluyt summed up the labors of the pioneer voyagers in an authoritative form, and established the canon of travel.   In his hands and those of his friends the Spanish chronicle of discovery took its place in importance alongside of the literary works which were at the same time being translated by Sir Philip Sidney, David Rowland, and Richard Carew.   His contemporaries occupied themselves with the romance, with the novel, and with treatises of practical art and science.   They were busied with history and the study of language.   Paralleling their efforts at their highest, Hakluyt's work is conspicuous in the most active period of Elizabethan translation, and represents the Spanish influence in its own sphere in its fullest development.

The circumstances of the parents of Hakluyt

were such that it was possible for him to
obtain a good education. He attended Westminster School while very young, and was
elected to a studentship at Christ Church,
Oxford, in 1570. There he took his bachelor's
and master's degrees four and seven years
afterward, respectively, and there he became
associated with some of the choicest spirits of
his time. When Hakluyt entered Christ
Church, Philip Sidney and Richard Carew
were students in that college; Lyly and
D'Oylie, the lexicographer, had already come
to Magdalen; Thomas Lodge and Edward
Hoby presently enrolled themselves in Trinity.
For five years of Hakluyt's stay at Christ
Church, Thomas Rogers, the translator of
Estella, was among his colleagues, while before
his retirement Antonio de Corro had begun
to read lectures with great acceptance in the
presence of students of various halls, and to
gather around him a flock of young admirers.
Corro and Hakluyt were undoubtedly contemporaries at Christ Church. All of these persons connected themselves in some positive
manner with Spanish literature. Carew, Sidney, Hakluyt, and also Fulke-Greville were

especially intimate. It was in common with them and simultaneously with Lyly, Lodge, Hoby, and their circle that Hakluyt acquired his first knowledge of Castilian.

The incentive which roused Hakluyt to obtain a knowledge of the peninsular tongues was his lively interest in the romance of the new world. He reared himself on stories of great and adventurous deeds. While at Oxford he read, as he says, but of course with a healthy contempt of the college curriculum, all the printed or written accounts of voyages and discoveries that he could lay his hands upon in Greek, Latin, Italian, Spanish, Portuguese, French, or English. These chronicles seemed to him to be as entertaining as the merchants had found them, and he commenced to lecture on them. It was the object of Hakluyt to put the science of navigation in England upon the same basis that it was in Spain. Charles V. had established lectures at the *Casa de Contratacion* at Seville, and the writings of Alfonso and Gerónimo de Chaves and Rodrigo Zamorano, mathematicians and cosmographers of that city, were studied by the Englishman. In 1582 he published his

first collection of voyages on America. This
won him the patronage of Lord Charles Howard of Effingham, the lord admiral, through
whom he secured an appointment as chaplain
to Sir Edward Stafford, when that gentleman
went to France as the royal ambassador in
1583. Hakluyt disposed his leisure at Paris
as profitably as his employer did his labor, and
continued his researches uninterruptedly. The
most important of the three works that were
the direct result of his sojourn at the capital
was the *De Orbe novo* of Peter Martyr Anglerius, which he edited and published in the
original Latin there in 1587. Martyr is remembered as an Italian scholar and ecclesiastic,
who crossed over into Spain in 1487, as his
namesake at the invitation of Cranmer subsequently crossed to England, and rose high in
the diplomatic and educational circles of Spain,
becoming a member of the Council of the
Indies, to which the supervision of the colonies
was intrusted. In this office Martyr amassed
the information which he preserved in his
history. The publication of this book was
begun at Alcala in 1516. Personal acquaintance with the prime movers in the war of

conquest and discovery lent great authority
to it, and the redaction by Hakluyt, though not
without many competitors, among others the
previous partial English translation by Richard
Eden, was a work of lasting value.

After he returned from France with Lady
Douglass Sheffield, subsequently the wife of
Leicester, in the year of the Armada, Hakluyt occupied himself with the composition of
the monumental *Principal Navigations of the
English nation.* The first edition of this
famous compilation appeared at London in
1589, and the second and definitive edition
in 1599 and 1600. The *Principal Navigations*
is by the nature of its subject rich in allu-
sions to Spain. Besides English accounts of
voyages to the coasts of the Spanish and Portuguese colonial possessions, and letters from
English residents in the peninsula, there are
over fifty sections in the work which are
translations from peninsular authors, some of
which are accompanied by reprints in the original tongue. Official documents in Spanish,
ruttiers, letters intercepted on the high seas
by English ships, or obtained through continental agencies, personal interviews granted

to Hakluyt by Spaniards imprisoned in England, and chronicles both of obscure and standard authors, make up the divisions into which these selections naturally fall.

The initial volume is devoted to accounts of voyages of the English to the north, and the second, which is given up to discovery to the south and east, is the first in which peninsular writers are largely drawn upon. Here the *Tratado dos descobrimentos* of Antonio Galvão and the *Chronica da vida do D. João* of Garcia de Resende are briefly quoted.[1] The last volume, however, is still more dependent upon Spanish and Portuguese sources, in spite of the fact that Hakluyt's object was only the rehearsal of the achievements of his countrymen. But no adequate view of America was then obtainable from English sources. The *Decades* of Martyr, the *Historia general* of Gómara, the *China* of Gonzalez de Mendoza, the *Historia natural y moral* of Acosta, the *Discourse of the West Indies*, captured with its

[1] Hakluyt appropriated the labors of his predecessors Eden and Willes. Galeoto Pereira's account of China, printed in Italian from a Portuguese Ms., and published by Willes in his revision of Eden, occurs in Part II.

author, Lopes Paz, a Portuguese, at sea, and the
Relaciones of Francisco Vazquez de Coronado,
Francisco de Ulloa, and Hernando de Alarcon,
dignitaries in the new world, were laid under
contribution.   To these there must further be
added the Japanese letters of the Portuguese
Jesuit, Luiz Frois, contemporary letters and
reports, the account of the customs of the
port of Seville by the pilot Pedro Diaz, and
many documents of a similar nature, which
were useful to Hakluyt in completing his
collection.

Unlike his predecessors for the most part,
Hakluyt did not bring these materials from
abroad himself: some were placed before him
by the English navigators on their return from
their marauding expeditions to the southern
seas.   In this manner many letters which he
might read and captives whom he might question were made accessible.   Other works from
Spain found their way across the channel
through Italy and France, sometimes in alien
dress, as in the compilation of Ramusio.   Yet
others were imported from the peninsula directly, and Hakluyt would even send thither
for the purpose of obtaining books which he

especially desired. The marked encouragement that he received at court enabled him
to take advantage of every means of information which was offered. While he was yet in
Paris, Elizabeth had nominated him to a prebend stall at Bristol in recognition of his second
book which she had read in manuscript. Other
preferments soon followed. In the enjoyment
of these Hakluyt completed the publication of
his great work, and in 1601 brought out the
Discoveries of the world vnto the yeere 1555, a
translation of the *Tratado dos descobrimentos* of
Antonio Galvão, a Portuguese.[1] It was succeeded in 1609 by a second book transferred
from the same idiom. This was encumbered
by an unwieldy title, *Virginia richly valued by
the description of the maine land of Florida.*
The work is an account of the ill-starred expedition of Fernando de Soto to Florida, set

---

[1] This book was translated, says Hakluyt, "by some
honest and well affected marchant of our nation, whose
name by no meanes I could attaine unto, and that as it
seemeth many yeeres ago. For it hath been by me above
these twelve yeeres." Hakluyt sent to Lisbon for a Portuguese copy in order to correct the translation, but was
unable to procure one. See his preface in the reprint by
the Hakluyt Society, p. vi.

down by a native of Elvas in east Portugal,
who accompanied De Soto through his perils
and wanderings.

Hakluyt became the centre of the group of
men who were intent on the subject to which
he was devoting his energies. The eminent
acceptability of his work to the queen and the
court, as well as his superior industry, designated him as the leading historian of travel.
He stimulated his friends to research and was
assisted by them in turn.   It was "at the
earnest request and encouragement of my wor-
shipfull friend Master Richard Hakluit, late of
Oxforde," [1] that Robert Parke translated the
Historia de la China of Fray Juan Gonzalez de
Mendoza, a book that has the distinction of
having introduced the characters of Chinese
chirography into Europe. This Parke dedicated his history to Thomas Cavendish, the
navigator. Hakluyt's first work was supplemented by a woodcut map by Michael Lok,
mercer and patron of Frobisher, which Lok
dedicated to Philip Sidney. Lok also published
a translation of the Parisian edition of the *De
Orbe novo* at London in 1612. He was much

---

[1] Parke. *Historie of China*, preface of the translator.

N

interested in discovery, for in the same year he
bought out an enlargement of Eden's *Decades of
the newe worlde*.   Michael Lok was the eigh-
teenth son of Sir William Lok, the favorite
mercer of Henry VIII.   The advantages of such
respectable birth presented him with opportunities of mingling with the adventurous spirits of
the day.   He was a member of the London
Muscovy Company, an uncle of Henry Lok, the
poet, and a brother of Thomas Lok, who took
such a prominent part in the Spanish trade,
and who was the principal of Nicholas and
Nichols in their negotiations in the peninsula.
These connections gave Michael Lok an entrance into many grades of society.   Through
him and others of his stamp, Hakluyt grew to
know the lesser travellers, the factors of the
merchants, whose experiences were scarcely on
the heroic scale.   He was familiar already with
the great men like Hawkins and Drake.   It
was therefore possible for him to collect the
personal relations of the chief actors in the
exploits in foreign lands, in the manner that
Peter Martyr had done in the Spain of Ferdinand and Isabella.   He edited, while sitting
with his family at home, the accounts of those

who had returned across the sea. His established position in London made him able to give them a wider circulation than obscurer persons could assure them. In this manner Hakluyt drew together in his volumes the stray works of obscure and unknown writers. Among the persons who described Spanish or Portuguese territories, Robert Baker and Nichols have been rescued from utter oblivion through the incorporation of their works in the *Principal Navigations.* And many others have been saved by this means from a similar fate.

The entire movement of translation of Spanish chronicles of the new world into English is, therefore, virtually summed up in Hakluyt. It is true that the bulk of the work of the geographer, which was immediately derived from the Castilian, is scarcely so great in proportion to that of his complete works, as that of the miscellaneous translations from that language by other hands is to the total volume of travel and discovery published in the sixteenth century in England. But the portion that was admitted into Hakluyt is all that has lived, excepting only the *Decades* of Eden. The other works have been forgotten. Those who made them public lacked both literary skill and authority. What they did was thus in itself ephemeral. Their works hovered on the border line of literature. As they lived in the midst of the events that they described, much that they wrote, owing to the absence of historic perspective, had only the value of news. Hakluyt possessed a master hand that endowed the subject-matter which he touched with something of a permanent interest, and therefore he and his writings had no real rivals in their own field.

CHAPTER VI

MYSTICISM AND PROTESTANTISM

I

THE translations of the works of the Spanish mystics and Reformers which were printed during the sixteenth century, belong to the latter half of the reign of Elizabeth. They began to usurp the position that had been occupied by the treatises of Vives, Osorio, and other peninsular scholars, at the time in which the chronicles of the new world rose into popularity. The accentuation of the religious differences with Spain after the death of Mary, precipitated theological controversy. Vives had largely avoided it; Osorio had openly entered into it; but the writers of younger generations felt its effects most strongly. The efforts of the scholars who essayed to refute the doctrines of Osorio, and those of the papists

who strove to maintain them, came at last to be
supplemented or opposed by the endeavors of
English Reformers who used the works of Spaniards in support of Protestantism, and by those
of other Catholic writers who followed for the
most part in the steps of the Castilian mystics.
On the Protestant side these men were the successors of Haddon and Foxe, but they failed to
acquire such credit as their elders had done.
The Spanish heretics had no such name as
Osorio among them, to command recognition
in the North, and hence remained but little
known.   Among the Catholics, other conditions prevailed, and the contemporaries of the
earlier papistical controversialists, Shacklock
and Fenne, achieved more substantial fame.
This was due to the merits of the mystics to
whose writings the Catholics went; as these
were not in any sense occasional, but possessed a popular value that was greatly enhanced by the reputation of Luis de Granada
about whom they centred, they became widely
esteemed.   They were the first religious writings in the peninsular vernacular to be generally read in England.   It was not long
before Granada was welcomed there with a

warmth that recalled the cordiality once shown toward Osorio and Vives.

The transition from the older to the newer age was first shown in the field of theology amid the group of Spanish refugees which was domiciled in London, and among the men who acted as their interpreters. As the persecutions in England drove fugitives to the continent, so the horrors of the Inquisition forced many independent spirits to leave Spain. In spite of the strenuous efforts of Charles V. to keep the faith of his subjects pure, the virus of the Reformation penetrated into that country. The intercourse of the peninsula with its heretical dependencies made this result inevitable. Books were printed in Castilian in Geneva and the German towns, and smuggled into the country under the very eyes of the authorities. When the emperor resigned the crown to Philip II., they were so generally disseminated that measures had to be determined upon for the suppression of heresy at the first favorable opportunity. This offered itself when Philip II. brought his wars against France and Rome to a successful conclusion. It was in 1558 that the Spanish Inquisition first began its crusade against Christians, which it prosecuted with relentless and merciless severity until every vestige of heterodoxy had been stamped out in the land.

Throughout the twelve succeeding years in which the Spanish Protestants, irrespective of rank or station, were hunted to the ground, the Reformers who were able to elude the vigilance of the Inquisition made their way to England. There they met with a hospitable welcome. From the security of their asylum, they might send out tracts and sermons to sow their opinions through the peninsula and the Lowlands, so far as they were able, with perfect impunity. Impelled by this purpose, fugitives from the Inquisition began to arrive in England in 1559. During the summer of that year, Rodrigo Guerrero was offered a chair at Oxford. There was nothing irregular in proffering a lectureship to a foreigner, from the English point of view. Spaniards had taught at the university since the opening of the century, excepting only in the reign of Edward VI., without exciting opposition. Vives, De Soto, and Villa-García furnished precedents sufficient to justify the installation of Guerrero. But to Philip II. a danger presented itself in the cases of the Catholic scholars which

had not been feared by Charles V., — Guerrero
might be used to build up a heretical school
among the Spanish subjects in England. Thenceforth this possibility never ceased to cause the
king and his ambassadors annoyance. In 1562
the apostasy among the Spaniards resident in
London was alarming; De Quadra complained
in vain that a large house belonging to Grindal,
the bishop of London, had been given to the
heretics, who preached there with the approbation of the queen, no less than three times a
week.[1] The protests of Guzman de Silva were
not more favorably received, but he flattered
himself that his promises and cajoleries had
won the refugees themselves. Speaking of one
of the most prominent of them, who had con-
sented to accept a pardon and return to Spain,
De Silva wrote in April 1565: " The Conventi-
cal of Spanish heretics here is on its last legs.
. . . They make much of an heretical Spaniard
everywhere in order to pit him against . . . who
are not heretics. This man was held in high esteem, and if affairs are managed skilfully I hope
his example will be followed by the submission of
the greater number of them, because such are the

[1] Froude, *England*, VII., p. 412.

evil designs of these heretics, that more of them (the Spaniards) are held by fear than ignorance of the truth." [1]   De Silva soon learned his mistake, for immediately after his withdrawal, his successor, Guerau de Spes, complained loudly of the continuance of the evil. The hundred and fifty Spaniards imprisoned at Bridewell during the trouble which grew out of Elizabeth's seizure of the treasure borrowed from the Genoese bankers on its way to Alba, were compelled to submit to the ministrations of an heretical Spanish preacher.   Copies of blasphemous books were also distributed among them.   Of these books, one by the preacher was current in three modern languages and freely circulated; another, *La Doctrina christiana* of the Calvinist Juan Perez, published in London in the original Spanish, though bearing the imprint of Venice, was particularly objectionable, as it could not possibly be intended for English readers.[2]

Elizabeth cared nothing about Spanish Prot-

[1] De Silva to Philip II., April 2, 1565, *State papers*, *Sp.*, *Eliz.*, I., p. 425.   A portion of the second sentence quoted is undecipherable.

[2] De Spes to Philip II., April 2, 1569, *Ibid.*, II., p. 140.

estantism, and she cared absolutely nothing about its individual exponents. She welcomed them only in order to annoy Philip II., whose troubles with the Turks, the Flemings, and the Dutch severely taxed his energies. When Guerrero was in England, she had just refused the hand of Philip, and Feria, exasperated at the coldness with which he had been treated, had just left the country; when De Quadra remonstrated against the use to which Grindal's house had been put, Elizabeth was aiding the Huguenots with arms and men; when De Silva was striving to undermine the "conventicle," the relations between the nations were most strained; and when the Spanish prisoners stood to lose their souls as well as their liberty in Bridewell, the English ambassador had been expelled from Madrid, all property of either nation in the other had been sequestrated, and commerce totally suspended.

But the Spanish heretics were heartily welcomed by the English Reformers as desirable recruits on ·religious and not on political grounds. That a Spaniard, the most orthodox of men, should profess the Reformed doctrines, seemed almost to demonstrate their validity.

Hence there was a willingness in many quarters to look kindly upon the strangers. There was a tendency to exalt them a little above the station which their talents entitled them to occupy. This was noticeable at the universities, from which the influence of the Spaniards was chiefly disseminated. The common hostility of that age toward strangers would not permit approval to degenerate into adulation. Opposition and rancor were not wanting, nor were they afraid to speak, but they did not prevail against political and religious affinities, in the universities at least.

Antonio de Corro and Cipriano de Valera were the only Spanish Reformers whose writings were frequently printed in England during the sixteenth century. This distinction which they attained is attributable to the fact that no other persons of the same nationality, who professed authorship, were long resident in the country. Both were born at Seville, that hotbed of heresy, and there both received an education. Upon the outbreak of the persecution against Christian heterodoxy, Valera at once emigrated to England. It was in the year of his arrival there that Rodrigo Guerrero was

offered a professorship at Oxford. Valera,
however, sought to enter as a student at the
other university, in which he was admitted B.A.
by special grace in 1559 or 1560. He then
became fellow of Magdalen College, commenc-
ing his M.A. in 1563. Three years later he was
incorporated in that degree at Oxford, after his
conversion had been certified by Cambridge.

Valera's literary labors were apparently confined exclusively to publications in the Spanish
tongue. The evident object of his writings
was the conversion of his compatriots. With
this end in view, he caused a variety of religious
works to be printed between 1588 and 1602.
These were of three kinds: in the first were
two treatises directed against the pope and the
mass, together with an exposure of the false
miracles performed by one María de la Visitacion, and tracts addressed to papists as well as
to the Christian captives of the Moors in Bar-
bary; in the second, Spanish translations of the
Catechism and *Institutes* of Calvin; and in the
third, translations of the New Testament and
afterward of the whole Bible. This version of
the Bible was a reproduction of that which
Casiodoro de Reyna had printed at Basle in

1567–1569, in which the Castilian had been carefully based upon the Greek and Hebrew texts. The character of these publications sufficiently attests the fact that Valera was not aiming to reach an English audience. His purpose was evangelistic; at times he was polemical. Only his polemics, of course, had any interest for the subjects of Elizabeth. Under these circumstances Valera's first and original works, the treatises against the pope and the mass, were alone translated by John Golbourne in 1600.[1] There was an edition in Spanish dedicated to Sir Thomas Egerton as early as 1588, but as Valera produced nothing else but translations that had already found an English dress, the weighty but unpolished *Dos Tratados* represent his contribution to English religious literature.

Antonio de Corro did not land in England until a later date. In 1568, according to Wood, one " Ant. Coran," who had been born in Spain, was preaching in the Italian church in London.[2]

---

[1] Two years previously one J. G. had published *A most fragrant Flower*, an exposition of the Lord's Prayer, by Luis de Granada. As Granada was not a polemical writer, he may well have appealed to the admirer of Valera, John Golbourne.

[2] Wood, *Athenæ*, II., p. 578.

This person was undoubtedly Antonio de Corro, as in 1569 Geoffrey Fenton translated an epistle sent by him to the "Pastours of the Flemish church in Antwerp." Corro afterward often appeared in the London pulpit. In 1571 he was appointed reader of divinity in the Temple through the good offices of Dr. Edwin Sandys, bishop of London, and the Earl of Leicester recommended him to Oxford University in March 1575. Despite the fact that Leicester was chancellor of the university, considerable opposition was manifested to the stranger. He was openly and energetically attacked by one John Rainolds as a heinous heretic. But Corro had the authorities to support him. He consequently was set up as reader in divinity to the students of Gloucester, St. Mary's, and Hart Halls. He was living as a student in Christ Church in 1579, in which college he was *censor theologicus* from 1581 to 1585. John Lyly, Richard Hakluyt, Thomas Lodge, Sir Edward Hoby, Thomas Pie, and probably John Thorius were in attendance at Oxford during Corro's activity there. Hakluyt and Rogers, moreover, were enrolled in Christ Church, not improbably, when Corro entered that institution

Corro's disposition urged him to treat in his writings a wider range of subjects than Valera had done. He was not to be satisfied with making the Bible more conveniently accessible in Spanish. Perhaps the blood which descended to the preacher from his father, who was a doctor of laws, inclined him to impatience and to controversy. Hence his admonition to the pastors of the church in Antwerp, and his *Supplication exhibited to the moste mightie Prince Philip, king of Spain.* For these epistles, the first of which was in French and the second in Latin and French, were not without interest in those times. It was for this reason, indubitably, that Geoffrey Fenton, a pronounced, but happily not a typical, Puritan, who would seem to have had no direct relations with Corro whatever, translated the Antwerp letter so successfully in 1569 that it was reprinted in the next year.

Nevertheless, the bulk of Corro's published work consisted of paraphrases and commentaries on the Bible. Three of these appeared during the years that he spent at Oxford. Corro was a more skilful writer than Valera, and impressed himself with greater power upon the students

with whom he came in touch. The fact that
he devoted himself to composing in Latin and
French rather than in Spanish was greatly in
his favor, yet it is not adequate to explain his
success. This must have sprung largely from
personal causes. Corro's religious writings
consisted of selections from the Bible, augmented by his exposition or paraphrase of the
passages, apparently compiled by his students
from notes of his lectures. In 1575 an exposition of the *Epistle of St. Paul to the Romans*,
"gathered and set together out of the readings
of Ant. Corranus of Sevilla, Professor of Divin-
itie," was published anonymously at London.
The book had appeared in Latin in 1574.
Five years later a similar work appeared, his
*Sapientissimi Regis Salomonis concio de summo
hominis bono . . . In Latinam linguam ab Antonio
Corrano hispalensi versa, et ex eiusdem præ-
lectionibus illustrata. Lond., . . . expensis ipsius
authoris.* It was dedicated to Lord Chancellor
Bromley. Corro's *Sermons on Ecclesiastes* were
abridged by Thómas Pitt and printed at Oxford
in 1585, and during the next year Thomas
Pie, B.D., printed *Solomon's sermon*, translated
from the *Sapientissimi Regis Salomonis concio*,

o

at the same place, with a dedication to Lady Mary Dudley.

Both Pitt and Pie were, undoubtedly, associated with Corro at Oxford. Pitt's name, it is true, is not recorded in the archives of either Oxford or Cambridge, but the publication of his *Ecclesiastes* at the former university while Corro was teaching there is sufficient to raise the presumption that Pitt was connected with the institution in some way, and to leave no doubt whatever that he was thrown in contact with Corro there. Pie, as a writer of considerable prominence on ecclesiastical subjects, is less involved in obscurity. This divine matriculated at Balliol College, Oxford, in December 1577, while Corro was in the midst of his career as a reader at the university. In 1581 he became chaplain of Merton College, and received degrees in divinity in 1585 and 1588. He is said to have been an eminent linguist, but his published works are all in English or in Latin. Pie died in 1610 on his living in Surrey, at the age of fifty years.

Corro, however, exercised his talents in another than the religious field, and undertook the task of publishing a Spanish grammar. His

political and religious writings were none of
them in his native tongue, nor did the more
valuable of them have any relation whatever
with Spain. But by the nature of the case,
this could not be true of a grammar designed
for teaching Castilian, which was thus an exception to his rule. The date of the composition
of this book[1] is placed at 1586. The book was
printed by Joseph Barnes, the university printer.
It is noteworthy, apart from its importance here,
because it was one of the first publications to be
issued by the Oxford press after its suspension
for a hundred years. An English translation
appeared in London in 1590, and was supplemented by a Spanish dictionary compiled by
John Thorius, to be used as a key to the grammar. This Thorius was not a cleric, but he was
like Pie an Oxford man, having matriculated at
the age of eighteen at Christ Church in 1586.
Corro had been enrolled as a student in that college as late as 1585, but though his connection
with the university does not seem to have been
continued after that date, it is to the circum-

[1] *Reglas gramaticales para aprender la lengua espanola y
francesca, confiriendo la una con la otra, segun el orden de
las partes de la oration Latinas*, Oxon., 1586.

stance of Thorius having studied at Christ Church that his translation of the grammar is to be ascribed.

During the four years immediately following his admission to Oxford, while he was still resident at the university, for he claims to have been a graduate, Thorius published two other translations from the Spanish ; namely, Felipe's *Counseller* and the *Serjeant major* of Francisco de Valdés. Thus before he was twenty-three, Thorius had turned three books from Spanish into English. Such a feat indicates extraordinary interest in the peninsular idiom. To account for this the influence of his father, John Thorius, "Balliolenus Flandrus," may perhaps be added to that of Corro in fixing the attention of the translator upon the language, as the elder Thorius was a physician, and in those days the medical profession in Spain was still held in some repute. The translator, on leaving Oxford, seems to have gone up to London. His master died in that city in 1590, just after Thorius had come before the public. The latter, however, continued his career with some success. Three years after that date he made his final essay in literature, and issued a volume contain-

ing a number of letters and sonnets to Gabriel
Harvey. These, if not of signal merit, at least
procured him some reputation as a poet, and rescued his name from oblivion for a season.

Antonio de Corro and, in a lesser degree,
Cipriano de Valera, were the sum and substance
of the abortive Spanish Reformation in so far
as it affected sixteenth-century England. Although the strength of that movement was
insignificant beside the comparatively vigorous
Protestantism which flourished among other
nations, the Spanish Reformers were indeed
much neglected by the Elizabethans. The
mutually hostile attitude of England and the
peninsula induced both Corro and Valera to
take refuge in the former country; once domiciled in the North, their writings obtained a
certain vogue by the accident of the personal
contact of their authors with the English.
Only two Spanish Reformers, indeed, secured
a hearing without this adventitious aid. The
first of these was Reginaldo Gonzalez Montano,
who had published a book entitled *Inquisitionis
hispanicæ artes aliquot detectæ, ac palam traductæ*
at Heidelberg in 1567. The second was the
Calvinist Juan Perez de Pineda.

The persons who introduced these authors to English readers have barely survived by name. They were certainly ardent Protestants, and Vincent Skinner, the translator of Montano, served as secretary to the royal council. As Skinner printed his *Declaration of sundry subtill practices of the Holy Inquisition* in 1568, at a time when Elizabeth was deliberately aggravating Philip II., and when the irritation on the part of both sovereigns was most acute, his work must have been inspired at court. It caused ambassador De Silva considerable annoyance, for he took the trouble to write to Philip about the *Declaration* in July, three days after its appearance, complaining of it "as a quarto nearly two inches thick," published anonymously. He furthermore asserted that it had even been fixed in a number of public places in the city.[1] This was a literal exemplification of the proverb "he who runs may read," and is in itself enough to determine the political character of the book.[2]

[1] De Silva to Philip II., July 3, 1568, *State papers*, *Sp.*, *Eliz.*, II., p. 50.

[2] The book marts of both kingdoms were, at the time, assiduously watched for offensive matter by the Spanish and English ambassadors. In that year, for example, Dr. Man

John Daniel, the translator of Perez de Pineda, was, then, the only Englishman who dealt with works of Spanish Protestantism possessing no more than religious import. His *Excellent Comforte to all Christians*, from the *Epistola consolatoria* of Perez, and his *Jehovah, a free pardon granted to all Christians*, both published in 1576, are to be regarded as purely devotional literature. In view of the nature of the translations from Corro, Valera, and Montano, which were all either occasional, by virtue of their subjects or through the circumstances of their appearance, these consolatory epistles stand quite alone in kind. Perez had been successively secretary of Charles V.'s legation at Rome, master of an orthodox college at Seville, for he was an Andalusian, and a Calvinistic writer at Geneva and Basle. Daniel, perhaps, came in contact with him at Geneva, or, perhaps, his attention was directed to the Reformers abroad by the Spaniards in England. The latter is not improbable, for Valera, indeed,

complained against the *Historia pontifical* of Gonzalo de Illescas, and in 1565 Richard Eden wrote home from Spain to Cecil of a book " by some mad Englishman," perhaps Roger Bacon, that a physician of Philip II. was reading. *State papers, for.*, *Eliz.*, VIII., p. 459 ; VII., p. 486.

reprinted the Spanish Bible of Perez's close
friend Casiodoro de Reyna, though at a much
later date. It can only be considered singular
that when Peter Martyr, Bernardino d'Ochino,
and other Italians were so widely read in England, but one Spanish continental Reformer was
accorded a hearing in the country. It is most
remarkable that Juan de Valdés, the friend of
Martyr and Ochino, and an author whose commentaries on *Romans* and *First Corinthians* had
been edited by Perez at Geneva, remained unnoticed until the last decade of the century,
while English and Spanish Protestantism met
in literature in the works of Corro, Valera,
Montano, and Perez de Pineda alone. The
writings of these men were set by their admirers in London against the productions of
the peninsular leaders of the Catholic reaction,
which commanded a following both abroad and
at home.

II

The Jesuitical seminaries on the continent
were the most efficient organization of the
English refugees either for political or religious
purposes. They did not reach the full height

of their power until the seventeenth century, but the literary activity of which they came to be the centre began to be felt in London during the latter years of the Tudor dynasty. The pensioners and supporters of Philip II., who had been compelled to leave their homes, flocked to Flanders for an asylum; some found their way to France, others to Rome, and still others, for political reasons, to Spain. The Earls of Westmoreland and Northumberland, Sir Francis Englefield, the Pagets, Throckmortons, and Arundels were only the most prominent of those who fled abroad. The university town of Louvain, especially, and Douay, Brussels, Nieuport, Antwerp, Arras, St. Omer, Rheims, and Paris were the headquarters of the movement in the North. They swarmed with English Catholics, who, could their strength have been utilized in united action, would have been a most dangerous menace to the state.

When the seminary at Douay was opened, this strength was partially brought into action in religious conspiracy. It was founded like all its fellows by the efforts of the English themselves. In 1568 Dr. William Allen, with the approbation of chancellor Galen of Douay

University, hired a large house near one of
the theological schools, and the first session
of the new college was begun soon afterward
with six students in attendance. The number
rose to one hundred and twenty in 1576, and
increased continually.   Pope Gregory XIII.
granted an annual pension of one hundred gold
crowns. In 1578 the college removed to Rheims,
in consequence of the momentary understanding
between England and Spain. It did not, however, lose its political importance. After its
return to Douay in 1593, the systematic education of priests for the English mission was carried on uninterruptedly for two hundred years.

The success of this college soon led to the
establishment of similar institutions in neighboring towns. These, however, were only of
inferior rank. The missionary colleges upon
the continent were without exception the offspring of Douay. In 1570 a preparatory school
for boys was opened at Esquerclin, a few miles
from that city, and Father Persons founded
another at St. Omer in 1583. The latter was
subsequently reorganized and turned into a
college. Besides the schools at St. Omer and
Esquerclin, two other English religious institu-

tions existed abroad, with which Douay was
associated either intimately or by the accident
of propinquity. These were the Jesuit College
at Rome, set up by Gregory XIII. in 1576,
which was recruited from Douay, and the Bridgettin Convent of Sion House, which consisted
of an independent company of nuns, originally
organized in Middlesex in 1413, that led a
cloistered life in various towns of France and
the Low Countries while the religious strife
was hottest. It was to this society of nuns that
John Fenne was confessor. It removed to Lisbon in 1594, and then to Mocambo, where the
company was permitted to remain without further molestation. These institutions, although
to an extent dependent upon the subvention of
Spain, were chiefly supported by contributions
which were forwarded across the channel by
Englishmen. The Catholics, indeed, took an
eager interest in their welfare, and it became a
religious duty with the papists to secure their
prosperity. So untractable a person as the Irish
Earl of Tyrone professed concern about Douay.
Only the system of fines and the severity of the
persecution inaugurated to nullify the labors of
the Jesuits, were able to diminish the revenues

which the seminaries derived from home. But the strength of the recusants was such that even these primitive measures could not cut off the supply of recruits sent from Oxford to be prepared for the mission, nor could they abate appreciably the efficiency of the institutions. By the year 1580 Douay had sent eighty-four priests into England; Campion and Persons followed within the twelvemonth.

But the seminaries had other functions than the sending of missionaries across the channel. Such an extensive movement as that of the English continental Catholics, which enlisted the sympathy of a multitude of communicants destitute of any means of publicly expressing their convictions at home, necessarily had its literary side. The recusants were forced to champion their doctrines in opposition to the Protestant leaders; and this, because of the vigilance of the Elizabethan government, they could only do abroad. Consequently, many works from English pens came from the presses of Rheims, Paris, Rouen, Douay, Louvain, and the neighboring cities during the latter half of the sixteenth and opening of the seventeenth centuries. Translations from

various Catholic writers were published.
Among the earliest of these works were the
controversial treatises of Osorio, englished by
Shacklock and Fenne; the most notable of
them was the famous Douay Bible, the authorized English version of the Romish Church,
which appeared in 1609, but by far the most
popular were the writings of the Spanish
mystics. It was in them, and especially in
the works of Luis de Granada, who summed
up the peninsular mystical movement in the
eyes of sixteenth-century Europe, that the
literary activity of the refugees found its most
striking expression. The non-theological character of these treatises recommended them to
the adherents of opposing faiths, and their
deep religious feeling assured their success.
Had mysticism been regarded by its leaders
as a theory instead of an experience, the English would not have welcomed it so willingly.
But the opposition of the prophetic and
priestly, of the mystical and scholastic elements in religion, is traditional and was plainly
apparent in orthodox Spain. That country
was the mother of the Jesuits and the birth-
place of the great reaction. It was because

of the conflict between the dreamer and ecclesiastic within its borders, that the con-
trast between the showing of Italian and
Spanish Catholicism arose in the North.   Few,
if any, Catholic works from the Italian were
published in English dress during the latter
half of the sixteenth century; thirteen editions of the books of one Spanish mystic were
either licensed or printed in that language
during twenty years of that period.   This con-
trast was brought about by Granada and his
co-workers.   If the intellect of the peninsula
was fettered, its spirit was yet free.

The mystics were celebrated quite as much
for their style as for the breadth and depth of
their religious feeling.   Style has placed their
prose among the classics of the Castilian tongue.
No writer, indeed, has owed more to his manner
than Granada.   Some of the mystics wrote with
simplicity, but Granada was essentially oratorical
and eloquent.   He was fond of superlatives.
He attempted to stimulate emotion by a profusion and concord of words rather than by the
expression of significant and discriminated ideas.
Grandiosity, verbosity, elaboration of the obvious, and utter subordination of thought to

phrase, are continually discernible in his pages.
In Spain these qualities heightened the effect of
his words and secured them a hearing among a
public which would not lend so ready an ear to
the less exaggerated though not less true feeling
of Diego de Estella. In England, where affectation in style became so common in the last quarter of the century, they procured for him a
unique welcome. His reputation rose with that
of Lyly, and was based upon the same fundamental grounds. It was three years after the
appearance of *Euphues* that a work of Granada
first appeared in English. Lyly became the
leader of a fashion, and Granada the most
popular peninsular author translated during the
closing years of Elizabeth's reign. One was
animated in his work by a strong moral sense,
the other by a religious ecstasy; but the preëmi-
nent vogue of both was due to the cultivation
of an exaggerated style.

Granada was born in 1504 in the city whose
name he assumed. While very young he joined
the Dominican order of preaching friars, and received his education in their college at Valladolid. He became successively the head of the
solitary Convent of the Escala Cœli in the Si-

erra de Córdoba and of a convent at Badajoz, and later provincial of the Portuguese Dominicans. In 1572 he retired into the Convent of Santo Domingo at Lisbon and there passed the remainder of his life in quietude, honored by persons of every rank in Spain, — Andrea Doria and bloody Alba among the rest. It was while presiding over the Convent of the Escala Cœli that he occupied his leisure with the composition of his *Meditaciones para las siete dias y siete noches de la semana*, and his *Tratado de la oracion y consideracion*, and during his retirement in Lisbon he indited his *Memorial de la vida cristiana*. These three treatises were translated into English by Richard Hopkins, who worked directly from the Spanish originals. In the popularity of his translations, this writer surpassed all the other refugees. Hopkins was favorably known as a scholar and a gentleman in many quarters. His success, however, is to be attributed quite as much to the reputation of Granada as to any accomplishments of his own. He entered St. Alban's Hall, Oxford, when about seventeen years of age, and remained in residence there until 1563. For reasons that are not now clear, he removed from

St. Alban's without a degree shortly after that date, with the intention of studying law in the Middle Temple; but the change did not prove satisfactory. Having tired of the heresy of the place, Hopkins crossed to Louvain in 1566. There he contracted a friendship with Dr. Thomas Harding, but afterward went into Spain, and studied in one of the principal universities of that country. On his return he again made his abode in Louvain, where he was settled with his sister as early as 1579. It was then that he began to produce his translations from Luis de Granada, with whose works he had undoubtedly become acquainted during his stay in Spain.

Hopkins published the *Tratado* and the *Meditaciones* at Paris in 1582, and it was later issued both at Rouen in 1583 or 1584, and at Douay in 1612. The first part of the *Memorial de la vida cristiana* appeared at Rouen in 1586 and 1599, and subsequently at Douay and St. Omer in 1612 and 1625. Paris and Rouen had been frequented by Hopkins during the years of his study of Granada, and he must have become known to the Catholic exiles resident in those localities. Cardinal Allen, indeed, entertained a favorable opinion of him, and to the Spanish authorities in the Lowlands he appeared to be an exemplary man, as he combined the two fundamental characteristics of Philip's ideal subject, —faith in the true God and zeal for the king. Two years before Hopkins' death, which occurred in 1594, his translation of the *Meditaciones* was finally published in London, as a part of his version of the *Tratado de la oracion y consideracion*, under the title of *Granada's exercises*. This book was relicensed in 1598, and republished posthumously at Edinburgh two years after that date, and in London, with dedications to William Dethick and John Banister the physician, in 1601.

Richard Gibbons printed at Louvain, in 1599, a treatise called a *Spiritual Doctrine*, which was a translation from Granada, and supplementary to Hopkins' *Memoriall of a Christian life*. It was not, indeed, the only work for which Gibbons went to a Spanish source, but it is the only one which appeared in the reign of Elizabeth. Gibbons was born in 1549, and after studying at Louvain and the German college at Rome, he entered the order of Jesuits in 1572. His brother, John Gibbons, was a co-laborer of the translator John Fenne, and engaged with him in the composition of Latin treatises. Gibbons subsequently became professor of philosophy and mathematics at Rome, and taught Hebrew and the canon law in France, besides filling chairs in educational institutions in Spain and Portugal. In 1590 he was an inmate of the English college at Valladolid. It was in the peninsula that he, like his predecessor, became acquainted with the writings of Granada. Moving in educated circles there, for other nobles than Feria countenanced the refugees, he could not well have remained ignorant of the religious writers of Castile. Spain, however, was not the place in which to print English books. It was not until his return to the north that he published the results of his studies. Gibbons' translation did not achieve the success that Hopkins' had won, yet he yielded to Hopkins in little but in age. He gave place in Jesuitical zeal to no man, for he even dedicated his *Spiritual Doctrine* to Sir William Stanley, who had betrayed Deventer to the Spaniards during Leicester's disastrous campaign.

Among the Catholics of the sixteenth century Hopkins and Gibbons were the only translators of the works of mysticism from the Spanish directly into the English language. One G. C., however, evidently an exile, also printed a book without any mark of place in 1584, called the *Contempte of the world and the vanitie thereof*. This was a version of a treatise originally written in Spanish by Diego de Estella, although borrowed by the translator from the Italian. It was issued by a continental press, and republished at St. Omer in 1622. Estella did not possess the qualities to rival the popularity of Granada. He was, it is true, confessor to Cardinal de Granvelle, and preacher to Philip II., but his unaffected style failed to attract extraordinary attention. His works did not appeal to other than a religious interest, and hence commanded a smaller sale than those of the Andalusian mystic, which had the advantage of adventitious aids.

Spanish mysticism, therefore, was expressed among the English Catholic refugees in the works of Granada and Estella as englished by this anonymous translator, by Richard Hopkins, and Richard Gibbons. Spanish scholarship was represented by the works of Osorio and Loarte, done out of the Latin by Richard Shacklock

and John Fenne.   Though the mystical writers
have stood the test of time much better than
the Latinists, the attention which was bestowed
upon them both by the refugees, was not dis-
proportionate amid the conditions of the sixteenth century.   These men were not only
exiles for religion, and hence apt to be ready
in dispute, but they were residents of the Low
Countries and the adjacent provinces of northern France.   Many of the writings of Osorio
and Loarte were printed at Paris and Rome,
and were consequently more accessible than
books that were purely Spanish.   The mystical
writers were, for the most part, translated by
persons who went to Spain, and obtained
knowledge of them there.   The *Contempte of
the world* was brought up from Italy like the
treatises of Loarte, and was the sole exception
to this rule.   Had the headquarters of the
English Catholics been in the peninsula, the
body of religious translation would have been
quite different.   Had the country not been too
remote to serve as a convenient asylum, an
organization of the Catholic exiles there would
have been sooner attempted.   But this was not
deemed desirable until the Armada had been

defeated. Then the English College of St. Alban at Valladolid was founded in 1589. St. Gregory's at Seville and St. George's at Madrid were established within the next five years, through the efforts of the Jesuits and the generosity of sympathetic Spaniards. But these institutions were not large, and that at Valladolid alone grew to be robust and flourishing. None of them attained to any influence during the sixteenth century, least of all in letters. Had the colleges in Spain been set up less tardily, when the complete success of the papal cause seemed imminent, it would scarcely have been possible that Juan de Avila, San Juan de la Cruz, Santa Teresa de Jesus, and Luis de Leon, the contemporaries of Granada, should all have remained strangers to the England of Elizabeth.

III

Appreciation of Spanish mysticism was in no sense confined to the exiles at Douay or other continental towns. The group of English refugees who were engaged in its dissemination was paralleled by a group of Protestants in London who essayed the same task. In the

last fifteen years of the sixteenth century
preachers of the Established Church, irrecon-
cilably opposed to the tenets of the Jesuits and
seminary priests who thronged the continent
and stole furtively across the channel, — men
committed to the Reformation by sympathy
and by vow as positively as Haddon or Foxe
had been, and participators in a manner in the
labors of Corro and Valera, — bestowed their
approval upon the works of Estella and Granada,
the identical authors who had elicited the fullest
admiration of the exiles at Douay. The depth
of the comparatively untrammelled religious
feeling of the mystical writers which created a
demand for reprints of Hopkins' translations in
Edinburgh and London, resulted also in translations by Protestant hands. The qualities of
style which made Granada to be widely read
on the continent, became quite as much admired in England. The activity of the Protestants increased with that of the Catholic
refugees. Indeed it was complementary to it.
Had only the translations which the latter
produced found their way across the channel, had these merely been reprinted in English
cities, the mystical movement would have ac-

quired little power. When these versions were
supplemented by others prepared in the country
itself, the interest in Granada became a force,
and the movement vigorous and complete.

Thomas Rogers and Francis Meres were the
principal Protestant translators of the Spanish mystics. Rogers obtained his education at
Christ Church, Oxford, while Hakluyt and
Philip Sidney were attending that college, and
Antonio de Corro was teaching in the university.
He entered in 1571, and did not take his M.A.
until 1576. After leaving the university, he
was appointed chaplain to Richard Bancroft,
who succeeded Whitgift in the see of Canterbury. In 1581 Rogers became rector of Horn-
ingsheath in Suffolk, where he died in 1616.
He left behind him a reputation as a religious
writer, the foundation of which he had laid in
the training that he received in assisting Bancroft in his literary work, and which he perhaps
realized most fully in his Sabbatarian controversy with Dr. Bound. The most notable of
his works were his *English Creed*, which appeared from 1579 to 1587, and a translation
of Thomas à Kempis' *Imitation of Christ*. In
1586 Rogers' version of Diego de Estella's

De la Vanidad del mundo was printed, just twelve years after the original Spanish had been published at Seville.[1]

Neither Rogers' association with Bancroft nor his bent toward the discussion of creeds, suggest in any way the possibility of his acting as the translator of the work of a pronounced Catholic and a monk. It was the vein of mysticism which was in the man, that inclined him to look favorably upon Estella. The disposition that induced Rogers to study Thomas à Kempis, enabled him also to give the Navarrese confessor of Philip II. his due. It was but a step from the one to the other, and the transition was not difficult, for Rogers was no extremist. His equability exposed him to the displeasure of both friends and foes. He was a moderate man, and found the infallible touchstone of the true faith in the spirit of Santa Teresa de Jesus, Luis de Leon, and Diego de Estella, reformers not of doctrine but of life, persecuted and reviled for heresy ostensibly,

[1] A Latin translation of the *Vanidad del mundo*, by P. Burgundo, was published at Cologne in 1585. As Rogers' version followed so closely upon that of Burgundo, the latter was probably its immediate source. Rogers translated other works from Latin, but no others from the Spanish.

but for a militant sense of purity and right in reality.

The appeal which Spanish mysticism made to Francis Meres, was not the same as that with which it had influenced Thomas Rogers. Meres was both a preacher and a literary man. He was born in Lincolnshire in 1565. His immediate relatives were in straitened circumstances, but the generosity of John Meres, his kinsman and sheriff of the county, mitigated somewhat their poverty. Meres attended Pembroke College, Cambridge, and received the bachelor's and master's degrees from the university in 1587 and 1591, respectively. He was incorporated as master of arts at Oxford in 1593, and shortly afterward removed to London with the intention of taking up literature as a profession. But authorship did not prove as remunerative as he had anticipated. In fulfilment of his intention to give himself up to the ministry, Meres took steps to procure a living, and obtained the grant of the rectory of Wing in Rutland, whither he removed in 1602. He diversified his clerical duties by keeping school in the town. The best part of his youth was thus passed as a writer in London, amid an

environment that was by no means strictly theological. He was as well fitted to appreciate
the distinction of the style of the mystics as to
respond to the fervor of their earnest appeals.
He took particular pride in his own euphuistical way of writing, and any similar exaggerations of which the Spanish mystics were guilty
gratified him. The more ornate and rhetorical
the manner, the more it was fancied by Meres.
He preferred, therefore, the sonorous periods of
Luis de Granada, the most grandiloquent of
Spaniards, to the simpler sentences of Diego
de Estella and others of his contemporaries,
and two of his books are translations from the
Andalusian preacher.

The literary activity of Meres was chiefly
confined to the last few years of the reign of
Elizabeth. It is more curious than important,
and almost entirely of a didactic nature, for the
poems signed F. M. in the *Paradise of dainty
devices* which have been ascribed to him, must
be the compositions of another, as Meres was
only eleven at the time that miscellany was
published. His best-known works belong to
the year 1598. These are the *Palladis tamia*,
the second of a series of volumes on literary,

ethical, and religious topics, planned by Nicholas Ling the printer, *Granados devotion*, and the first part of the *Sinners guyde*, also translated from Granada. The second part of the *Sinners guyde* was not published until 1614, when it was brought out by Richard Field, with a dedication to Sir Thomas Egerton. One of these men was the printer and the other the patron of Cipriano de Valera, during his residence in England. Yet Meres gives no sign of having been acquainted with Spanish literature in other than a very casual manner. The evidence against his command of Castilian, though mainly negative, is convincing. Meres' *Comparative Discourse of our English poets with the Greek, Latin, and Italian*, contained in the *Palladis tamia*, when compared with the *Arcadian Rhetorike* of Abraham Fraunce, which was written precisely a decade earlier, shows a lamentable ignorance of Spanish letters. Fraunce offers a considerable number of citations from Spanish poets; Meres has none. It is true that the scope of Meres' subject did not require that he should treat the peninsular poets, but the only reference which he makes to them impeaches his knowledge of their works. This is the pas-

sage in which the name of Gonzalo Perez is
linked with that of Surrey.   Meres says: " As
Consalvo Periz that excellent learned man, and
Secretary to King Philip of Spayne, in translating the Ulysses of Homer out of Greeke into
Spanish, hath by good judgement avoided the
faulte of Ryming, although not full hit perfect
and true versifying; so hath Henry Howarde
that true and noble Earle of Surrey in translating the fourth book of Virgil's *Æneas.* . . ." [1]
This is the Perez who was a correspondent of
Ascham, from whom Meres has borrowed this
sentence almost literally.   That such a proceeding was allowable enough in the compilation of
a school book, which the *Palladis tamia* practically was, no one will be disposed to question;
but the coincidence of the language of Ascham
and Meres, in the latter's only reference to a
Castilian poet, supports the opinion that Meres'
knowledge of Spanish literature was neither
extensive nor first hand, if indeed it reached
beyond the French versions of Luis de Granada.

The penchant toward literature which was a
characteristic of Meres, was shared by Thomas

---

[1] Meres, reprint by Haslewood in *Ancient crit. Essays*,
II., p. 149.   See Ascham,*Scholemaster*, ed. Arber, p. 147.

Wilcox, another London divine of the latter part of the century, who undertook translation from the Spanish. Wilcox did not deal with the mystical writers, although he did translate from that tongue. He was educated at St. John's College, Oxford, where he was a student in 1564. On completing his studies, he retired to the metropolis and became, according to Wood, "a very painful minister of God's word." In this capacity he achieved great repute, which he increased by his religious writings and by translations from Théodore de Bèze and Bertrand de Loques. To these translations one other of a totally different kind must be added, for Wilcox prepared an English version of the first part of Montemayor's pastoral novel, the *Diana*, in 1598. This work, which was dedicated to the Earl of Southampton, is still in manuscript. It was evidently undertaken as a recreation. Since Valera went to Oxford two years after Wilcox had entered the university, it is possible that the Spaniard exerted some influence upon him, as perhaps on Rogers and Meres. The *Diana*, however, had been printed in French twenty years before Wilcox com-

pleted his version, and copies of both the
Spanish and French editions had then long
circulated in England. Bartholomew Yong,
who had editions in both languages at command, finished his *Diana* in 1583, though it
was not published until 1598. It is therefore
not so strange that another translation should
have been undertaken at the latter date, as
that it should have been the work of a cleric
like Wilcox. But the incongruity is no
greater than in the cases of some of his
contemporaries. In the perusal of Spanish
books the Elizabethans were not inclined to
read into them offensive doctrines even when
they might have been justified by the text.
These they were content to combat in open
controversy. Thus the spirit of Estella was
agreeable to Rogers, the eloquence of Granada
to Meres, and the romance of Montemayor,
incomparably freer than either from possibili-
ties of offence, because of its secularity, to
Thomas Wilcox.

The success of Luis de Granada was the
noteworthy feature in the translation of peninsular religious writers during the Elizabethan epoch. In the reign of Henry VIII.

the English gave much study to Vives, in the transitional period which was inaugurated by the marriage of Queen Mary, to Osorio, and in the latter years of the century to the Spanish mystics. The Latin authors yielded to those who wrote in the vernacular. No Spaniard assumed a commanding rôle in the eyes of the Elizabethans in the field of scholarship. Corro, Arias Montano, and Ximenez de Cisneros all received a hearing, but none of them left a deep impression. It was Granada alone who took fast hold of the English mind and won acknowledged popularity. He occupied during the last quarter of the century, in so far as the changed conditions would permit, the position that Guevara had filled from the days of Lord Berners, and no other Spaniard in that age, save Guevara, was so often translated or so widely read in England.

Guevara had assumed the attitude of a moralist in his most successful books; Granada always wrote from the religious point of view; but neither pursued a method which emphasized unduly differences of doctrine. Both were greatly assisted by their use of style. Neither was in the habit of weighing his words, of adjusting the word to the thought; both played with them as if they had no weight.   The earlier writer was distinguished by the balancing of word, phrase, and clause against other words, phrases, and clauses, either in parallelisms or antitheses, in such a manner as to preserve one cadence throughout, frequently emphasized by the recurrence of the same sounds or rhymes. Far-fetched allusion and, to a less degree, rhetorical question were characteristics.   The later writer habitually succumbed to rhetoric in his periods and attempted to stimulate emotion by the employment of a profusion of words in place of ideas.   He was exuberant.   The earlier was petty and had his parallel in euphuism; the later was grandiloquent and more nearly approached the Arcadian style of Sidney.   Both made an appeal to a similar taste.   The popularity of Guevara was on the decline in England when the works of Granada began to appear in English, although the *Epístolas familiares* and the *Aguja de marear* were just being translated, but it revived simultaneously with the rise of the latter author.   During the twenty-three years previous to the translation of the former's *Meditaciones* in 1582, the *Golden Boke* had been

Q

but three times reprinted; in the next five years an equal number of reissues appeared. A new edition of the *Diall of princes* was also published in 1582, and the *Monte Calvario* was translated for the first time in 1595–1597. This was the only purely religious work of Guevara to appear in English, and its publication at the height of the popularity of Granada, which was in the religious sphere, cannot have been a mere coincidence. These authors were admired when the English affectations were at their height.

The revival of Guevara, however, did not rival the interest in the mystical writers. He was replaced by his English imitators. Granada, on the other hand, was widely read. Ten separate translations from his works were either printed or licensed to be printed in English during the twenty years beginning with 1582. The number of editions to which there is similar reference was sixteen. Because of their freedom from pettiness of device, they continued to appear in the next century after the decay of euphuism. Yet Granada did not acquire the reputation in England that his predecessor had possessed. Both the character of his own work and the complexion of the times united to prevent that he should. The courtier had availed himself of such adventitious aids as pseudo-historical interest to obtain success, but the mystic remained within the limits of religious literature. The great activity of the press had further produced a change in literature since the death of the earlier writer. Books had become more plentiful, and the literary forms of the great impending period were momentarily differentiating themselves. Many models had been set before courtiers and popular authors which were better suited for general imitation than religious works. Hence the phenomena of the earlier were not repeated in the later epoch. The works of Granada, instead of becoming the common dower of the intellectual world, remained the special property of men of piety.

CHAPTER VII

TRANSLATORS OF ELIZABETH'S COURT

NEITHER the trading class nor those persons who dwelt abroad solely in the cause of religion, occupied themselves at all with books that lay beyond the provinces of history and theology. The chronicle of adventure attracted the merchant, and the religious treatise, whether controversial or mystical, commended itself to the partisans of the Roman and Anglican factions. Though Spanish literature of an æsthetic character had been introduced into England by the courtiers of Henry VIII., it did not assume its due place in the volume of Elizabethan translation until the agency of the English ambassadors in Spain and the political refugees in the peninsula had become effective in the dissemination of culture. The best blood of England flowed in the veins of the emissaries and gentlemen travellers whom she sent into Spain. There those who deemed themselves the pro-

spective rulers of England congregated; there
they waited for Philip II. to restore them to
their own. In the ample leisure of which they
were masters, they found time for the study of
literature. Their friends carried romances, novels, and even poetry to the North, as the traders carried chronicles of discovery, or the
Catholics the writings of the mystics. By the
endeavor of ambassadors and gentlemen of education who visited the peninsula, the general
interest in Spanish books in England, never
entirely quiescent since its birth at the time
of Lord Berners, was stimulated and in a
measure satisfied. The agency of no other persons in the latter part of the century was so
potent as theirs in distributing the culture of
Spain.

During the reign of Elizabeth the English
were represented by four ambassadors at the
court of Castile, — Sir Thomas Chamberlain,
Sir Thomas Challoner, John Man, and Sir John
Smith. Chamberlain's embassy in Spain lasted
from January 1560 to December 1561. Challoner was ambassador from November 1561 to
April 1565; Man from March 1566 to July
1568; and Smith for ten months, beginning in

September 1576.   Each thus resided some time
in the country.   Smith was essentially a soldier
and not a man of letters.   An indiscreet and
hot-headed gentleman, he habitually yielded to
an impetuosity that would have cost him dear,
had he been other than the nephew of Jane
Seymour.   His rash temper forced him to leave
Spain, after an undignified quarrel with the
Archbishop of Toledo in 1577, and it afterward
got him into prison when he spoke intemper-
ately of Lord Burghley.   It was in December 1563, fourteen years previous to his embassy, that Smith first visited Spain.   He had
come from Italy, travelling with six horses in
fine style, and at Monçon "alighted at the lodg-
ing of Don Francisco de Castillo, whom he had
known in London."[1]   Not improbably Smith
learned Spanish from such friends in the English capital, for he was already familiar with the
language during his stay in Hungary.   He may
have picked it up among the Spaniards among
whom he fought in various places on the continent.   His association with these men enabled
him to obtain a command over Castilian, so that
he wrote the language with facility.   At his

[1] *State papers, for., Eliz.,* VI., p. 632.

death he left a manuscript called *Collections and observations relating to the condition of Spain,* the material of which he gathered during his stay in the country.   This was chiefly in Spanish, and in the nature of a diary, but it does not properly belong to literature.   The other writings of Smith were military tracts, and, like others of that sort, the work of a professional soldier.   It was, of course, inevitable that military treatises, composed by men who had served with the celebrated Spanish troops, and been drilled in their tactics, should show the influence of such service.   But this also, though important, is not a literary influence.   If Smith and his contemporaries bore themselves " with a Spanish port," the consequence to literature was Shakspere's Don Armado and Jonson's Bobadil, but nothing more.

Dr. John Man was stationed for two years in Spain.   Guzman de Silva summarily described him on the occasion of his appointment, calling him "a worthy person who speaks Italian." [1]   Man, however, was something more.   Formerly chaplain to Archbishop Parker, he had become dean of Gloucester,

[1] De Silva to Philip II., *State papers, Sp., Eliz.,* I., p. 517.

and was recognized as a Reformer of a pronounced type. Scarcely more tactful than Smith, he speedily alienated the good-will of the Ferias, upon which the English ambassadors were dependent to a great extent. This piece of foolhardiness was notably unfortunate, for Man, being a married prelate, had been coolly received from the beginning, and there was much question in the country whether it was lawful to speak with him. He was the victim of systematic annoyance, and, since he was ignorant of the language, opposed by the Ferias and their clique, and disliked even by the trading class, who saw the progress of their suits impeded by his unpopularity, he lived in endless trouble. The latter part of his stay he spent at Barajas, a neighboring town to Madrid, where he was practically confined under the eye of the Bishop of Pampeluna, who was occupying the house next door. Under these conditions Man returned home unmoved by the attractions of Spanish literature. He was lucky to have escaped the hand of the Inquisition. The danger in which he stood was much greater than that which had threatened Sir Thomas Chamberlain, who had been

sent to the peninsula soon after Philip's return
from the North, and dwelt in Spain at a time
when the hostility of the Holy Office was not so
pronounced as in Man's day. Had Chamberlain
not constantly been in the care of the physicians, he would not have occupied an unusu-
ally difficult position. Not unpopularity, but
illness, kept him from the court and deprived
him of the opportunity to bring his scholarship into play in the peninsula.

Of the four ambassadors accredited to Philip
II. during the reign of Elizabeth, Challoner
was the only one to whom fortune was at all
propitious. Like the others, Challoner was a
university man, and as a Latin poet he ranked
high among his contemporaries. He had contributed to the first edition of the *Mirror for
magistrates*, and was regarded with deference
by a large circle of admirers. When, at the
age of forty, he arrived in Spain, he was at the
height of his power and influence. Though
not recognized at court for over five months
after his coming, he succeeded in establishing
amicable intercourse with the Ferias and with
the English residents in the centres of trade.
It was with the assistance of these men that

he performed his duties, for he was none too welcome to the king. Challoner was dependent upon interpreters, though he had accompanied Charles V. to Algiers in 1541, and had served Sir Henry Knyvet in the peninsula at the opening of 1542. He retained William Phayre for his knowledge of the Spanish tongue and because of his familiarity with the diplomatic usage of the country. When Bartholomew Withipoll, who had learned much of the language during his stay in the country, left Challoner in 1562, only a steward and secretary remained who were acquainted with Spanish. The ambassador cared more for Italian and French. Sir Thomas Smith corresponded with him about Ronsard, and Henry Killigrew about French verses of the latter's own making. He sent a number of Italian books home, — among others one by Giorgio Siculo to Elizabeth, — and Killigrew mentions stanzas which had been translated by him from Ariosto. It was in Spain that he wrote the poems *De Motu gallico* and *De Republica anglicana*. Challoner was, in fact, a persistent poet, for the *De Republica* contained upward of six thousand verses, samples of which he would now and then forward to England for the benefit of Dr. Wotton, Sir John Mason, or John Challoner, sometimes sending word that if they liked them they might show them to the queen.[1] In 1563 Challoner went so far as to send verses to one of the Spanish universities. This was the University of Alcala. The verses were returned to him by "Edmund Tanere," chaplain, who wrote that the praise that they had there could not be declared.[2] He also enclosed epigrams by two young men in commendation of them. Challoner was greatly pleased by the reception of his verses, though he did not as a rule have a very good opinion of the judgment of Spaniards. He questions their sanity in other matters. "Generally, the air of Spain," he wrote a year previously, "is evil for hurts on the head, and Alcala peculiarly noted for one of the worst places."

The great productivity of Challoner emphasizes the singular neglect of peninsular

[1] The correspondence and official documents of Challoner's embassy in Spain are contained in the *State papers, for.*, *Eliz.*, IV.–VII. Challoner was accustomed to write freely of his literary work. For the above, see V., p. 394; VI., pp. 248, 499; VII., p. 149.

[2] *Ibid.*, VI., p. 409.

literature by the resident ambassadors. With
the one exception of the work of Lord Berners,
the neglect was complete. Wyatt was absolutely uninfluenced by his stay in Spain.
Emissaries in other countries were accustomed
to send some of the notable books published
in them to members of the council or to
friends at home. No such books were sent
from Spain. Only on one or two occasions
does any Spanish production appear to have
been noticed by the ambassadors. One was
when Nicholas Hawkins saw an old book by
a Spanish bishop at Barcelona, whose doctrines
all Spain could not answer; one was when Sir
Philip Hoby made a memorandum that he had
heard a sermon of the Bishop of Granada; and
another when Dr. Man objected to Gonzalo de
Illescas' *Historia pontifical*, asserting that it
slandered Henry VIII. and Elizabeth.[1] This
silence was due in the instances of Smith and
Man to the hostility which they aroused and
felt. In the cases of Chamberlain and Challoner, it was partly due to isolation and partly
to the handicap of unfamiliarity with the lan-

[1] *Letters and papers, for. and dom., Hen. VIII.*, VI.,
p. 388; XIII., pt. 2, p. 415; *State papers, for., Eliz.*, VIII.,
p. 459.

guage. Chamberlain was, besides, annoyed by sickness, and Challoner occupied with other literary interests. The climate and the enmity of the people invariably made the lot of the ambassadors unenviable in the extreme. Chamberlain's parting witticism was repeated by Challoner, "Spain? quoth he; nay, rather pain." It is apparent, however, that there were compensations that even ambassadors could not ignore; for Challoner expected to take home with him a *cuero* or two of such good wine that when he drank it he should make verses *extempore*.

The total indifference of the English ambassadors to Spanish literature must be accounted for on personal grounds, since the merchants, many of whom had resided a longer time in the country than they, and the travelling class, many of whom remained but a brief time, often assumed a different attitude. Some attention was paid to Spanish books, even by the special emissaries of the queen. Sir Henry Cobham, who was more than once despatched to the peninsula, when congratulating Challoner on his reported recall in 1563, desired him to bring some Spanish

books on his return.[1]   Thomas Wilson, twice
commissioned to Portugal, kept up a correspondence with persons in Lisbon, and several
works from the Spanish were licensed by the
Stationers' Company in London under his
hand.   But it was the young gentlemen who
travelled in the peninsula, either as guests of
the ambassadors or of the Catholic refugees,
who busied themselves with translations.   A
group of translators consequently appeared at
court.   Those who went abroad in the opening decade of Elizabeth's reign, came in contact with Challoner in Spain; others were in
a way related to him in his capacity of classical poet; therefore, though the ambassador
was not properly the centre of any group, for
he died immediately after his recall in 1565,
yet the translators at court were not unbound
to him.   His wide circle of friends, which included Haddon, Cheke, Richard and Thomas
Sackville, Burghley, John Mason, the Cob-
hams, and Bishop Grindal, made him an important figure.   Only his neglect of Spanish
literature prevented him from becoming a

[1] Cobham to Challoner, December 21, 1563.   *State papers,
for.*, *Eliz.*, VI., p. 637.

potent force in furthering translation. As it
is, the ambassadors stand to translators in a
generic rather than a personal relationship.
The connection is one of circumstance, of
common literary affiliations.

In May 1562, Barnaby Googe returned to
England from Spain, bearing with him two
wooden coffers of "*gwadamessillez*" hangings
for Sir Thomas Chamberlain, with two little
silver candlesticks, one salt-cellar, gilt, with the
cover, a basin, an "ewell silver parcel," gilt,
and a little fardel of linen napery. As the
kinsman of Burghley, he had been hospitably
entertained by Sir Thomas Challoner, for whom
he carried these presents home, at the end of
his sojourn of a year in the peninsula. Previous to going abroad Googe had studied at
New College, Oxford, and at Christ College,
Cambridge, and had also entered Staple Inn,
becoming a retainer of Burghley. He remained
but a brief time at each of these places, for he
left England at the age of twenty-one. While
Googe was yet in Spain, his friend, L. Blundeston, put a volume of his poems into the printer's
hands, without the knowledge of the author.
Googe had already published a translation of the

first six books of Marcellus Palingenius' *Zodia-
cus vitæ*, but had not appeared in the rôle of an
original poet. Finding that it was too late to
prevent the printing of his verses, he completed
the last selection of the published volume, called
Cupido's conquered, for Blundeston, and the
book was issued in 1563 under the title *Eglogs,
epytaphes, and sonettes*. Among the poems that
it contained, two of the eclogues, the fifth and
seventh, are translations into verse of prose
passages of the *Diana* of Montemayor. The
fifth eclogue is a free adaptation of the story of
Felismena in the second book of the *Diana*, and
follows the general outlines of the original,
though some of the speeches are closely translated. The seventh is a tolerably faithful rendering of the scene between the shepherds
Silvanus, Sirenus, and Selvagia, in the first
book. The *Diana* was not printed until 1559,
or about a year before Googe arrived in Spain,
and in these eclogues it was probably introduced
to England. It certainly made its first appearance in English literature in this volume of
Googe's verse. The sixth eclogue also contains a few lines borrowed from the Spanish of
Garcilaso de la Vega, the lyric poet. Sanna-

zaro had described, in the eighth *prosa* of his
Arcadia, various idyllic methods of bird-catch-
ing, which the shepherd Carino and a woodland
nymph had practised together in a pastoral re-
treat. These had been versified by Garcilaso,
with but slight changes, in his second eclogue,
in which they constitute the greater part of the
lament of Albanio, the central feature of the
first half of the poem.   Googe extracted from
this long relation, written with all the charm
of the Toledan poet, merely an account of snar-
ing a flock of birds, by the device of letting
loose one of their fellows bearing a limed line
among them : —

> " Sometime I wold betraye the Byrds
>   that lyght on lymed tree,
> Especially in Shepstare tyme,
>   when thicke in flockes they flye,
> One wold I take, and to her leg,
>   a lymed Lyne wold tye,
> And where ye flock flew thickest, there
>   I wold her cast awaye,
> She strayght unto the rest wold hye,
>   amongst·her mates to playe.
> And preasyng in the mydste of them,
>   with Lyne and Lyme and all,
> With cleving wyngs, entangled fast
>   they downe togyther fall." [1]

[1] Googe, *Eglog VI.*, ll. 143–156.

R

This passage is not reminiscent, in Googe's eclogue, of the happiness of a former love, as it was in Garcilaso and Sannazaro, but is the principal feature of a brief rehearsal of the sports whereby one may forget love and keep it from the mind. The English poem, therefore, resembles its Spanish and Italian prototypes in the incident alone, and not in the spirit in which it is given. It contains the only lines of Spanish lyric poetry, except the lyrics included in the *Diana*, which were translated into English in the sixteenth century. Total neglect of the genre would not have been so remarkable as this scant recognition of it. It is a strange phenomenon that the Spanish lyric, when it once entered England, should have done so in but a dozen lines, which were not only a paraphrase of an Italian author, but of slight importance in themselves.[1]

[1] There can be no doubt that Googe translated this passage from Garcilaso and not from Sannazaro, for he imitates the Spaniard, not only in his conciseness, but in his petty modifications of the Italian. Thus Sannazaro speaks of capturing three birds, while Garcilaso and Googe speak of but one. The Spanish verses, which Googe follows very closely, surpass both the English and the Italian in merit. See Garcilaso de la Vega, *Egloga II.*, ll. 248–259.

Googe was married shortly after the appearance of his poems, but only after Burghley and Archbishop Parker had interceded for him with the lady's father. In 1574 he obtained an office in Ireland, where he resided for eleven years. Meanwhile, versions of Kirchmayer's *Regni papistici* and Herebachius's *Husbandry* came from his pen, and in 1579 he published his translation of the versified *Proverbios* of the Marquis of Santillana, with the paraphrase by Pedro Diaz de Toledo, a scholar of the reign of Juan II. of Castile. This was the first translation of a collection of Spanish proverbs into English, and the only one printed during the sixteenth century.

The principal friends of Googe who engaged in authorship belonged to the group which flourished during the first seven years after the accession of Elizabeth, translating the tragedies of Seneca into English verse. Alexander Neville, an inmate of Parker's house, Jasper Heywood, John Studley, Thomas Nuce, prebend of Ely, and Thomas Newton were the leading members of this group. Alexander Nowell, dean of St. Paul's, and Thomas Phaer, the translator of the Æneid, were also much

esteemed by Googe. The religious tone of this
society is its most obvious feature ; Neville,
Nowell, Nuce, and Newton had theological
affiliations, and Heywood afterward became a
Jesuit. The relationship in which the group
stood to the ambassadors in Spain was also
marked. Phaer, like Challoner, had been a
contributor to the *Mirror for magistrates*. The
latter's friend, the critic of his verses, Sir John
Mason, was a patron of Heywood. Parker was
the chief adviser of ambassador Man. Googe,
besides having travelled in the peninsula, had
been at Cambridge while Cipriano de Valera
was at the university, and may have been at
Oxford when the Spanish scholars were lecturing there during the reign of Mary. But this
possibility is a matter of little significance, for
the important consideration is the direct communication between the members of the group
and Spain. Through this contact they were
enabled to bring many till then unknown Spanish books into England. The *Diana* was undoubtedly brought to the notice of London by
Googe by letters from Spain, and in person on
his return from his travels. It is scarcely possible that the selections which he made from it

should have been completed in England before
his departure for the peninsula in the winter of
1561–1562, where it had appeared only in the
preceding year.[1]

Thomas Newton was another of this group
to translate from the Castilian. Newton is remembered as a writer both of English and Latin
verses, as well as a translator of literary, historical, and medical works, chiefly from the
Latin. It was in the year 1580 that his version
of Pedro Mexía's *Pleasaunt Dialogue concerning
phisicke and phisitions* appeared. The original
formed a portion of the *Diálogos* of Mexía, a
Sevillian of considerable learning, who rose to
be chronicler to Charles V. Newton, however,
dealt with no other Spanish author, and was
principally known by his more important works.
Among these was the *Thebais* of Seneca, which
he translated to complete the volume of the
tragedies of that author rendered by Neville,
Nuce, Heywood, and Studley, that he published
in 1581. His ability as a Latinist drew those
men to him, for it was his chief distinction.
Like Googe, who was some two years his senior,

[1] Fitzmaurice-Kelly is of the opinion that the *Diana* was
published in 1559 ; Brunet places the first edition at 1560.

Newton had studied at both Oxford and Cambridge, and had followed Googe, approximately, at the interval of a year at both universities. Retiring from Oxford, Newton returned to his home at Butley in Cheshire, where he practised medicine, and is said to have taught school. He was patronized by the Earl of Essex at a later date, and in 1596 Elizabeth presented him to a living in Little Ilford, Essex, whither he then removed. As one of the most prominent of the older Elizabethan writers, Newton was associated in one way or another with many of the notable figures of the time. He dedicated books to Walsingham, Challoner's friend Lord Cobham, and Admiral Charles Howard of Effingham. He was especially indefatigable in composing prefatory and commendatory verses for his contemporaries. Anthony Munday, Jasper Heywood, and Thomas Tymme, the editor of Bryan's *Looking-glasse for the courte*, were among those to whom Newton addressed his complimentary lines.

William Blandy was not the least of the men who obtained the commendation of Newton. Blandy had been elected fellow of New College, Oxford, during the year in which Newton re-

turned to Trinity after a short residence at
Queen's College, Cambridge.   At that time
Richard Hopkins, and Thomas D'Oylie the
lexicographer, were students at Oxford, and
Thomas Wilcox, a translator of the *Diana*, was
about to enter the university.   Blandy continued his studies until he obtained his degree
in 1566, when he was charged with Romanism,
and was summarily removed from his fellowship.   The apprehensions of the authorities
on this point were undoubtedly not without
foundation, for he removed to Newberry, after
allying himself with the Middle Temple at
London, and in 1576 brought out the *Five
Books of Hieronimo Osorius, contayning a discussion of ciuill and Christian nobilitie.*   This he
dedicated to Leicester.   As this was not a controversial work, Blandy was not obliged to take
refuge on the continent as Shacklock and
Fenne had done.   He served in the Low Countries, however, but with the English troops, and
sought the patronage of Sidney, when publishing his dialogues with Geoffrey Gate in 1581.
Blandy was a representative of the class of
Catholic sympathizers, of which the Sidneys,
the Herberts, and the Howards were prominent

members, which by its moderate bearing lived peacefully under the Protestant régime, but which was disposed by its sympathies to welcome the old doctrines, if unaccompanied by the threat of Spanish domination. It was partly to satisfy the demands of this element that Blandy undertook his translation; but admiration of Osorio was by no means confined to any particular sect. Editions of that author's *De Gloria libri V.* were published in the original Latin at London in 1580 and 158.(.), and met with success similar to that of the controversial tracts of the Portuguese bishop. Speaking of Osorio, Newton says: —

> " Ille, ille est nostri Phœnix et Tullius ævi,
>   Alpha disertorum dicier ille potest.
> Numine Blandæus Phœbæo concitus, hujus
>   Scripta Latina docet verba Britanna loqui." [1]

These lines truly indicate that the cause of the popularity of the book was twofold, and resided in the esteem in which the translator was held as well as in the merits of the original author.

Another scholar, William Patten, who had been associated with Burghley in his younger days, compiled a volume called the *Calendars*

[1] See Wood, *Athenæ*, II., p. 11.

of Scripture, largely from a Spanish source, in 1575. This book purported to give the "Hebru, Chaldean, Arabian, Phenician, Syrian, Persian, Greek, and Latin names of nations, contreys, men, weemen, idols, cities, hils, rivers, and of other places in the holly byble" with their English equivalents. It was founded by Patten upon the *Complutensian Polyglot* published at Alcala under the direction of Cardinal Ximenez in 1517, and also upon a work by Joannes Arquerius, of Bordeaux. The compiler was a cleric and prebend of St. Paul's, and he appears chiefly as an adherent of Lord Burghley. It was probably due to Burghley, whom he accompanied to Scotland in Warwick's command in 1548, that he was appointed teller of the exchequer. He corresponded with Sir Francis Walsingham, and his intimacy with the ministers, his office, and his history of the Scotch campaign, which is his best-remembered work, distinguished him as one of the court set. He was a friend of Sir Thomas Challoner, and the uncle of Sir William Waad, the diplomatist, who was sent as special ambassador to Madrid when Elizabeth dismissed Bernardino de Mendoza from her court in 1584.

The *Concejo y consejeros de príncipes* of Federico Furió Ceriol, a well-known writer of Valencia, was translated by Thomas Blundeville,
another member of the group of classicists.   A
native of Newton-Flotman in Norfolk, where he
resided, Blundeville early acquired an enviable
reputation as a translator of Plutarch.   For many
years a great variety of works on such diverse
subjects as logic, astronomy, horsemanship, geography, and navigation appeared from his pen.
Few of them were original.   Blundeville was
the recipient of the favor of Leicester, who acted
as his especial patron, and was addressed in
verse in complimentary terms by Ascham and
Jasper Heywood.   His translation of the treatise
of Furió Ceriol appeared in 1570, when he was
at the height of his career.   Blundeville tells
how he came upon the book in some prefatory
remarks, in which he says that it was " first written in the Spanishe tongue by a Spanyard called
Federigo Fvrio, and afterward translated into the
Italian tongue by another Spanyard called Alfonso d'vlloa, but not with so good grace as I
believe it had in the Spanishe, which indeede I
never sawe, and therefore though my friend
Mayster John Baptist Castiglion, one of the

Gromes of hir Highnesse priuie chamber . . . de-
liuered me the saide book at my last being at the
Court, earnestly requesting me to put the same
into our vulgar tong, yet I would not altogither
trāslate it, but thought it best to make a brief
collection of the substance thereof, cutting of all
superfluous talks. . . ."[1] The testimony of this
preface is important because it demonstrates that
there was common talk of Spanish books in the
circle of Blundeville's friends.   The translation
of the treatise of Furió Ceriol was, of course,
purely the result of chance; but it is evident
from the report about the inferiority of Ulloa's
version which was in circulation, that some of
the members of his set were better informed
upon Spanish literature than he himself could
pretend to be.   Blundeville, while working from
an Italian copy, was nevertheless still within
the sphere of the direct peninsular influence.

It was in the midst of similar forces that Edward Hellowes, the last of the English translators of Guevara's secular works, lived.   Nothing
is known of the career of this man beyond the information that he gives of himself in his books.
According to his own assertion, Hellowes served

[1] See Brydges, *Censura*, V., p. 371.

under Sir Henry Lee as groom of the leash in
the year 1574, if not previously, and he continued to hold that office until he resigned to become groom of the chamber in 1597.   The three
translations which make up the total of his literary work, were drawn from the writings of
Guevara, and they all appeared within a period
of five years after Hellowes first came into notice.   The *Familiar Epistles* were published in
1574, and the *Chronicle conteyning the liues of
tenne emperoures of Rome* and the *Inuention of
the arte of navigation* in 1577 and 1578, respectively.   Hellowes dedicated the *Familiar Epistles* to Sir Henry Lee.   The *Chronicle* and the
Arte of navigation, which were two of four
treatises by Guevara published together at Valladolid in 1539, had not been hitherto done into
English, though the two companion treatises
had been translated by Bryan and North.[1]   The
name of Charles Howard of Effingham, the
patron of Hakluyt, appeared on the title page

[1] Thomas Tymme, minister, and emendator of Bryan's
Dispraise of the life of a courtier, was affiliated with this
group of translators.   He dedicated his version of Augustin
Marlorat's commentary on *St. Matthew* to Sir William
Brooke, Lord Cobham, the friend of Challoner and brother
of Sir Henry Cobham, the diplomatist and Spanish student.

of Hellowes' last work, and furnishes the only
clew whereby the relationship of Hellowes to
other students of Spanish may be traced. It,
however, leads nowhere, for the *Arte of navigation* was very probably inscribed to Howard
merely because he was lord admiral at the time.
All the associations of the book are thus nautical.

The *Familiar Epistles* were supplemented
within a year after their publication by the
Golden Epistles of Sir Geoffrey Fenton. The
Golden Epistles were apparently designed as
companion pieces to Hellowes' work, and they
purported to be "gathered as well out of the
Remaynder of Guevaraes workes as other authors, Latine, Frenche, and Italian." There is
no evidence to show that Fenton possessed an
acquaintance with Castilian. The portion of
his collection for which he was indebted to
Guevara was borrowed from the version called
Les Épîtres dorées, by the Seigneur de Guttery,
three books of which had been published at
Paris in 1565. Fenton certainly resided in that
city two years after that date, and it was there
that he became acquainted with the *Histoires
tragiques* which François de Belleforest had
translated from Bandello, upon the English

version of which Fenton's reputation chiefly
rests. There, also, he undoubtedly obtained the
Épîtres dorées of Guttery, and began the task
of turning them into insular idiom. Fenton
was furthermore known as a translator of religious and historical works from the French,
and he englished the Latin epistle written by
Antonio de Corro to the Flemish church in
Antwerp, mention of which has already been
made in the discussion of the works of Corro.
The details of Fenton's early life, which does
not exhibit the repulsive side of his character
so plainly as his later years, are, like those of
Hellowes', to be ascertained chiefly from his
books. He seems to have been a kinsman
of Burghley and Leicester. This connection
opened a political career to him. Fenton accordingly gave up literature to accept office
in Ireland, as Barnaby Googe had done, and
sailed for that country in 1580. There he met
Edmund Spenser; there he was employed on
official business with Sir William Fitzwilliam,
and others with whom Googe was associated;
and there, not improbably, he came in contact
with Googe himself, as they both claimed relationship with Burghley and had mutual ad-

mirers, among whom was the poet George
Turberville.   It is evident, therefore, that
Fenton's personal relations with the group of
Patten, Googe, and Newton, though they did
not lead up to his translation of Guevara,
illustrate by an additional example the existence of an appreciable interest in Spanish
literature among the writers of the court,
whether at first or second hand.   A similar
interest attaches to the *Forest or collection of
historyes*, translated by Thomas Fortescue from
Claude Gruget's French version of Pedro
Mexía's *Silva de varia leccion*.[1]   Whether this
Thomas Fortescue is identical with the brother
of Sir John Fortescue, chancellor of the exchequer, who bore the same name, or not, is a
matter of conjecture.   Sir John, however, was
the dedicatee of this collection of stories.   The
Fortescues long manifested sympathy with the

---

[1] In addition to the works of Mexía, translated by Newton
and Fortescue, that author's *Historia imperial y cesárea*
was licensed to be printed in English at London on December 10, 1601.   It does not appear, however, to have been
published before 1604.   The translator, William Traheron,
was dependent upon an Italian version for his knowledge of
the original.   Singularly, Edward Grimstone's *Historie of
the Indies*, translated from the Spanish of José de Acosta,
was first licensed and published in the same years.

Catholic cause, the most prominent members of the family having been attainted with Cardinal Pole. It is in itself quite likely that Thomas and Sir John Fortescue were brothers, but the fact that the former did not use the original text of Mexía makes it improbable that he is the Thomas Fortescue who was in debt in Spain at the opening of the year 1561. The *Forest of historyes* was, indeed, taken from a French version of an Italian translation. It consequently emphasizes, like Fenton's work, the translators' independence of any one source for the material which they used. There is no better instance of the roundabout way by which books sometimes travelled from the peninsula. The work found its way into England in the course of the movement that introduced the Italian *novelle* into the country. Unlike the great bulk of its nationality, it was not the product of the direct influence of Spain.

The *Silva* of Mexía was, indeed, quite generally known in London during the first half of the reign of Elizabeth, and even at a later date. Before Fortescue had undertaken his translation, it had been laid under contribution by the author of the *Palace of pleasure*. William

Painter, the compiler of this celebrated collection, was born in Middlesex about the year 1540, and entered St. John's College, Cambridge, in 1554, while Blundeville must have been studying at the university. He afterward taught school, and received an appointment as clerk of the ordnance in the Tower of London in 1561. He occupied this post until his death in 1594, before which he had acquired a considerable fortune at the expense of the state by collusion with his patron and official superior, Ambrose Dudley, earl of Warwick, the brother of Leicester.

Painter borrowed but two chapters of his work from peninsular sources. Neither he nor his master seem to have been thrown in the way of the Spanish influence. Anne, countess of Warwick, however, was subsequently the benefactress of Lewkenor, the translator of Acuña. The *Palace of pleasure* may be traced to Italian writers almost in its entirety. The story for which it was indebted to the *Silva* of Mexía was obtained through the version which existed in that language. It was entitled "The mariage of a man and woman, hee being the husband of XX. wiues and shee the wife of

8

XXII. husbandes," and was the twenty-ninth
story of Painter's first tome, which appeared in
1566. In the second volume, which was published during the next year, five of Guevara's
supposititious letters of Plutarch and Trajan
were inserted in the place of a tale, as the
twelfth selection. Painter was indebted to
Spain in no other way. The influence of that
country did not really impress itself upon him,
or his imitators Pettie, Whetstone, and Turberville, though all but Turberville were sensible
of it. It did not come to these men in its full
vigor direct from Spain. When it reached
them, it was denationalized in so far as it could
be so. It was more like a general and impersonal force.

It was as such that it reached Christopher
Marlowe, who was also under obligations to the
work of Mexía. *Tamburlaine*, Marlowe's first
tragedy, was founded upon the relations which
purported to give the history of that prince in
the *Silva* and in Pietro Perondino's *Magni
Tamerlanis vita*, published at Florence in 1553.[1]

[1] Faligan, *De Marlovianis fabulis*, p. 111. The story
of Tamburlaine also occurs in Newton's *Historie of the
Saracens*.

The exploits of Tamburlaine in the version of
Mexía, were probably familiar to Marlowe in
Fortescue's *Forest of historyes*, as the play was
not composed until 1587.   There is no warrant
for supposing that he was acquainted with the
original.   Marlowe was long known chiefly as a
student of the classics.   It is only in a broad
sense that he can be said to have felt the influence of Spain.   Nevertheless the recognition of
that country by the dramatist as by the translators of the *novelle*, though casual, is significant.
It is true that the plots of the Spaniards, and
not their spirit, were borrowed by these men.[1]
Externals only were concerned, and these at
second hand.   Yet this devious invasion of
England through Italy, was an important means
by which the literature of Spain widened the
scope of its influence, when it had once acquired
reputation among the people of the North.

[1] Faligan draws a parallel between the bearing of Tamburlaine and Amadis of Gaul, in order to assert that Marlowe
was affected by the method of the romance of chivalry.
The suggestion, however, that Marlowe knew Paynel's
Amadis is highly improbable, and impairs the argument
irretrievably.   See Faligan, p. 116.

CHAPTER VIII

SIDNEY AND OXFORD: PATRONS OF LEARNING

I

THE number of literary forms that appealed to the court groups of translators has already been pointed out. The courtier was more catholic in his tastes than the tradesman or the controversialist, because of the many-sidedness of his interests, and the diversity of their origin. In the groups of Eden, Googe, and Fenton, all the strands of Spanish influence that were known to the first half of Elizabeth's reign were interwoven. The modes in which this influence expressed and strengthened itself were so various and so closely conjoined, that in estimating the precise character and antecedents of the court groups, it is futile to attempt to determine the specific effect of each. The consequence of the presence of Philip II. in England, and the results of the teaching of Spanish friars and Reformers at

the universities, are discernible in the latter
half of the sixteenth century. Frequent communication with the peninsula, both through
independent travellers and the agency of the
queen's ambassadors, the indirect ingress of
Spanish books through French, Italian, and
Flemish channels, and the residence of Spanish ambassadors and otherwise accredited representatives at London during a period of
twenty years, combined to put Spain and its
literature prominently before the English mind.
The conditions which had obtained in the days
of Katherine of Aragon were repeated on a
larger scale, if in a modified form. After the
attention of the English had been concentrated
again upon the peninsula by the marriage of
Philip and Mary, it was never afterward quite
diverted.

In the last quarter of the century Castilian
was read in the higher social circles. During
this period three Spanish grammars were printed
within two years in London. The earlier
court group of translators, that of Googe and
Fenton, was composed of persons employed
in official capacities, and was largely the crea-
ture of the connections of its members with

Sir Thomas Challoner, Barnaby Googe, and
others who had been in Spain; but the later
groups were less exclusively dependent upon
influences of any particular class.   The followers of Sir Philip Sidney and the Earl of
Oxford, or the antiquaries of Archbishop Parker's society, depended upon all the sources
of Spanish culture in varying proportions.
This is an evidence of the fact that these
groups were the last to develop, the most
mature and comprehensive in kind.   Knowledge of Spanish was with them a matter of
course, not the result of casual acquaintanceship with statesmen and travellers.   It was an
element of general culture.   With Hakluyt in
travels, with Hopkins and Meres in religion,
with Sidney and Oxford in letters, the Spanish
influence enters upon the period of its full maturity in England.

    There is no need to review at this time the
position of Sir Philip Sidney in English letters.
The services of both himself and his sister, the
Countess of Pembroke, to literature, and the
close and generous friendships which they cultivated with the leading writers of their day
have been amply elucidated.   They have added

to the reputation of one whose personal qualities have made his name the synonym for the
perfect knight. About Sidney and the Countess in London, or on other occasions in their
country homes at Penhurst and Wilton, Fulke-
Greville, Sir Edward Dyer, Constable, Daniel,
Drayton, Whetstone, Harvey, and Spenser gathered, each in his time. Among foreigners, Sidney was on familiar terms with Giordano Bruno
and Hubert Languet. Among students of
Spanish history and literature, Richard Carew,
Abraham Fraunce, and Hakluyt were personally connected with his set; Nicholas Lichfield,
the traveller, and many other translators from
the Castilian invited his patronage by placing
his name on their title pages; and Thomas
Moffett, the Paracelsian, who had visited the
peninsula, later maintained relations which were
of an intimate nature with the following of the
Countess of Pembroke. Throughout the Sidney and Pembroke circles, which may be considered in the present connection as one, there
was an evident familiarity with peninsular literature. References to Spanish books are too
frequent to be casual. Sir Philip himself translated from Montemayor. Fraunce in his *Arca-*

dian Rhetorike presupposes an acquaintance
with Castilian in the reader. That language,
together with the pastoral of Montemayor, according to the testimony of Bartholomew Yong,
was well known to Lady Rich. Despite the
fact that Sidney at twenty had such a con-
temptuous opinion of the Spaniards, neither
he nor his adherents held the literature of the
peninsula cheap.

No families of Elizabethan England were open
to influences from Spain at more points than
the Sidneys and Herberts. When Philip II.
attempted to cajole the confiding Mary in order
to obtain the mastery of the country and the
crown, the Earl of Pembroke was the most
trusted of his northern followers. It was Pembroke who led the promised aid to Philip on
the continent in the war with France. Sir
Henry Sidney was scarcely less devoted to the
cause of the king. He and Lady Sidney were
among the most untiring plotters who secretly
visited De Quadra at Durham Place, when the
stability of Elizabeth's government was not yet
assured. De Silva was intimate with Henry
Sidney, and was entertained at the country
home of his brother-in-law, Sir William Dormer.

When Antonio de Guaras, the merchant who acted as representative of Philip II. in London after the expulsion of Guerau de Spes, was thrown into the Tower, it was Sidney who had to be called all the way from Ireland to explain De Guaras' case.   Leicester was guilty of complicity in these plots; indeed, they were designed to promote his advancement.   The Haringtons, a family into which a sister of Sir Henry Sidney had married, kept up open communication with their cousins, the Ferias, in Spain.   Lady Margaret Harington had removed to that country with the Duchess of Feria. William Harington and William Burlace, a dependant of Leicester, and one of the Dormers at least, visited the peninsula for the purpose of conferring with their relatives.   George Fitzwilliam, another connection, successfully carried through the plot by means of which Philip II. was induced to grant John Hawkins letters of nobility for his pretended treason to the queen, and to liberate his sailors imprisoned in Spain.

This event took place in the year that Sir Philip Sidney left college.   It was not only in his own family that Sidney came in contact with Spanish influences.   At Oxford he was the contemporary of Richard Carew, Thomas D'Oylie, Thomas Rogers, and Hakluyt, all subsequently at least familiar with Spanish. When Sidney matriculated, Cipriano de Valera must have been in residence at the university. The incentives which urged Carew and his friends to study the language, cannot have been escaped by Sidney. They were powerfully reënforced by other associations in after life. The friendship of Sidney with Drake and Michael Lok and other men of action and affairs opened before him stores of information that the sea-dogs and tradesmen brought from the colonies and the home ports of Spain. It was only the year before his death, when on his way to carry out an intention of embarking with Drake, that he fell in with Dom Antonio del Crato, the Portuguese pretender, at Drake's house in Devonshire. Dom Antonio at once wrote to Elizabeth that he would like to go on the expedition simply to keep Sidney company.[1] The letter, though over-polite, is an interesting memorial of Sidney's later dealings with the Spaniards.

The bulk of Sidney's translations from the

[1] Mendoza to Philip II., October 8, 1585, *State papers, Sp., Eliz.,* III., p. 550.

Castilian is insignificant. It consists only of the second and third lyrics of the first book of the *Diana* of Montemayor. These songs are the only Spanish lyric poetry, except some lines of the sixth eclogue of Googe, which were translated into English, independently of any prose setting, before the accession of James I. Bartholomew Yong retranslated them somewhat later into spiritless verse when making his version of the *Diana*, completed in 1583. Yong's songs, however, did not appear apart from the prose of his *Diana*, with the exception of twelve which were reprinted in *England's Helicon* two years after the appearance of the complete translation. Sidney's distinction is, therefore, almost unique. His translations were printed at the end of the *Arcadia*, and the second song is also contained in *England's Helicon*.

Sidney did not appropriate the prose of Montemayor, but he was not uninfluenced by it. There is a striking parallelism between the opening passages of the *Arcadia* and the *Diana*. Furthermore, both novels are mixed pastorals combining elements proper to the eclogue and the romance of chivalry. Montemayor made free use of letters, combats, and enchantments,

which had until then not been considered
proper to the pastoral. He was followed and
far outstripped in the employment of these
devices by Sidney. The courtly and thoroughly
aristocratic tone of the *Diana*, which is particularly obtrusive in the additions of Alonso Perez
and Gil Polo, dominates the *Arcadia*. It is
also evident in Sidney's style, but it would be
injudicious to attempt to father the affectations
of which Sidney is the best-known representative upon Montemayor. There is a similarity
in the exaggerated manner of both writers, and
particularly in the length and in a certain lan-
guor of the sentences; but Montemayor is much
simpler than Sidney. His affectation is due to
the sentimental artificiality of the life of his
shepherds; with him the expression is not
strained beyond the conception. In this respect
the Spanish differs from the English pastoral,
which was indebted to its prototype for something of its conduct, but not deeply enough
influenced to owe anything to its style.[1]

[1] The attempt to connect the style of Sidney with that of
Montemayor has failed. Dr. Landmann, the chief exponent of the affirmative view, who was very positive about
the indebtedness of Sidney to the Spaniards in 1882 (*New
Shakspere Society transactions*, 1880–1885, pt. II., p. 264) is

Abraham Fraunce is now remembered as a tireless advocate of the English hexameter, but in his own day the intimate terms on which he associated with the Sidneys, whose protégé he was, greatly added to the importance of his work, for Fraunce was one of the inner circle of the men of letters who surrounded Philip Sidney. Sir Edward Dyer, Gabriel Harvey, Thomas Watson, and Spenser were among his closest friends. He obtained his education at St. John's College, Cambridge, where he remained from 1575 to 1583, and then began his career as an author, which he pursued jointly with the practice of law for the next ten years. At the expiration of that period Fraunce induced the Earl of Pembroke to recommend him to Burghley for the office of queen's solicitor in the court of the marches of Wales. This suit had a successful issue. Fraunce received

much less sure of his ground in his later preface to the first part of *Euphues*. The truth is that the alliterative, euphuistical, and arcadian styles had started on their course before 1580, when the *Diana* was as yet not widely read in England. Yong, in translating that book, was given to ornamenting and elaborating the style of the original; *e.g. Diana*, London 1598, pp. 129, 131, 139, etc. He was, indeed, conforming it to a standard which it had not set, and whose requirements it did not fully meet.

the appointment he desired, withdrew from
literature, and devoted his abilities to the duties
of his office, which he continued to hold for
over forty years.

The writings of Fraunce cover a variety of
subjects, but an element of unity is introduced
into almost all of them by his predilection for
classical metres.   Translations from the Latin
poets, from Vergil down to Thomas Watson, as
well as from the Italian of Tasso, are an important part of his work.   Many of these are included in the *Countess of Pembroke's ivychurch*
which exhibits Fraunce in the rôle of pastoral
poet.   His treatise upon heraldry on the one
hand and his *Lawier's logic* on the other, indicate the range of subjects treated by him.   It
is only his *Arcadian Rhetorike*, however, that
shows a knowledge of Spanish writers.   The
Rhetorike, which was published at London in
1588, enjoys the distinction of containing the
only selections from Spanish lyric poets that
were printed in the original tongue in England
during the supremacy of the Tudors.   Fraunce
introduced Boscan and Garcilaso de la Vega
to readers north of the channel.   The complete
indifference with which these poets had been

regarded from the time of Wyatt and Surrey,
who, as they were cultivating the Italian manner
in England while the Spaniards were introducing it into the peninsula, might very well
have assumed a sympathetic attitude, can only
be regarded with surprise. Garcilaso outstripped
the early English Petrarchists so completely
that his merits should have met with ready
recognition. They were already attracting the
attention of the French. Du Bartas in his
Semaines, in enumerating the four chief supporters of the principal modern languages,
coupled the names of Boscan and Garcilaso
with those of Guevara and Granada.[1] England
had already expressed approval of the prose
writers indicated by Du Bartas, and in the
Arcadian Rhetorike she made the acquaintance
of the poets. But although it passed through
a second edition, Fraunce's book lacked the
essentials of popularity, and exists now in a
unique copy. It was one of the dullest of the
critical treatises which followed closely upon
Webbe's *Discourse of English poetry*, for avoid-
ing questions of general interest as far as possible, the book treats of the bewildering array

[1] Du Bartas, *II. Jour. de la II. Sepmaine*, l. 605.

of rhetorical figures so assiduously discussed by Elizabethan critics, and attempts an exhaustive classification of them.

In support of the precepts which he advances Fraunce adduces numerous passages from Homer, Vergil, Tasso, Du Bartas and Sidney, Boscan and Garcilaso de la Vega. The number of lines Fraunce borrows from the Spanish in the *Arcadian Rhetorike* is two hundred and sixty-three. Two hundred and twenty of these, apportioned in thirty-eight selections, are taken from the three books of the poems of Boscan, but of these the narrative poem *Ero y Leandro* was evidently Fraunce's favorite; only forty lines divided into seven selections, and all but one of them from eclogues, are drawn from Garcilaso. This small collection of quotations, of which the longest includes only forty verses, together with the songs of the *Diana*, represents the acquaintance of the Elizabethans with Spanish lyric poetry. The fact that these authors were cited in the original, even were there no confirmatory proof, would make it plain that knowledge of Spanish was not rare among men of letters. But the bulk of quotations from the Spanish is noticeably less than that of the passages from any of the other languages except the Greek. Fraunce thus tacitly, and perhaps unconsciously, confesses a preference for Vergil, Tasso, Du Bartas, and Sidney as models for the English writer. This preference shows his sanity; but to rank Boscan before Garcilaso is a madness only credible in a partisan of classical metres. Garcilaso also precedes Du Bartas in merit, but then Du Bartas was a favorite with Fraunce. It is quite likely that Fraunce based his scheme of illustration, certainly on its Spanish side, upon the classification of authors in the *Semaines*, for all of his representatives of the modern languages are cited in that work. But the English would not indorse the judgment of the Frenchman. The lyric poets of Spain commanded no audience, and the popularity of Guevara and Granada was not paralleled by that of Garcilaso and Boscan.

Whether the inference based upon the use of Spanish in the *Arcadian Rhetorike*, rightfully attributes a knowledge of the language to the circle of Sidney generally, or only to individuals comprised within its limits, it is undeniable that an interest in Spanish literature was manifested by many of its members. Spenser may or may

T

not have understood the citations of his friend
Fraunce, but he read *Lazarillo de Tórmes*.
This famous novel of Don Diego Hurtado de
Mendoza, who had served as imperial ambassador to England from May 1537 to September
1538, was translated by David Rowland of
Anglesey, and published in 1576, if not, as is
probable, in 1568, when it was first licensed by
the Stationers' Company. Two other editions
were issued before the close of the century, besides a translation of the anonymous second
part by William Phiston in 1596.[1] Rowland
had studied at Oxford, and spent his life as a
teacher. After leaving the university, he travelled through Italy and Spain as tutor to a son
of the Earl of Lennox, a Catholic partisan, and
on his return settled in London, giving instruction in Greek and Latin. Here he published a
school book for students of the Latin language,

[1] William Phiston, author, was a resident of London. He
translated from the Latin, French, Italian, and Spanish, and
attracted the attention of Alexander Nowell, Edmund Grindal, and Robert Radcliffe, earl of Sussex, a patron of Thomas
Tymme. The *Relaciones*, englished from Jean de Montlyard's French version of the treatise by Antonio Perez, bore
the initials W. P. upon their title page, it has been said ; but
the real translator seems to have been one P. Ol.

and here possibly he may have become acquainted with Spenser when the poet returned from northern England in 1578, for in that year Spenser sent Harvey a copy of *Lazarillo* along with one of the jest-book, *Howleglas*, the *Til Eulenspiegel* of Thomas Murner. Rowland and Spenser possessed a common friend in the poet Turberville, who furnished commendatory verses for *Lazarillo*. The translator, however, was not one of Sidney's immediate followers; he appears to have courted especially the favor of Sir Thomas Gresham, to whom *Lazarillo* was dedicated most appropriately, for few men were better qualified by experience to know the actual life of Spain.

Others who had travelled quite as extensively in the peninsula as Rowland had done, however, attached themselves to the Sidney group. Among these was Nicholas Lichfield, a man of gentle birth, who had spent much of his life abroad and seen military service in foreign lands. Upon his return to London Lichfield published a book upon the art of war, to which he gave the title *De Re militari*. It was a translation of a similarly named Spanish work by the once famous Captain Luis

Gutierres de la Vega, of Medina del Campo, and was dedicated to Sidney. In the same year an English version of the first part of the *Historia do descobrimento e conquista da India*, by Fernão Lopes de Castanheda, was issued. This Portuguese work Lichfield dedicated to Sir Francis Drake, promising that the second and third books would follow if the first met with approval. The judgment of the public was apparently adverse.

The Silkwormes and their flies, a didactic poem by Thomas Moffett, met with a more auspicious reception. Moffett enjoyed the acquaintance of many of the principal persons of the time, both at home and abroad; for he was not only a Cambridge man, but had been a student of medicine in several of the German cities, in which he had published several theses, and subsequently became a practitioner of the first rank and celebrity in London. In 1583 he accompanied Sir William Waad and Peregrine Bertie, grandson of María de Salinas, on an embassy to Elsinore, and there met Tycho Brahe. Taking up his residence in London, Moffett soon numbered the Knyvets, the Duchess of Somerset, Essex, and Walsingham among

his patients. He also came to know Drake and
Henry Herbert, earl of Pembroke. It was at
the time that Fraunce abandoned literature for
the law that Moffett became a dependant of the
Countess of Pembroke, in the service of whom
he passed the latter years of his life at her
Wiltshire home. While Moffett was accepting
a pension from Pembroke, he published his
poem in London. The observations upon which
it was based had been personally made by him
when making a tour of Italy and Spain. He
wrote of the silk culture, which was for a brief
period the especial industry of the latter country, where silk was a staple product of the Moors,
from the vantage ground of actual experience.
Moffett was not himself a man of letters, but he
was one of the most prominent of the set of the
Countess of Pembroke who manifested an interest in Spain.

The literary movement of which Sidney had
been the head was not affected disastrously by
his death. Among the writers to whom it owed
its vitality, Fraunce and Moffett remained with
his sister and enjoyed her patronage, but Antonio Perez, the fugitive Spanish diplomat, and
Bartholomew Yong wrote under the encourage-

ment of the Earl of Essex and of Lady Rich.
The personal bond that had united the Sidneys
and Herberts on the one hand with the Dev-
ereuxs and their friends on the other, through
the attachment of Sidney and Penelope Devereux, was renewed by the marriage of Essex
and Sidney's widow, Frances Walsingham.
The members of these families had grown up
amid the same environment and continued to
be subject to the same general influences until
the end.   Identical social forces operated to
draw them together.   Nevertheless the death
of Sidney emphasized the line between the followers of the two houses.   The rise of the
power of the Earl of Essex secured for him
political eminence, and it also made him more
sought after than he had been formerly, as a
patron of learning.   There was thus an obvious though not a radical distinction between
his followers and those of the Countess of
Pembroke.

Antonio Perez arrived in London in the
summer of 1593, and at once sought the protection of the young favorite.   Antonio del
Crato had been entertained by the English
because of his claim to the Portuguese throne;

Perez was welcomed because of his knowledge
of statecraft and, more particularly, because of
his familiarity with the secrets of Philip II.[1]
He had been arrested in Spain in 1579 by the
order of the king, upon the charge of having
procured the murder of Juan de Escobedo, the
emissary of Don Juan de Austria at Madrid.
This charge was in fact but a subterfuge, for
the real offence of the favorite minister had
been an intrigue with the Princess d'Eboli,
widow of Ruy Gomez, at one time the chief
adviser of the king. Perez suffered imprisonment for eleven years in Castile, and at the termination of that period he escaped to Saragossa,
where he was again apprehended. The independent spirit of the Aragonese refused to
abet the unconstitutional process by which he
had been condemned, and he was freed by
the people and escaped into France. He had
scarcely been in that country a year when he
was summoned to the court at Tours by Henry
of Navarre and despatched to London to secure

[1] Mignet's *Antonio Perez* is the best monograph upon the
life of the fugitive Spaniard. The Anthony Bacon papers,
published by Birch in his *Memoirs of the reign of Elizabeth*, are essential to the understanding of the relations
of Essex and Perez.

the coöperation of Elizabeth in the war which
was then being waged against Spain.

It was during the summer of 1594 that Perez,
while still residing in London, published the
original edition of his *Relaciones* in Spanish,
and accompanied it with a dedication to Essex,
in which he assumed the pseudonym, Rafael
Peregrino. This book at once created a sensa-
tion. It contained narrations of the adventures
of Perez in Spain and of the insurrection of the
Aragonese in his behalf at Saragossa, besides a
description of the judicial system of Aragon
and of the defence which he had prepared to
meet the charges that the king had brought
against him before the *Justicia* of that province.
The personal nature of the matter that was
at the heart of these troubles was such that
even the partial explanation of it which the
Relaciones offered, laid bare the secrets of
Philip II. before the eyes of Europe. Assas-
sins were accordingly hired to put Perez to
death; yet had they succeeded, it would have
been too late to undo the mischief that had
been done. The book was translated into
Dutch in the year of its publication; it was
presently reprinted in Leon, as well as at Paris,

and a French version was made by Jean de
Montlyard by the year 1598. It was in France,
indeed, that the *Relaciones* met with the greatest
success, for it was in that country that Perez
found a permanent asylum. Spanish books had
been freely translated into French throughout
the sixteenth century, and they had found
their way across the Pyrenees to some extent
previously, but it was not until the *Relaciones*
and *Cartas* of this author appeared, that the
Spanish influence became prominent in French
letters.[1] To hold that these works originated
that influence would of course be an extreme
view, but there can be little doubt that
the auspicious position and talents of Perez,
which caused him to be sought out in the
highest circles in the land, concentrated the
attention of the French on peninsular literature, upon which it had before been only
quietly and desultorily fixed.

The publication of the *Relaciones* was not an
event of the same moment in England that it
was south of the channel. They added nothing
to English letters. There was, however, an
English translation by one P. Ol., in 1598,

[1] Chasles, *Études sur l'Espagne*, p. 238.

which was made from Montlyard's French version, and was dedicated to Fulke-Greville. Perez exerted no more influence in London than did Antonio del Crato, whose misfortunes called forth a number of tracts and pamphlets. The *Relaciones* were a passing wonder, the effects of which were inconsiderable when compared with those of the antecedent translations of the *Diana* or of *Lazarillo*. Upon the first appearance of the Spanish edition, Perez sent copies of the book to Burghley, Essex, Lady Rich, Southampton, Mountjoy, Harris, Hatton, and Sir Robert Sidney. All these persons countenanced him for a season at least.[1] He was a correspondent of Lady Knollys and a constant companion of Francis Bacon.[2] The welcome that those persons extended to Perez was dictated by political expediency. Most of them were members of the circle of the Earl of Essex.

[1] Perez, *Cartas*, Pt. I., nos. 20–35 ; Pt. II., no. 91.

[2] The intimacy between Perez and Francis Bacon was so great that it aroused the fears of Bacon's mother, who wrote to her son Anthony : " Tho' I pity your brother, yet so long as he pities not himself, but keepeth that bloody Perez, yea a coach-companion, and bed-companion, a proud, profane, costly fellow, whose being about him I verily fear, the Lord God doth mislike, and doth less bless your brother in credit and otherwise in his health, surely I am utterly discour-

When Perez arrived in London, Essex had been advocating an aggressive policy against Philip II., and an offensive and defensive alliance with France, against the more cautious and passive plans which were favored by the Cecils. The adoption of this radical plan of action was what the Spaniard most desired, both for the further-ance of his ambitions and the gratification of his spites. He therefore lost no time in securing the good-will of the young favorite, to whom his accomplishments and experience especially ap-pealed. Essex presented him at court and obtained for him an annual pension of one hun-dred and thirty pounds from the queen. He also introduced his guest among his private friends with great freedom, and carried on a correspondence with him in Latin, even after his return to France. Because this alliance was one of mutual advantage only, Perez met with a chilling reception during his second visit in

aged . . . to maintain such wretches as he is, that never loved your brother but for his own credit living upon him.'' This letter is a sufficient confutation of the contention that Bacon was the scapegoat of a new and higher morality. It also shows that there were other persons in England than Burghley, to whom the essential weakness of Perez was perfectly clear. See Birch, *Memoirs*, I., p. 143.

the summer of 1596. Essex was then at Plymouth preparing for the raid upon Cadiz, and was too strong to care further for aid from Henry of Navarre. His former dependant was therefore obliged to return disgruntled to Paris, where he died in 1611, in his seventy-second year, but not until a final attempt to reëstablish himself in England during the reign of James I. had ended in humiliating failure.

The explanation of the continued ill-success of Perez north of the channel lies in the character of the society into which he was thrust. His literary labors had been anticipated by the Elizabethan translators, and the limitations of his practical usefulness were plainly understood even by Essex. Like Sidney, Essex had been led to give his attention to peninsular affairs by educational, political, and social influences. His grandfather and great-grandfather had been connected with the set of Lord Berners, and the latter had accompanied Dorset to Guipuzcoa. He himself had sailed with Dom Antonio in the Counter Armada of 1589, and he again led the forces against Cadiz in 1596. Like the Sidneys, he had correspondents in Spain, and friends, who were familiar with the country, in London.

Anthony Standen, for example, a protégé of the earl, had spent three years at the court of Madrid, and was well acquainted with the later English merchants, such as Edmund Palmer, who sent information of the affairs of Philip II. to Elizabeth, and with the English gentlemen resident in the capital, such as Anthony Rolston, who secretly watched over the interests of their countrymen abroad.[1] The friends of the Ferias did not stand apart from the set of Essex. Perez was to him, therefore, but another instrument by means of which he might strengthen and better his position. The mission of the Spaniard to England was purely political, and the results of his dealing with the subjects of Elizabeth are to be studied in the political sphere. Perez obtained no firmer foothold in society than Guzman de Silva had done. He did not acquire a name as durable as that of a successful artist. He came and was forgotten. The brief repute that he enjoyed was the consequence of Essex's policy of entering for his own purposes into the affairs of Spain.

Bartholomew Yong, the translator, was purely a literary man, and the follower of Lady Rich.

[1] Birch, *Memoirs*, I., pp. 94, 95 *et seq.*

Few non-original writers of the Elizabethan age were better known by their contemporaries. The facts of his life are, however, involved in obscurity. According to his own statement Yong was a member of the Middle Temple, London, and possessed a working knowledge of French, Italian, and Spanish. The patronage that he sought was that of Sidney's Stella, Penelope Devereux. Yong, consequently, was not far removed from the Sidney set. Like her lover, Lady Rich had some knowledge of Spanish, and she shared an admiration for the *Diana* with him. That Yong knew Sidney personally is not probable, for he was the especial protégé of Lady Rich at a later date, though happily before the breath of scandal had blighted her name. Among her friends he found the same interest in peninsular literature that permeated the circle of Sidney. It was owing to his association with these people, as well as to the popularity of the author whom he translated, that Yong's merits came to be recognized, and, indeed, overestimated, when the century closed.

The literary work of Yong includes the fourth book of Stefano Guazzo's *Civile conversation*,

the three preceding parts of which had been
done into English by George Pettie, a version
of the *Fiammetta* of Boccaccio, and the first
English translation of the *Diana*. This translation was complete. It embraced the original
Diana of Montemayor, published in Spain
about 1560, just before the death of its author;
the continuation by Alonso Perez, published in
1564; and the *Diana enamorada*, — another second part, though usually printed as a third, —
written by Gaspar Gil Polo in the same year.
The tale of the Moor Abindarraez, according
to some authorities inserted in the Spanish editions from the *Inventario* of Antonio de Villegas,
also occurs. Yong's translation was finished in
1583, though not printed until 1598, the year in
which Thomas Wilcox completed his translation of the first part of Montemayor. It is
painstaking and remarkably faithful, barring
slight exaggerations in the false taste of the
time, but it is not readable. The verses are
particularly unfortunate.

Yong returned from Spain about 1579, after
having spent nearly three years in the country
in study and on business. He shortly afterward made the acquaintance of Edward Ban-

ister, of Idesworth, Hampshire, who presented
him with a copy of the first and second parts
of the *Diana* of Montemayor, advising him to
translate it from the Spanish in order to refresh
his knowledge of the language. Yong had
never before heard of the book, but he determined to act on Banister's advice. He therefore secured copies of the French versions of
the first part by Nicholas Colin, and of the
second and third by Gabriel Chapuis, all of
which had been recently printed, but finding
the portion done by Chapuis to be unsatisfactory, determined to rely entirely upon the Spanish originals. This he accordingly did. He
closes the preface to the *Diana* by expressing a
wish that Edward Paston, Esq., who had englished certain passages of the book for his own
amusement, had made a complete translation,
which, Yong says, "for his [Paston's] travell in
that countrey, and great knowledge in that
language, accompanied with other learned and
good parts in him, had of all others, that ever
yet I heard translate these Bookes, prooved the
rarest and worthiest to be embraced." [1]

This paraphrase of Yong's preface makes it

[1] Yong, *Diana*, preface.

clear that it was possible for a person of education and serious tastes to spend considerable time in Spain without becoming even moderately acquainted with its literature. For the success of the *Diana* had been instantaneous; it was among the most popular of books when Yong was in the peninsula. It is also clear that there were persons in England who were much better informed of current Spanish literature than many intelligent Englishmen in Spain. Upon Yong's return his friends at once produced copies of the *Diana*, of which he had never heard abroad, and Edward Paston perhaps was already translating passages of the pastoral.

This Edward Paston was the posthumous son and heir of Sir Thomas Paston and god-son of Edward VI.[1] He was, therefore, the head of the Paston family of Norfolk, which the letters of its earlier representatives have since made famous. The family was on intimate terms with the Dormers during the reign of Mary, and in 1559 a Mrs. Paston was among the ladies who accompanied Jane Dormer to the estates of the Duke of Feria in Spain, with the intention of taking up her residence in that country.

[1] See *Norfolk archæology*, IV., pp. 3, 45.

U

The Pastons were also intimate friends of Sir Thomas Challoner at the period of his embassy. There can, therefore, be no question of the title of Edward Paston to a knowledge of Spain at first hand. Though there is no record of the date at which he travelled in the country, it is plain that he fulfilled the intention which Sir Henry Sidney expressed, and visited his relatives at the hospitable residence of the Ferias. Whether Edward Banister, the other friend of Yong who read Spanish, had close ties with the peninsula or not, is uncertain. He was, however, a gentleman of culture, and a lover of works of art. In his will, mostly written in Yong's hand in 1600, he speaks of his books, instruments of music, painted tables, cloths, and pictures, white marble, porphyry, serpentine, and other stones, carvings of wood, and things in glass, thus establishing his title to be considered one of the pioneer collectors of curios in England. Possibly he was the Edward Banister mentioned in the will of the Duchess of Northumberland in 1553, — a lady who was prominent at court in the time of Philip and Mary.[1] The name of Banister occurs, more-

[1] See Hunter, *Shakespeare*, I., p. 191.

over, in the correspondence of the embassy of Sir Thomas Chamberlain. It is most probable that as he was a man of culture and a lover of the beautiful, he had, like the Sidneys and so many of the members of their set, personal and direct relations with the Catholic refugees and malcontents in Spain.

II

Although the variety of influences which entered into the groups of translators from the Spanish during the last quarter of the sixteenth century, was the common characteristic of them all, it manifested itself under different aspects in different spheres. The translators of the circle of Sidney were chiefly under obligations to the set of the Ferias, whose predominance dwarfed all other influences among them. Those of the circles of the Earl of Essex and Countess of Pembroke also acknowledged an immediate indebtedness to the Spaniards. The friends of the Earl of Oxford, however, were collectively dependent in quite equal proportions upon almost if not quite all of the agencies whereby Castilian books and culture penetrated England. Robert Baker, George

Baker, and Anthony Munday all felt the spell
of the peninsula, yet they were strikingly differentiated each from each.   Some travellers,
some translators, a principle of unity was lacking among them.   De Vere himself was the
only tie that bound them together.   He went
abroad for three years in 1575, but he does not
appear to have visited Spain.   His sympathies,
however, were with that country, for he gave
his father-in-law, Lord Burghley, much trouble
by espousing Norfolk's cause at the time of that
nobleman's rebellion in 1571, and later he was
among the converts of Campion and Persons
at the first landing of the Jesuits.   He was in
a position to inform himself easily of Spanish
affairs.   Robert Baker, the voyager, and George
Baker, the physician, had visited the country
and were in his service; but nevertheless his
interest in the peninsula was apparently slight.
Sidney's group studied Spanish literature, they
seemed to care for it, and to know it better than
it was commonly known; Oxford's possessed a
casual interest in the subject, such as might
very well be shared abroad.   Sidney's group
were familiar with the Castilian originals;
Oxford's with French and Italian translations.

Oxford, though one of the principal patrons of those who were swept into the stream of Spanish influence, was not attracted by writers because they moved in that stream, nor did he grant to any his favor because of a predilection for Spain.

George Baker obtained recognition as a surgeon of unsurpassed excellence. Born in 1540, he was admitted to membership in the Barber Surgeons' Company while yet young, and became its master, by election, in 1597. He easily achieved a position among that notable group of London practitioners, the fame of which has survived not only in his own books, but in those of his friends John Banister, John Gerard, and William Clowes. For Baker, in common with the others, was an original writer and a translator, publishing versions of medical works by Guido, Conrad Gesner, and Giovanni da Vigo. It was in the year 1574 that he issued his *Composition or making of the most excellent and pretious oil called oleum magistrale*, which, the title goes on to state, was "first published by the comandement of the King of Spain." This was his first work as well as his only translation from the Spanish. At the time of its appearance Baker was already well established in London, and connected with the household of the Earl of Oxford. The details of his life are not familiar, and the occasion of this translation is a matter of conjecture. As it was then usual for physicians to study on the continent, Baker, who was thirty-seven when the treatise was printed, perhaps met with the original in Spain.

Anthony Munday, the most prolific of Elizabethan writers, suffers much in comparison with his friend, the professional, dignified Baker. The son of a London draper, Munday seems to have led an irregular life in his youth. He first comes into notice as an apprentice to John Allde, the stationer. In 1578 he was sent abroad, at the age of twenty-five, for the purpose of obtaining damaging testimony against the English seminaries on the continent. On this mission he visited France and Italy, and met the traitor Thomas Stukeley while inspecting the college at Rome.[1] After an absence of a year Munday returned to England and entered the service of the Earl of Oxford, in

[1] Stukeley, having failed in his plots in Spain, sailed with Dom Sebastian, and perished in the battle at Alcazar.

whose company he enrolled as a player, having had experience on the stage before going abroad. Oxford soon introduced the young actor to George Baker and others of his followers. Munday was not content, however, to remain long in the company of the earl. He saw an opportunity to advance his fortunes in the excitement aroused in the country by the preaching of Campion and Persons. Always the enemy of Catholicism, he entered into a virulent crusade against the Jesuits, which, though it must have alienated him somewhat from his patron, who was among the earliest converts of the priests, yet inured to his immediate advantage. Having resigned from Oxford's company of players, he was soon rewarded by an appointment to take bonds of the recusants in the interest of the public safety, and later was advanced to be a messenger of Her Majesty's chambers. The emoluments of this office he supplemented for a time with the proceeds of the sale of his books, though he subsequently took up the trade of his father. Munday was facile and careless. Nothing, not even his absence on the foreign tour of Pembroke's actors, blighted his fertility. The period of his greatest productiveness was, however, that between 1580 and 1602. Between these years he collaborated in drama with Middleton, Drayton, Webster, Chettle, Wilson, and Hathaway, translated romances, made ballads, contrived pageants, and issued pamphlets with almost equal success. The variety of his works brought him prominently before the principal men of his time, and gave him besides an extraordinary reputation among persons of humble talents and scant education.

Munday appealed to the uneducated through his translations of the French and Spanish books of chivalry. Paynel had introduced the peninsular romances into England, but in Munday's versions they achieved popularity.[1] It was shortly after his return from Rome that Munday seems to have directed his attention to preparing the cycle of the Palmerin romances for the press. On February 3, 1581, *Palmerin of England* was entered for publication in the stationers' register, and before the end of the decade *Palmerin d' Oliva, Palladino of England, Amadis of Gaul, Primaleon of Greece,*

[1] John de Vere, earl of Oxford, the father of Sir Edward de Vere, had been, it will be remembered, a patron of Paynel.

and *Palmendos* followed quickly, in the order
named. With one or possibly two exceptions,
all of these works were translated through the
medium of the French. When that language
furnished Munday with no text, the immediate
source was Italian. Despite the certainty with
which the versions which were used in preparing the English translations have been identified,
the bibliography of the subject is in great confusion. Many romances were licensed years before the publication of any copy now known.
Sometimes the number of parts translated was
specified on the stationers' register, sometimes
it was not. The difficulty of clearing up the
subject is enhanced by the episodic character of
the stories, which were circulated without any
regard to the sequence of the parts. Translations were made with absolute contempt for the
proper sequence. Thus the order of the original Spanish series of the Palmerin cycle is:
Palmerin de Oliva, *Primaleon*, *Polindo*, *Platir*,
Flotir, and *Palmerin de Inglaterra;* in the
Italian series, however, *Platir* preceded *Polindo*,
and *Flotir* was moved to the foot of the list.

Palmerin of England was undoubtedly not
only the first of Munday's romances to be

licensed, but the first to be printed as well.
The earliest known edition of the first two
books belongs to the year 1596; but as the
third book was printed in 1595, there can be
no doubt that the original edition of 1581 existed, though it has quite disappeared. *Palmerin of England* was translated from Jacques
Vinant's version of Luis Hurtado, but the third
book, the composition of Diogo Fernandes de
Lisboa, was borrowed from the Italian of Mambrino de Roseo. *Palmerin d' Oliva* followed
Palmerin of England, the first part appearing
in 1588, the second in 1597. It is supposed
to be the work of the daughter of a carpenter
of northern Spain, but as there is difference of
opinion about the location of the home of the
authoress, some placing it in Burgos in Old
Castile and others in Ciudad Rodrigo, a city
of the ancient kingdom of Leon, the final judgment has yet to be pronounced. The English
is based on a French version of the initial book
by Jean Maugin, and also upon the complete
Italian rendering of Mambrino de Roseo. *Palladino of England*, the third of the Spanish
series, was published in the same year as *Palmerin d' Oliva*, having been drawn from the

French of Claude Colet, a friend of the poet
Jodelle. After a twelvemonth, *Primaleon of
Greece* was licensed to be printed in seven
parts, and shortly after there is an entry
authorizing the publication of the first and
second books. These had evidently been sub-
divided for convenience at the earlier date.
No copy of *Primaleon* that is older than 1595,
however, is extant. The third part, which is
entitled *Palmendos*, was issued in 1589 when
the others were licensed. It is therefore probable that the first two parts were ready in that
year. The text used by Munday was not the
original Spanish of Francisco Vasquez, but that
of François Vernassol for the opening book, for
which Vernassol was partly indebted to the
Italian, and that of Gabriel Chapuis for the remainder, which had been transcribed by the
Frenchman. The fourth and concluding book
of *Primaleon*, entitled *Darineo de Grecia*, was of
purely Italian origin, but it is entered on the
stationers' register in 1598, where the initials H.
W. are given as those of the translator. *Platir*
and *Flotir* are accounted greatly inferior to the
rest of the series in every particular, and never
made their way across the channel into England.

The romances of the *Palmerins* were published in the peninsula mostly at Salamanca and Toledo, between the years 1511 and 1587. It was in 1508 that the progenitor of the novels of chivalry, *Amadis de Gaula*, appeared at the former city in the arrangement of García Ordoñez de Montalvo. It is now established that this famous work was current in some form in Spain in the days of the Black Prince, as it is mentioned with disapproval in a poem of Pedro Lopez de Ayala, who was taken prisoner by the Black Prince. Montalvo's arrangement was in four books. Three of these, however, were furnished him from the Portuguese adaptation by Vasco de Lobeira. The success of the revised *Amadis* was instantaneous. Many additional wonders were soon affixed to the original adventures of Amadis by numerous imitators. The romances became the reading of kings as well as of the people. The favorite books of Charles V. were the *Chevalier délibré*, a French romance, and *Don Belianis of Greece*.[1]   It is

---

[1] Both of these romances appeared in English during the sixteenth century.   Sir Lewis Lewkenor translated the *Resolved Gentleman* from the Spanish version of Hernando de Acuña, in 1594.   Lewkenor was a friend of Anne Russell, countess of Warwick by marriage with Ambrose Dudley.

said that Francis I. was fascinated by the *Amadis* while a prisoner in Spain after the battle of Pavia, and that, on returning to his own dominions after attaining his liberty, he immediately commanded Nicholas de Herberay to translate the *Amadis* into French. Herberay obeyed the mandate of the king. Eight books were turned into French by him, and printed at Paris between 1540 and 1548. These were the volumes which were known to Anthony Munday. The first and probably the second book, were published in English at London in 1588–1589, both appeared in 1595, and all the original four of Montalvo in 1619, but, as is stated in the preface, after longer delay than had been intended.[1] The edition of 1619 was completed at an honorable lady's request and with her support. It was dedicated to Philip

The three families were all implicated in Wyatt's treason, and the Lewkenors were largely Cambridge men, though the name of Sir Lewis does not occur in the records of the university. A Sir Lewis Lewkenor was master of the ceremonies to James I., and was undoubtedly identical with the translator, whose political interests induced him to publish the *Estate of English fugitives under the King of Spain*, in 1595. *Don Belianis de Grecia* was englished in 1598 by L. A., a writer whose initials also appeared upon the seventh, eighth, and ninth books of the *Mirrour of knighthood*.

[1] Brydges, *Brit. Bibl.*, II., p. 561.

Herbert, earl of Montgomery. Munday asserted in the preface to that edition that the fifth, sixth, seventh, and eighth books were then all well advanced in translation; but the fifth book had, however, been licensed as early as 1592, and all from the second to the twelfth inclusive, in 1594. It is certain that if these entries on the register were anything other than formalities, which is, in view of Munday's declaration, exceedingly unlikely, the translations were by another hand.

The popularity of the romances of chivalry in Spain was coincident with the duration of the sixteenth century. At first their readers included persons of high rank, but with the development of printing, the romances became readily accessible to the humbler people. In Cervantes' time they were the favorite reading of innkeepers. If the tradition of the authorship of *Palmerin de Oliva* is correct, the series of the Palmerins was plebeian in the beginning. As the books of chivalry multiplied, the plots grew wilder and more preposterous, the style lost its purity and became ill suited to a cultivated taste. The success of the romances among the people ultimately produced a reac-

tion against them at court.   They had never
striven for the graces of a court style, and
when they began to be written for the general
public, the result was the aggravation of their
faults.   These became intolerable.   Hence when
the books of chivalry were brought into competition with the masterpieces of the Spanish
golden age, nothing could avert their decline,
which, accomplished among the better element,
waited only for the ridicule of Cervantes to be
complete.   Hence the failure of Paynel's translation in England.   It was undertaken at too
late a day.   The Spaniards of the higher classes,
it is true, had not yet forgotten the romances;
they even held them before the eyes of the
Elizabethans.   When Elizabeth seized and appropriated the treasure which the Genoese
bankers were carrying up the channel to the
Duke of Alba, and it was considered prudent by
her advisers to find counter-grievances to forestall any objection on the part of Philip II.,
Don Guerau de Spes was put under arrest, and
among the principal charges against him was
that of wanton disrespect to the queen, in
referring to her as the Lady Oriana.[1]   De Spes

[1] *State papers, Sp., Eliz.,* II., p. 118.

extricated himself from this predicament by
asserting that in Spain it was still considered a
compliment to address the queen by that name.
But such events did not suffice to ensure the
success of the *Amadis* at court, though they
did result in its translation by Paynel.   It
failed to please the nobility, and native and
Gallic romances, written or adapted either
anonymously or by authors who revealed only
the initials of their names, continued to occupy
the popular field.

But at the time of the return of Munday
from the continent, the Spanish romances of
chivalry achieved their first success in England.
In that year Margaret Tiler published a translation of the first part of the *Espejo de príncipes*,
one of the most extravagant and fantastical of
the books of chivalry.   Two years later *Palmerin of England* was licensed, and the other
translations by Munday followed at brief intervals.   The translation of *Espejo de príncipes*
introduced a new element into English literature.   With the exception of the interlude
founded upon the *Celestina* by Rastell and the
Amadis of Paynel, the translations from Castilian had heretofore been confined to four classes

of books: the court morality of Guevara; court and pastoral romances, such as the *Cárcel de amor* and *Tratado de Arnalte y Lucenda* of San Pedro, the *Historia de Aurelio y Isabela* of Juan de Flores,[1] and the *Diana* of Montemayor; religious writings; and books upon travel and the art of sea-faring. Guevara had been translated exclusively by the home-staying courtiers; the court romances, chiefly by gentlemen who had travelled in the peninsula; the clergy had been the sponsors for the third class; and merchants employed in the Spanish trade, for the last. The literature of the courtiers then, it is evident, was purely aristocratic and sophisticated, a far remove from the spirit of the

[1] Claudius Hollyband (Claude Desainliens) translated *Arnalte and Lucenda* from the Italian version of Bartolomeo Maraffi, in 1575. The English and Italian texts were published together for students of Italian, and reprinted in 1597, 1608, 1616, and 1619. Hollyband taught school in St. Paul's Churchyard, and issued other polyglot publications, among which was the *French Littleton*. The *History of Aurelio and of Isabell*, of Juan de Flores, an amorous tale of the early years of the reign of Charles V., was translated into English anonymously, and printed in parallel columns with the original Spanish, the Italian of Lelio Aletiphilo, and the French of Giles Corrozet at Antwerp in 1556, and at London in 1588. It also appeared at London in 1586, the Spanish being omitted.

x

Amadis. Guevara had been translated for forty-
six years when the *Mirrour of knighthood* appeared, the courtly romances for half that
number ; and yet the books of chivalry were
represented only by the abortive attempt of
Paynel. *Amadis* and *Palmerin* were losing
ground steadily, and their chances of attracting
attention grew less every year. It was therefore
certain that if they were to be translated at
all, it was to be through the common people.
The aristocracy had utterly ignored them. In
1577 the merchants first manifested an interest
in Spanish literature. Two years later Margaret
Tiler's translation came from the press, and
through the rest of the century the publication
of chronicles of discovery and of books of chivalry went on side by side.

Munday became familiar with the books of
chivalry, of course, during his sojourn on the
continent. He translated from the French and
Italian versions because they were current in
the countries which he had visited. Whether
the idea of publishing *Amadis* and *Palmerin*
in English occurred to him abroad, or was
suggested to him by the example of Margaret
Tiler, is a matter of little importance. The

significant fact is that both set themselves almost simultaneously to make the Spanish romances accessible to the people. For in spite of the dedication of the *Amadis* to the Earl of Montgomery and of *Palmerin d' Oliva* to Drake, neither was looked upon with favor in the upper circles. The reading of romances was deemed to be a loss of time. Meres expressly condemned both Palmerins, *Primaleon of Greece*, *Palladino*, *Palmendos*, *Don Belianis*, Emanuel Ford's *Castle of fame*, the *Mirrour of knighthood*, and various Arthurian romances, in his *Palladis tamia*.[1] But his protests hardly reached the ears of those whom they might have benefited, for the Spanish romances crowded out the earlier group which had been fostered by Caxton, and are said to have been the common reading of milkmaids in the next century.

Munday appreciated the moderate requirements and intelligence of the audience to whom he catered. Always a careless writer, in his romances he paid slight attention, says Southey, to the language, actions, or evident meaning of

[1] Meres, *Palladis tamia*, reprint in *English Garner*, II., p. 268.

his originals.   Southey is further of the opinion
that the greater part of *Palmerin of England* was
not the work of Munday, but of some inexperienced person to whom he assigned his task.[1]
Munday cared nothing for the romances or for
literature, but he did value his assets, and he
regarded the romances as marketable property.
He dealt in them as he did in the news of the
day, as in his account of the *Ligue* of the Guises,
or of the false Dom Sebastian of Portugal, who
was believed for a time to be the hero of Alcazar.[2]   It was not only the pamphlets that he
published, but the romances as well, that have
caused him to be remembered as the "Grub
Street Patriarch."

[1] Southey, *Palmerin of England*, I., p. xlii. Southey
advances the view two pages later, that Sidney, Spenser,
and Shakspere all imitated *Amadis of Greece*, the ninth
book of the Amadis series.

[2] Munday translated a *Discourse of Dom Sebastian* from
the Spanish of José Teixeira through the French in 1601.
Five pamphlets upon the supposed return of Dom Sebastian were licensed within three years, — one in February 1599, one each in March and April 1601, and two on
September 27, 1602.   The last two entries are those of Munday's *Discourse*, which was in two parts, and the entry of
March 30, 1601, refers to the same tract. The *Wonder of
the world*, of April 12, was a ballad, and not connected with
the *Discourse*.

Thomas Lodge, the imitator of Lyly[1] and Greene, though personally attached neither to Sidney nor Oxford, moved on the confines of their groups. He was an exponent of forces which Oxford's set embodied, not exclusively, but notably. The group represents the general

[1] John Lyly (1554?–1606), the "high priest" of euphuism, invited the patronage of the Earl of Oxford, whose friendship he afterward enjoyed, when Munday entered the theatrical troop of that nobleman. He therefore lived in touch with the peninsular influence. Lyly had studied at Oxford from 1569 until 1575, at the period when the maximum number of writers who subsequently translated Spanish books were at the university. Thomas D'Oylie, the lexicographer, studied with him at Magdalen, and at the same time Sidney, Hakluyt, Rogers, Carew, Lodge, and Sir Edward Hoby attended Christ Church or Trinity. Lyly did not come into the circle of the Earl of Oxford until the expiration of the three years which he spent in the country on the eve of the completion of his *Euphues*. How far this much-discussed book is the result of the extravagant tendencies of English sixteenth-century humanism, and how far it was inspired by Guevarism, is yet to be determined. The radical theory of Dr. Landmann concerning Lyly's indebtedness to Guevara, is well known. The most conservative scholarship admits that in matter and manner *Euphues* bears occasional resemblance to Berners' and North's translations of the *Libro áureo*. If Lyly's style was indeed formed upon that of Pettie's *Palace of pleasure*, on the other hand, as Pettie is conceded to have known parts of the gallicized Guevara, the stream of euphuism does not in any case move far from Spain.

Spanish influence in letters. Lodge was
the second son of Sir Thomas Lodge, lord
mayor of London and a merchant of standing,
who had fitted out many voyages to foreign
parts, among which were those of Robert Baker
and Sir John Hawkins, in 1562. The younger
Lodge was sent to Trinity College, Oxford,
about 1573. There he became the servitor of
Sir Edward Hoby, then a student in that college,
and there he was the contemporary of Hakluyt,
Rogers, and Antonio de Corro, to mention a few
of his colleagues who were about to become
distinguished in the world of letters. After
enrolling as a student in Lincoln's Inn, Lodge
abandoned law for literature, writing plays and
novels, following the model set by his friends,
Barnaby Rich, Lyly, and Greene. His first
romance was dedicated to Sidney. This, as
well as his succeeding novels, belonged to the
type of the love pamphlet, which was so happily cultivated in England after the manner of
the Italians. Lodge presently turned from letters to more adventurous pursuits, and em-
barked on voyages with Captain Clarke to
Terceira and the Canaries, and with Thomas
Cavendish to South American ports. It was

on this voyage that Lodge claims to have written a *Margarite of America*, a euphuistical romance, the material for which he asserts was obtained from a Spanish work in the library of the Jesuits at Santos on the coast of Brazil. A number of Cavendish's men under Captain Cocke, remained in that town upward of five weeks in the winter of 1591–1592, and the captains and a number of gentlemen lodged in the College of Jesus.[1]

The Spanish influence in the *Margarite* has commonly been overestimated. Lodge landed in England after parting from Cavendish in 1593, three years before the *Margarite* was published. In this interval his pen was by no means idle. The *Life and death of William Longbeard*, a *Fig for Momus*, the *Divel conjured*, and several lyrics, for example, belong to the period. Lodge undoubtedly held back the *Margarite* for the sake of adding the finishing touches. Many of the songs which it contained are open imitations of the lyrics of Dolce and other Italians. It is not likely that these were written in the South Atlantic; they were prob-

---

[1] Hakluyt, *Principal Nav.*, III., p. 842 ; Laing, *Acc't of Lodge*, p. xxxv.

ably inserted afterward. The romance itself, according to Lodge, was composed in the Straits of Magellan. The *Margarite* presented no style that was new to English, and the attempts to connect its peculiarities directly with the Gongorism of Spain are fantastical. The book is in Lodge's usual manner and does not read like a translation. It was not unusual in the sixteenth century for authors to claim foreign originals for the offspring of their own imagination. Both Guevara and the Spanish and Italian authors of the books of chivalry had pursued this course. In view of these facts, together with the internal evidence, the statement of Lodge cannot be understood to apply further than to the design of his story.

When the *Margarite* appeared, Lodge was already a convert to Catholicism. Once more abandoning literature, he went abroad to take up the study of medicine. The degree of M. D. was conferred on him at Avignon in 1600, whereupon he returned to London and acquired an enviable reputation as a physician, during the latter part of his life. Henceforth his works were of a didactic nature, dealing mostly with medicine and religion. The first books by

Lodge, licensed after his return from Avignon, were translations from Luis de Granada. There are two entries of this sort in the stationers' register: the *Flowers of Lodowicke of Granado gathered out of his spirituall workes*, on April 23, 1601, and the *Paradise of prayers gathered out of the spirituall workes of Lewis of Granado*, May 22, 1601. It is possible that these entries both refer to the same work. Only one translation by Lodge from Granada has been identified by bibliographers. In translating the works of Granada, Lodge coupled his name with that of the most popular Catholic religious writer whose books were known in England at the close of the reign of Elizabeth. He came under the influence of this writer at Avignon, as Richard Hopkins had done in Spain. Though engaged in the same task as Lodge, Hopkins, being a political exile, was obliged to restrict his sphere of action to the continent. His works were admitted to England upon sufferance. Lodge, though a Catholic, was at the same time essentially an Englishman, and beginning his sectarian propaganda on the threshold of King James' reign, occupies a position in the van of the Catholic reaction.

This movement, though mainly inspired from Italy, thus owed something in its infancy to Spain.

The avenues, indeed, through which the higher types of literature reached England from the peninsula were two in number during the reign of Elizabeth.   Many Spanish books were imported from France and Italy throughout the century in common with the literature of those countries. Spanish works were sometimes sought out in French and Italian versions because of the interest which existed in Spanish affairs, and sometimes they found their way to England unheralded, as if they had been the production of the latter peoples themselves. It was in this manner that Fortescue, Fenton, and Munday obtained the books of which they made use. In the same way, at an earlier date, Berners and Bryan came into possession of the works of Guevara. The set of the Earl of Oxford is the best exemplification of the *modus operandi* of the French and Italian mediation during the latter half of the century. Its connection with the peninsula was slight. It expressed a general interest in Spain. On the other hand, the early group of translators at the court for the most part, and

the entire group which gathered about Sir Philip
Sidney, embody the peninsular interest in its
purest form.   The activity of these men was the
consequence of direct international communication, yet the translation of so many Castilian
writings into English was not merely the result
of commercial or political intercourse between
the English and Spanish people.   It was the outcome of the contact of the aristocratic classes.
The merchants did not bring the literature of
art to England; Googe and Challoner, associat-
ing in the peninsula with the Ferias, introduced
it into Elizabeth's court, through Newton, Patten, Hellowes, and Googe himself.   The family
ties between the Sidney group and the Countess
of Feria drew Paston, the Haringtons, the Dormers, and others to Spain, and produced the
translations of Sidney, Paston, Yong, and the
work of Fraunce.   The literary intercourse was
intimately bound up with the social, and did not
precede it.   It was necessary to be well received
at Madrid, and by the Spanish aristocracy, to
become familiar with the higher type of Castilian
literature.   When the English became firmly
established in Spain, the literature of that country was first made familiar to London.   The full

development of the Spanish influence in England dates from that time. The translation of works of æsthetic value from the Spanish direct, which only became customary in the last quarter of the century, and which was the sign of the maturity of the peninsular influence, was not possible until the contact of the upper classes of the nations had paved the way for the importation of the best culture of Spain directly into England.

CHAPTER IX

ANTIQUARIANS AND LEXICOGRAPHERS

I

THE court groups of translators, at the head of which Sidney and Oxford stood, were leaders in the advance of the Spanish influence; but the movement at the close of the century, which found its expression in pure literature in them, manifested itself also in the antiquarian society of Archbishop Parker and among the lexicographers of London. The antiquaries made the most considerable approach, collectively, to a scholastic, to a distant and impersonal interest in Spanish history and learning, that was made in the reign of Elizabeth. This interest, though it was impersonal, was at the same time real. Many of the members of the antiquarian society were intimately connected with the principal exponents of the Spanish influences. Richard Carew, the companion of Philip Sidney in his college days, Stow, the acquaintance of Munday,

and Hartwell, the friend of Hakluyt and Newton, maintained relations with those who were
familiar with at least one phase of Castilian literature. Many ties bound the antiquaries to
the sets at court; they were encouraged by
Burghley, Leicester, and Walsingham; Bancroft, Whitgift, and other churchmen were
among their stanchest friends. Sir Henry
Spelman patronized the lexicographer Minsheu,
and Parker rendered most valuable services to
John Day, Barnaby Googe, and Dr. Man. The
translations which were made by the antiquaries, however, were small in bulk, and almost
casual in character, for they had little direct
intercourse with the peninsula. The group was
permeated by the interest in things Spanish
that was abroad, perhaps in a more than usual
degree. The work which it accomplished paralleled, in a discreet and scholarly way, the productivity of the pamphleteers during the period
in which the latter were most assiduous in circulating news about Spain.

Richard Carew, the first gentleman of Cornwall, is remembered as an antiquarian, but he is
much better known as a translator and a poet.
The five cantos of *Jerusalem delivered*, which he

did out of Tasso, are more frequently mentioned in histories of literature than his other works, but the *Examination of men's wits* was by far more popular among his contemporaries. The book is a curious collection of psychological and physiological observations, regarding, partly, the education of children. It was written by Juan Huarte, and enjoyed great repute throughout Europe as late as the day of the critic Lessing, by whom a German translation was made. Carew was acquainted with it only through the Italian version of Camillo Camilli, which was lent to him by Sir Francis Godolphin.

Carew, although a country gentleman, had much occasion to be in the capital. He was twice member of Parliament, and the friend of Camden, Cotton, Spelman, and the other members of the antiquarian society. At an earlier period he was exceptionally intimate with Sidney and Hakluyt at Oxford. Carew entered Christ Church in 1566, remaining in residence about four years. At the age of fourteen or fifteen he contended in debate against Sidney, who was barely his senior, before Leicester and other nobles, until the authorities were glad to call a draw. Thomas D'Oylie, Rogers, Lyly, and Valera were also contemporaries of Carew at the university. The languages which he knew, however, he taught himself by dint of persistent reading. This was no slight task, for he was familiar with Greek, Italian, German, French, and Spanish.

Carew's translation of Huarte was immediately due to the influence of his Cornish surroundings. A powerful element in the family of his second wife, the Arundels, who were neighbors of the Carews, had been converted to Catholicism, and its members were properly counted by Bernardino de Mendoza among the most enthusiastic English partisans of Philip II.[1] Sir John Arundel involved himself so deeply in treason that he was sent to the Tower in 1586, while in the previous year Charles Arundel was banished and fled to Spain. Sir George Carew, the brother of Richard, had served in Ireland under Sir Henry Sidney, and

[1] In a statement forwarded from Paris by Mendoza to the king, August 13, 1586, the names of the Englishmen who had agreed to rise on the coming of a Spanish force are preserved. Those of Sir John Arundel and his son, Lords Henry and Thomas Howard, the Earl of Arundel, Lords Montague and Vaux, Sir Walter Aston, and the Throckmortons appear. *State papers, Sp., Eliz.,* III., 604.

there came into touch with the Spanish and Italian conspirators against the queen. It was Godolphin, the father-in-law of Sir George, who owned the copy of the *Exámen de ingenios*, from which Carew made his translation. Godolphin had married among the Killigrews, one of the oldest Cornish families, and his wife was the sister of Sir Henry Killigrew, a man evidently of some parts, for he was a diplomatist, musician, and painter, and the literary adviser of Sir Thomas Challoner. It is not surprising, therefore, as it at first sight seemed, that books by Spanish authors were circulating in Cornwall. The affiliations of the inhabitants with the persons who were best situated to be cognizant of peninsular literature, if somewhat complex, were numerous. They indicate the extent of the dissemination of its influence apart from the court, in the remotest corner of the kingdom.

Abraham Hartwell, the younger, was likewise a translator from the Italian. He eschewed general literature, for his mind had a pronounced historical bent. Indeed, Hartwell must have been a person of unusual force of character to have escaped being diverted to

Y

theology, for in his youth he had been secretary to John Whitgift, afterward archbishop of Canterbury and his faithful patron, and he also shared the friendship of Bancroft. That he was a relative of the elder Hartwell, the religious enthusiast, is probable, as Thomas Newton addressed him in verse on the occasion of the elder's decease. The names of both are of frequent occurrence on the books of the Stationers' Company.

The younger Hartwell attended Trinity College, Cambridge, receiving the customary degrees in 1571 and 1575. There he was the colleague of Thomas Moffett and George Clifford, subsequently earl of Cumberland, who both studied at Trinity, and probably also of Abraham Fraunce. These associations have left no discoverable traces in the works of his maturity. It was during these college days, however, that Hartwell attracted the attention of Whitgift, who was the dominant power in his life. Three of his works were dedicated to his patron, at whose request some of them were undertaken. The entire list of the writings of Hartwell is not long. Omitting several papers which he composed for the society of antiquaries, to which he was the last member admitted, it comprised a *History of the warres betweene the Turkes and the Persians* and the *Ottoman* of Lazaro Soranzo, both from the Italian; a tract giving an account of one Martha Brossier, a supposed victim of demoniacal possession, from the French; and a *Report of the kingdome of the Congo*, originally written in Portuguese by Duarte Lopes. These books were printed within the first decade of Elizabeth's reign, and all of them, setting aside the demoniacal tract, were borrowed from the same romance idiom, for Lopes' work was current in the Italian of Filippo Pigafetta. The translation was begun in compliance with the expressed desire of Hakluyt.

Carew and the younger Hartwell both moved in the company of men who lived in direct contact with the Spanish forces operating in England, and they resembled each other in the respect that they were indebted to friends who were not members of the society to which they both belonged, for their knowledge of the peninsula. Robert Beale, the third member of the group, duplicated their experience in this respect. Beale was born in 1541, and becoming a Puritan in his youth, joined the colony of Protestant refugees on the continent during Mary's occupancy of the throne. After the accession of Elizabeth he secured an office in the English embassy at Paris, where he ultimately became secretary to his uncle, Sir Francis Walsingham. He soon demonstrated his abilities in several positions of responsibility, and was sent to the Lowlands in 1576 with Admiral Winter, a thorough master of Spanish, on a mission to the Prince of Orange. He proceeded thence to Germany. At Frankfort he met Hubert Languet, who gave him a letter of introduction to Sidney. Beale served the state in civil, religious, and military affairs. Uniformly holding a high place in the councils of the nation, he was one of the envoys sent to treat for peace with Spain at Boulogne in 1600. Besides his friendships with Winter, Sidney, and Walsingham, he possessed an acquaintance with Henry Killigrew, as well as with Whitgift, with whom, indeed, he entered into open controversy.

Beale published a number of books on legal and historical subjects, but his chief work was his *Rerum hispanicarum scriptores*, printed in three volumes at Frankfort in 1579. This compilation, which presents some points of analogy with Eden's *Decades of the newe worlde*, may be set off against the chronicles of discovery that were at the time being translated by the merchants. It is a work of scholarship, based upon the writings of approved Spanish, Portuguese, and Italian historians of the peninsula, and chiefly upon those which were composed in the Latin tongue. The dominance of Spain in Europe, together with the impending breach between that country and his own, suggested the idea of such a compilation to Beale, for he possessed a lively interest in affairs. After the defeat of the Armada, he published a *Collection of the King of Spain's injuries offered to the Queen of England*, and a *Vindication of the queen against the objections of the Spaniards*. The materials for his history, however, came to his notice while he was travelling upon the continent, and the book was evidently arranged during the author's sojourn in Germany, which began in 1576. As his stay was not terminated until 1578, and the *Rerum hispanicarum scriptores* appeared at Frankfort in the ensuing year, the work can claim English parentage only.

Sir Edward Hoby lived in the midst of a similar environment. Though not himself a member of Archbishop Parker's society, Hoby was one of the group of which it may be considered the centre. As he patronized Camden and enjoyed the friendship of Sir George Carew, the influences which shaped it could not well pass him by. Hoby was the eldest son of Sir Thomas Hoby, the translator of the *Courtier* of Castiglione, and nephew of Sir Philp Hoby, formerly agent of Henry VIII. in Spain. He received his education at Trinity College, Oxford, whither he was sent at the age of fourteen. There he was the contemporary of Hakluyt, Rogers, and Thomas Lodge. After leaving Oxford he is said to have become a lover of learning and antiquities; but he also developed a taste for war, which he gratified by accompanying Essex on the expedition against Cadiz in 1596. The immediate fruit of Hoby's experience in that empty triumph was his translation of Bernardino de Mendoza's *Theoriqve and practice of warre*. This work has been adjudged to be the most valuable of all Spanish military treatises. It is imbued with the spirit of the able and uncompromising diplomat who organized and abetted the Catholic conspiracies against Elizabeth in her own country, on the eve of the great international conflict. In publishing the translation, Hoby ranged himself in the ranks of the martial writers of the reign, but the merit of his author guaranteed the book some consideration as literature. The translation was the natural outcome of his surroundings. To pass by the linguistic accomplishments of his father and uncle, Hoby maintained intercourse with persons who were in the stream of foreign influence. At Eton he read Latin with Sir John Harington and Thomas Arundel, and his friendship with Sir George Carew has already been pointed out. Charles Howard of Effingham, the patron of more than one translator, had married his wife's sister. Hoby himself published a translation from the French of Martin Coignet, in his twenty-seventh year. These circumstances all portray his contact with the cosmopolitan forces of the time. He inherited an interest in foreign affairs, that, though it might be directed by fortuitous events, did not owe its being to chance. In common with Beale, Hartwell, and Carew, he came into the path of a general culture in which the knowledge of Spain, if it was not a vitalizing principle, was certainly an ingredient.

II

The existence of a body of grammarians and lexicographers engaged in the study of Castilian, indicates most plainly the position which that language had attained at the time of the defeat of the Armada. It was the commercial recognition of the vogue of Spanish. Previously to the sailing of that ill-fated fleet, copy books illustrating the proper manner of writing the peninsular and other hands,[1] a few romances in parallel columns, a polyglot dictionary containing Spanish as one of its four languages, and a grammar and dictionary by Antonio de Corro had appeared in England.[2] Corro's work

[1] A *Newe Copie booke*, containing the Spanish hand among others, was printed at London in 1591. It seems to have been an enlargement of Jean de Beauchesne's *Trésor d'escripture*, originally published at Paris, in 1550, and issued in English dress at London, in 1570, 1574, and 1602. The first English edition does not appear to have contained the Spanish hand. The names of Thomas Scarlett and John Baldon have been mentioned in connection with this book.

[2] Attention has been called to Corro's work on p. 194, and to the romances of *Arnalte and Lucenda* and *Aurelio and Isabell* on p. 305. The polyglot dictionary referred to

was republished in English dress by John Thorius in 1590, and was immediately followed by the most important Spanish dictionaries that were prepared in the country during the sixteenth century. These were the compilations of Thomas D'Oylie, Richard Perceval, and John Minsheu.[1] The work of this group, which was the last of the kind to be done in the reign, stood on a higher plane of scholarship, certainly on the Spanish side, than that of its competitors. No opposition rivalled it for completeness, nor sufficed to avert the recognition of its authority.

The little group which was thus paramount in England upon questions of the Spanish

is the *Dictionaire colloques ou dialogues en quattre langues. flamen.ffrançoys. espaignol. et italien, with the Englishe to be added thereto*, which was licensed upon the stationers' register on September 12, 1578. It is possible that this never came from the press, as the home of the *colloquia* was the continent.

[1] William Stepney obtained a license for the *Spanishe Schoolemaster conteyninge 7 dialogues . . . proverbes and sentences, as alsoe the Lordes prayre, the articles of our belief the X. commaundementes, with diverse other thinges necessarie to be knowen in the said tonge*, on January 13, 1591. The ten commandments must have been favorite reading with beginners in Spanish, as they were licensed to be printed in that language as far back as 1568–1569.

language, bears the marks of the same influences that affected the littérateurs at court and their friends, the members of the society of Parker. To the antiquarians Spanish was merely a side issue, a topic that occupied a comparatively insignificant place in their minds, but, to D'Oylie, Perceval, and Minsheu, it was a bond of mutual interest. They were drawn together because their attention had already been independently concentrated upon the study of Castilian. In October 1590 D'Oylie obtained a license for a *Spanish Grammer, conformed to our Englishe accydence. With a large dictionarye conteyninge Spanish, Latyn, and Englishe wordes, with a multitude of Spanishe wordes more than are conteyned in the Calapine of x : languages or Neobrecensis dictionare.* It soon came to D'Oylie's notice that Richard Perceval had about completed a similar work which was much further advanced than his own. He therefore abandoned the purpose of publishing his own dictionary, and placed his material at Perceval's disposal, with the request that the Latin part which Perceval had not included in his scheme, should not be omitted from the book. With D'Oylie's assistance the *Biblio-*

theca hispanica was published by Perceval, in
two separate sections in 1591.   The grammar,
embracing passages " gathered out of diuers
good authors," filled the first part, and a dictionary in three languages, the second.   The whole
was asserted to be " very profitable for the
studious of the Spanish toong."   This dictionary at once became a recognized success, and a
second edition was called for, which appeared
in 1599. Perceval, however, had at that time
obtained political employment, which furnished
him with ample means of subsistence.   The
dictionary and grammar were therefore revised
and sent to the press by John Minsheu, a
teacher of languages.   A   third edition by
Minsheu followed in 1623.

Thomas D'Oylie was born in Oxfordshire
about the year 1548, and entered Magdalen
College at Oxford in 1563.   At this institution Lyly became his colleague six years later.
Leaving Oxford in 1571 to study abroad,
D'Oylie proceeded to Basle, where he obtained
his doctorate in 1581.   Thence he travelled
to the Low Countries, practising his profession, and returned to London in 1585, becoming a fellow of the College of Physicians.

D'Oylie had been at Oxford when the most distinguished of the translators from the Spanish had been in attendance at the university. While he and Lyly were at Magdalen, Sidney, Carew, Hakluyt, and Rogers were at Christ Church, and Wilcox was at St. John's. The incorporation of Valera into the university took place during the period of his residence. These associations evidently exercised a potent charm over D'Oylie, and one which his stay in continental seats of learning and among the combatants in Flanders served to intensify. The course of his studies offers an exact parallel to that of Hakluyt's, though in a different sphere. They studied together at Oxford. Both deepened the culture that they there acquired, by travelling abroad. Both enjoyed the patronage of influential persons, — D'Oylie that of Leicester, Sir Francis and Anthony Bacon, and Hakluyt that of Stafford and Lady Sheffield, then presently to become Leicester's wife. Indeed, the Bacons were connections of D'Oylie; Sir Robert Cecil befriended him. The life of the man was passed among the circles of the broadest culture in the land.

Richard Perceval, on the other hand, is supposed to have obtained such education as he possessed, at St. Paul's School and at Lincoln's Inn. He early developed an extravagant vein, married young, and fled to Spain to escape the consequences of indiscretions which had brought upon him the wrath of his father. There he remained four years, until the death of his wife. Returning to London, the knowledge of Spanish which Perceval had acquired during his residence in the peninsula procured him employment from Burghley, and he was called upon to decipher documents in that language, a task that Sir William Winter and Bernard Hampton had performed before him. It is Perceval who is said to have interpreted the despatch which brought the first news of the coming of the Armada. Thereafter his rise was rapid. Sir Robert Cecil took him under his protection, and he was forgiven by his father. In 1603–1604 he became a member of Parliament from Yorkshire, and subsequently a promoter of the London Virginia Company. After the death of his patron, Perceval retired with his second wife to Ireland, where he died in 1620.

It is not possible to fix the exact dates of Perceval's sojourn in the peninsula, as diplomatic agents were no longer maintained by the queen at Madrid at so late a day. His return, however, took place before the rupture of all intercourse, and coincided very well with that of D'Oylie from the Low Countries. Reëstablished in London, both authors began the labor of compiling their dictionaries, the materials of which they had gathered in their absence. Perceval had drawn his directly from Spain; D'Oylie does not seem to have visited the peninsula, but he was no novice in its tongue. If previous character counts for anything, the scholarship of the *Bibliotheca hispanica* can scarcely have been improved by the retirement of D'Oylie in favor of Perceval. The name of the latter had not been associated with long vigils by the student's lamp. His confrère, too, had made good the disadvantage of not having had knowledge acquired on the spot, by "the cōference of Natyve Spaniards." Warton's hypothesis that Perceval was the R. P. who translated the second to the sixth parts of the *Mirrour of knighthood*, accords better with what might have been expected of such a person as Perceval had shown himself to be in his early life, than does the compilation of a lexicon. But the translations of this romance by the pen of R. P. extended over a period of seventeen years, only ending with the century. Perceval, if the hypothesis be correct, must have returned to England about 1583, and have continued to occupy himself at intervals with the *Knight of the sun* until well in his prime. The incompatibility of such a pursuit with the later career of the man need not be remarked. Both the romance and the lexicon cannot be attributed to him, for Warton's suggestion is purely gratuitous. It is quite unlikely that a politician and a scholar dissipated his time on romances while enjoying his hardly won and much-menaced good fortune.

The last editor of this dictionary, John Minsheu, properly belongs to the next century. His principal achievement, the *Guide into tongues*, a lexicon containing words in eleven languages, and the first book sold by subscription in England, was not published until 1617. An English-Spanish dictionary with " speches and prouerbes together with delightfull and pleasant

Dialogues in Spaneshe and English " appeared,
however, in connection with his revision of
Perceval during the reign of Elizabeth. Minsheu was a teacher of languages who eked out
a scanty livelihood in London. He prosecuted
his studies through the generosity of Sir Henry
Spelman and of friends at the universities.
The relations which he must have entered into
with his predecessors appear to have been of a
purely commercial kind, as the difference in
the standing of Minsheu and D'Oylie and Perceval would indicate. But at the close of the
century, the peninsular influence in London
was sufficiently strong to be somewhat independent of social ties. Minsheu was able to
go about among the strangers who frequented
the capital. These lent him aid. In the compilation of his *Guide into tongues,* he enlisted
the services of a number of foreigners and
friendly disposed scholars. What he lost by
failing to secure the patronage of the nobility
or of the members of the highest circles, who
were at the time most familiar with peninsular
literature, he replaced by the help of agencies
less conspicuous, aristocratic, and exclusive,
which were rife among the foreigners resident

in the capital, whether preachers, merchants, fencing masters, or what not, who had been received by the English since the days of Henry VIII.

When Elizabeth's reign drew near to its termination, the English Renaissance had progressed so far that in the increasing dissemination of foreign culture the translators at the court but summed up influences which, instead of being confined to them alone, had come to be potent in all London. The long-continued intercourse with the peninsula then bore its fruit. The defeat of the invincible Armada, the ravaging of the Spanish and Portuguese seaboards by the soldiers and sailors of Essex and Drake, the campaigns of the Duke of Parma in northern France, and the threatened descent of the second armada, — events which succeeded each other in rapid sequence within the limits of a decade, — had riveted the minds of the people upon the Spanish nation. The course of history was paralleled in a modest way by the movement of literature. The full tide of translation set in, the sign of which was the sudden appearance of Castilian grammars and dictionaries in England. Spanish books

z

were printed in the original at Oxford and London. It became a common custom to insert sentences and quotations in that language into novels and plays of native or Italian origin. Swelling and boisterous words were borrowed freely by Nash and his contemporaries. The peninsular influence, reaching the point at which it was no longer inseparably dependent upon individuals in direct contact with Spain, became in some degree general and free. On the practical side, its typical representative was Minsheu, the scholar and home-student, as distinguished from the more cosmopolitan travellers who had preceded him, Thomas D'Oylie and Richard Perceval.

CHAPTER X

THE NATURE OF THE INFLUENCE OF SPAIN

WHEN Henry VIII. was casting about at the opening of the third decade of the sixteenth century to find plausible grounds to put Katherine of Aragon away and to crown Anne Boleyn queen in her stead, the literature of the peninsula was a sealed book to his subjects. No Spanish work had then been translated into the English language, none was familiar as yet to the people, or well known even to scholars. When James I. succeeded Elizabeth seventy-three years later, some hundred and seventy volumes, written either by peninsular authors or in the peninsular tongues, had already appeared at London or in other centres for the publication of English books. Taken in the mass, these were fairly representative of the life and letters of Spain. They covered the whole range of its literature, irrespective of form, with the sole exceptions of the lyric and the drama.

They embraced both popular and scholarly types, and included, indeed, much that seemed anti-Spanish in its essence, such as the tracts of the Sevillian Reformers. This variety of content was accompanied also by differences in the manner of presentation. Of the total number, perhaps thirty works remained in the Latin in which they had been indited, and twenty in the original Castilian of their authors. The others had all been translated, for the most part quite adequately, into the vernacular. Book by book they covered a wide field and pleaded many special causes. Now it was one interest to which they appealed, now it was another. Collectively, whatever the language in which they were couched and whatever the tenor of the views they set forth, they were one and all essentially the outflowering of the Spanish mind and its characteristic embodiment in the eyes of the English people.

As the interest of England in the peninsula was long bent chiefly upon the official acts of the peninsular government, the history of Spanish literature north of the channel, during the Tudor times, was a phase of the history of the hegemony of politics and trade in the intercourse of the countries, by which the domination of the practical in determining the development of the æsthetic arts was effected. The subordination of the latter was exhibited throughout the century in many ways. The manifestations of Spanish culture gained and lost in clearness according to the policies which prevailed under the different sovereigns. For each reign received it in a spirit quite its own. As the English under Henry VIII. were brought into relations with a limited number of the Castilian nobility in London, they derived from them a polite acquaintance with the Spanish court, but little knowledge of the Spanish people. The marriage of Philip and Mary at once left its stamp upon social and political conditions. It was signalized by glittering pageantry and impressive fêtes, which, though designed to astonish the intruders from Castile, produced no less an effect among the citizens of London themselves; the spectacle diverted the attention of the people in great part from the mere court customs of Spain, and awakened the imperial spirit in England through the study of the history of the southern empire. Under Elizabeth the increasing importance of

the countries to each other, the interchange of
commercial products and the strife of religious
and ecclesiastical ideas, which were unbroken
between them for so many years and determined
their mutual social attitude for so many more,
finally rendered the nation as thoroughly familiar with the Spaniards as it had been previously with the other and less isolated Latin
races.

The translations that were made from the
Spanish during these reigns gave evidence in
their sphere of the nature of the surroundings
which called them forth. This was to be seen
primarily in the part which the different languages played as mediums for the introduction
of the peninsular literature. With possibly a
single exception, the Spanish books which were
read in London in the days of Henry VIII. and
Edward VI. were obtained through the French
or the Latin. Those which were circulated
under the sceptre of Philip and Mary were
drawn, on the other hand, directly from the
Castilian or from the Latin of Spaniards who
either were or had been residents of England.
These translations were, of course, corollaries
of that unhappy alliance. The rupture of

the artificial union upon the death of Mary banished foreign advisers from the capital and again threw the English upon the French and Italians for their knowledge of their former allies, so that the number of translations from peninsular authors through the mediation of those two languages during the first half of Elizabeth's reign came to be equal to that from the Spanish alone or to that through the Latin. From the year 1578, however, when the nations had adjusted themselves to the new aspect of their fortunes, the immediate influence of the Spanish rapidly augmented, so that by the time of the queen's death, at the height of the movement, more than twice as many Castilian books had been derived from that language immediately as had been englished through other tongues.

The time between the original appearance of a work and its translation, furthermore, was dependent upon the operation of the same causes, and showed the same progression toward unhindered communication with Portugal and Castile. Setting aside the work of Vives and the scholars who did not write in the vernacular, and who often lived abroad and

may be well regarded as the property of Europe
at large, this interval, previous to the accession
of Queen Mary, was never less than five years
nor more than ten, except in the cases of works
of long-established reputation. The coalition
which was brought about in Mary's reign encouraged the study of chronicles of Spanish
history and discovery, rather than that of polite
literature. The exploits of the nation were
recorded most adequately in books of some age,
such as the *Decades* of Martyr. Consequently,
though old as well as new publications were
imported from the peninsula throughout the
century, the former predominated in this period
because it was the aim of the translators to cel-
ebrate the achievements of their allies, and to
make the history and wisdom of Spain at her
best commonly known. The return of normal
conditions at the opening of the reign of Elizabeth restored the *status quo* which had existed
under her father. The interval of translation,
indeed, became still greater than that which
prevailed under Henry VIII., and few books
reached London until they had already been in
circulation a dozen years. It was not until the
later days of Elizabeth that the recent publica-

tions of her enemies came to be reproduced at
her court within less than five years of their
first appearance, — the minimum time which
had prevailed at the opening of the century.
This celerity, however, was due only to the
industry of those persons who had travelled in
the dominions of Philip II., or who had friends
within the boundaries of his empire.   For the
rest, the interval of translation was not sub-
stantially modified.

The bulk of books by Spanish authors, finally,
afforded but another instance of the potency of
the same laws which fixed the manner and the
hour of their appearance.   The volumes of
Spanish origin which were printed in England
before Elizabeth scarcely equalled a score all
told.   They extended, however, over a period
of thirty years, being divided evenly between
the reigns of Henry VIII. and Edward VI.,
and the reign of Mary.   The activity of the
early Elizabethan era augmented the total number to fifty by 1577; but in the remaining years
of the epoch, when the means of communication
between the countries were more efficient within
their limits than ever before, fully two and one-
half times as many peninsular works were pub-

lished in England as had been made accessible
to the people since the inception of the movement with the interlude based upon the *Celestina*, just after Vives had been banished the
country for espousing the cause of Katherine
of Aragon. Throughout the whole century
the English had been, indeed, drawing nearer
to an understanding of the intellectual and
spiritual life of Spain. At its close very
nearly the whole literature of the nation was
duly represented and read in accredited exem-
plars in the North, and Spanish letters had
won a position quite independent of the political conditions which had nourished and fostered
them. The evidence of this fact was the great
increase in the number and variety of translations, in the shortening of the interval between
the date of their original and that of their foreign publication, and in the notably rising ratio
that the number of books borrowed immediately
from the Castilian bore to those which penetrated the country in French and Italian dress,
though these last did not become less frequent
but multiplied more rapidly than they had previously done. The catholicity of taste which
was exhibited in this movement, and the pro-

gressive complexity which marked its development through the groups of Berners, Eden,
Googe, Hakluyt, Sidney, Essex, and Oxford,
made plain the separation of the literary and
political strands, and the attainment by the
former of a significance exclusively its own.

But this independence was barely evident
before the death of Elizabeth, nor was it even
then complete.   It was the long wars of Spain
upon the continent and against the Turk, her
daring in the wildernesses of America, and her
enterprise in the immemorial cities of India
and Cathay, that crowned her banners with
glory.   Her power to do indubitably developed
and demonstrated her greatness, for her achievement was most certain and her influence most
profound in the practical sphere.   Hénce it
was that her statesmen and her courtiers, her
soldiers and her sailors, in familiarizing England
with themselves, taught her truly the best les-
sons that Spain could teach.   They preceded
the poets and scholars of their country in alien
lands.   The English Renaissance, though it
owed so much to all the nations of southern
Europe, acknowledged to each, indeed, a particular debt.   From Italy and France, to which

it went voluntarily in search of culture, it
learned scholarship and refinement; from the
superior strength of Spain, which it was now
compelled to reënforce in the field, and now
coerced to oppose in a struggle for existence
that was to be carried to the bitter end on sea
and on land, it obtained command of itself and
won the right to be free. It was through actual
contact, through the association of man with
man, through the immediate dissemination of its
methods and its imperial ideals, and not through
its books, that Spain quickened the nerve and
stiffened the fibre of the English nation. Thus
also the spread of its culture became dependent
upon political and commercial necessities, and
remained subordinate to them. When Spanish
letters were fully brought to the attention of the
country, and when the comparative maturity of
the Castilian genius had at last secured independent consideration on the ground of its
intrinsic merit, the natural consequence was
the deepening of the knowledge that was
already current about the peninsular peoples,
which was political in its origin and practical
in its application. For this reason such a large
proportion of the Tudor translations from the

peninsular tongues, was of a didactic nature, —
either histories, treatises of war, medicine, and
navigation, or religious writings.   All these
classes of books, like the Spanish grammars and
dictionaries, eame into demand in London solely
in response to social and material requirements.
For this reason also the translations, even when
grown numerous as in Shakspere's time, had
such small permanent significance in the land,
and contributed so little to English thought.
The general influence, the initiative or the
regulative force of Spanish in English letters,
was inseparable from that of the every-day
intercourse of the nations.   The chief office
of Spanish culture abroad was none other than
to deepen the impression which had been made
by Spanish enterprise and arms.   This was at
once the source of its limitations and of its
power.

The traces of this connection of peninsular
learning with achievement are at once apparent
upon a survey of English letters in the sixteenth
century.   They are far more prominent and
common than the signs of any influence that
was purely literary in its character.   The innumerable tracts and broadsides which were so

frequently the aftermath of current events in the history of Spain could only have been produced in England in response to purely political causes. The union of practical and imaginative strands was most clearly seen in occasional publications of a higher type. These were the "books with a purpose," and especially the controversial writings which were penned in reply to the professed opinions of peninsular scholars. Osorio da Fonseca's letters to Elizabeth, written upon the suggestion of the Portuguese king, and the treatises of Haddon and Foxe, which were similarly inspired at the English court, were the most famous examples of the kind. These books made an arena of the printed page, and cannot be considered apart from the circumstances out of which they sprang. They were the creations of the time, it is true, and purely ephemeral in character, but the elements that produced them wrought effects more general and enduring. These were patent in many quarters, and distinctly discernible within the pale of literature in criticism, in the drama, and in romance.

Spanish criticism had just made its real

beginnings at the close of the long rule of
Philip II., in the work of Rengifo and Alonzo
Lopez.[1] Hence it could have had no connection with the contemporary rhetorical treatises
in the North. But English critical writers did
not hesitate to take notice of Spain in other
ways. The *Arte of English poesie*, which was
published in the year after the Armada, is a
typical instance of the manner in which the
peninsula and its culture were regarded. The
author of this book had visited the courts of all
the Latin kingdoms, and if, as is probable, he
was Richard Puttenham, the nephew of Sir
Thomas Elyot, he could not have been without
friends at Westminster. The book abounds
in references to Spain. These are of two
kinds, — anecdotes of the Emperor Charles V.,
of King Philip II., and other royal personages,
and random remarks upon phrases and modes
of speech then affected in Castile. There are
only two passages in the *Arte*, however, which
indicate any acquaintance with the literature
of the country. One of these is an aside about

---

[1] The *Arte poética española* of Juan Diaz Rengifo was
published in 1592. Lopez printed his *Filosofia antigua
poética* in 1596.

two hundred crowns that Queen Mary gave to the poet Vargas as a reward for his epithalamium upon her marriage with Philip, and the other an incidental censure passed upon Guevara on account of his over fondness for the use of antithesis.[1] Thus, though the *Arte of English poesie* was exceptionally rich in allusion to Spain, the attention bestowed upon Spanish writers was so surprisingly small as to amount almost to neglect. Since political and social conditions were clearly predominant, this was perfectly natural, and the consequent disproportion, however glaring, must be viewed as inevitable.

In the evolution of the pastoral and other love romances of the sixteenth century, the same phenomena are discernible. The English romance grew out of the imitation of Italian models. The ultimate source of books of this type, it should be noted, was always the same, though the modes in which it was approached were not uniform. Thus the *Margarite* of Lodge and the *Arcadia* of Sidney were in part the result of Italian influence transmitted

---

[1] *Arte of English poesie*, Arber's *English Reprints*, VII., pp. 32 and 220.

through Spanish mediums. But such instances were exceptional. Apparently in every other work of the genus, this process was reversed, and the contribution of the peninsula was incorporated into the romances through the good offices of Italy. Barnaby Rich's *Don Simonides, a gentilman Spaniarde*, which was first issued in 1581 and completed three years later, was thoroughly Italian. The story of *Dom Diego and Genevora*, that was included by Whetstone in his *Rocke of regard* in 1576, and by Painter in his *Palace of pleasure*, although it was laid in Spain and contained Spanish words, was taken bodily, Castilian and all, from Bandello. The earlier *Historie of John lorde Mandozze*, written by Thomas de la Peend and published in 1565, was drawn from the same author. These romances were typical of their class. In yet others, in place of heroes professedly Castilian and quotations borrowed from that language, notable events in ancient or contemporary Spanish history were recounted, as in the story of the battle of Alcazar in Whetstone's *English Myrror* of 1586, or in the bald narrative called *Howe Kinge Rodorigo lost his kingdome*, which was

2 A

annexed to Lodge's *Longbeard*, published in
1593. Greene, the most representative of the
writers of this kind of fiction, visited Spain, if
his own word may be relied upon, but he took
home with him small knowledge of the country
and none of its language and literature. His
patriotic pamphlet entitled the *Spanish Masquerado* confirms this view.[1] Speaking broadly
and admitting scarcely an exception, the incongruity between the sense of the greatness of
Spain which was revealed in the English
romance, and the scant acquaintance with the
genius and culture of the country which was
there shown was unmistakable. It is impossible to resist the conviction that the romancers
knew the country only at second hand, and
even then derived their information from
strangers and not from the writings of its
sons.

The historical importance of Spain occupied

[1] The passage which is the authority for Greene's visit to
Spain occurs in the *Repentance of Robert Greene*, *Works*,
ed. Grosart, XII., p. 172. A brief portion of the Latin dialogue with Francis Hand which is prefixed as an introduction to the *Planetomachia*, is said to have been borrowed
from Joannes Jovianus Pontanus, a secretary of Ferdinand
of Aragon. See Morley, *English Writers*, IX., p. 225.

perhaps an even larger place in the minds of the Elizabethan dramatists.   The *Edward I.* of Peele, in which Eleanor of Castile was a central figure, his *Battle of Alcazar*, and the anonymous *Lust's dominion*, once attributed to Marlowe but probably identical with the *Spaneshe Mores tragedie* by Dekker, Haughton, and Day, which was entered by Henslowe in his diary on February 13, 1600, all testified to the might of the nation, even while they showed an almost complete ignorance of the true history and disposition of its people.   The Queen Eleanor of the play was an inhuman villain who retained only the name of a woman who has come down in history as one of the most charitable of queens; the Spaniards, Portuguese, and Moors of the other pieces are most inadequately characterized; and the death of the king in *Lust's dominion*, the details of which were suggested by the recent decease of Philip II., so circumstantially described by contemporary pamphleteers, was an empty distortion of an impressive and pathetic scene.   The drama called *Stewtley* by Henslowe, and acted by his company in 1596 when the popular interest in Stukeley's fantastic career in Spain and Africa was at its height ; Hathaway,

Day, and Haughton's *Conqueste of Spayne by John a Gaunt* of the year 1601, and Chettle and Dekker's *Kinge Sebastiane of Portingalle*, which was also brought forward in 1601, when the supposed return of the victim of Alcazar was agitating Europe, — though all lost, undoubtedly treated the events about which they revolved with as little regard for the facts of history as might well be. Anthony Wadeson's *Humorous Earle of Gloster with his conquest of Portugall*, of the year 1600, dealt with events that were purely imaginary. The *Comicall Historie of Alphonsus, king of Aragon*, of Greene, published in 1599, and Kyd's *Ieronimo* and its continuation, the *Spanish Tragedy*, both of which were completed between 1584 and 1589, also differed from the preceding dramas only in that they were obviously pseudo-historical. None of these plays had any connection with the localities to which they were assigned. Their subjects were all selected in deference to the position of Spain in the public eye at the time in which they were composed.[1]

---

[1] The play called a *Speneshe Fygge*, which was contracted for by Henslowe, and the *Phillipe of Spayne*, entered in his diary under the date of August 8, 1602, and thought by

The Spanish characters which were interspersed through the Elizabethan drama at large failed in a similar manner to cast a foreign atmosphere about them. Indeed, the Castilians of the Elizabethan stage exhibited the fixed unity of the types of comedy. They were either arrogant, boastful, pompously affected, or cruel, — to possess any of these traits along with a Spanish name was to be a Spaniard in the eyes of the Elizabethan playgoer. This was true in the days of Greene and Peele, and the attitude of audiences was not altered for the better in later years. Thomas Middleton's *Lazarillo de Tormes*, in his *Blurt, master constable*, published in 1602, was a far remove in almost every way from its famous namesake. This, too, was in spite of the fact that the name Lazarillo was suggested to Middleton by the success of the Spanish novel in Rowland's

Collier to be the same as *Lust's dominion*, were the offspring of the identical conditions which produced the plays mentioned in the text. The *Indes* which Haughton, Wentworth Smith, and Day were writing in 1601 cannot have omitted to represent the exploits of the Spaniards in the new world. See Henslowe's *Diary*, pp. 171, 201, 207, and 225. On the other hand the anonymous *Mucedorus*, whose hero was prince of Valencia, was purely fantastical.

translation. It seems to have become soon a synonym for unscrupulousness, and to have been separated from the taint of maliciousness and of essential vulgarity with which it was properly associated. In the drama of the reign of Elizabeth, perhaps the best portraiture of Spanish character is Shakspere's Don Armado, in *Love's labour's lost*. Yet Don Armado is more vainglorious than Spanish, despite the association of his weaknesses with the crazy Monarcho as well as with that people generally. The absence of any characterization of the race cannot truly be considered strange. Its outward manners and its eccentricities were at once apparent. They challenged imitation. Hence Elizabethan literature, whether occasional or pure, whether in critical, narrative, or dramatic forms, was not prone to pass beyond the surface of Spanish history and the externals of Spanish character. Objective features were readiest to its grasp, and impressions formed during a long and for the most part unfriendly intercourse determined its prevalent attitude.

Had the literature of the peninsula left no mark in the North that was distinctively its own and more important than a dower of

names, its history would have been an anomaly.
It is true that English culture, on account of
the remoteness of its home and the tardiness
of its Renaissance, contributed nothing to the
work of the contemporary Spanish writers.
Certain occasional publications, relative to the
court at London or to the interests of the subjects of the Tudors, were circulated in Castile,
and sometimes at the hands of Englishmen, but
these did not rise in significance above the
events which suggested them. Only one book
by a Briton secured any following in the country during the sixteenth century, and that was
Edward Lee's volume against Erasmus, through
the agency of which accusations were brought
against the Dutch humanist before the Inquisition.[1] The controversy in which Lee was involved, however, was a personal quarrel. On
the other hand, Spanish literature could but

---

[1] Pedro de Victoria, Luis Carvajal, Juan de San Vizente,
Diego Lopez de Zúñiga, and Sancho de Carranza were the
enemies of Erasmus in the peninsula. The three friars first
named acted against the Dutch scholar solely in response to
the promptings of Lee, who was their friend. Erasmus himself testified to the damaging effects of Lee's book, which
appeared in 1526. See Valdés' *Ziento i diez Consideraziones*
(*Reformistas antiguos españoles*), Madrid, 1863, p. 689.

leave its traces in the strictly literary work of
the Elizabethan writers, for it was readily accessible to the later Elizabethans both in the
original and in translation, and it was, until the
close of the Tudor epoch, relatively much more
forward than the work of the English themselves. The open-mindedness of the Anglo-
Saxon, so greatly augmented in the Renaissance
by the inferiority of his position, afforded him
opportunity to benefit by the progress and
superior advancement of other peoples. It inclined him above all to acknowledge insensibly
the fundamental resemblances in the character
of the insular and peninsular races. Both
nations were frugal, industrious, and especially
able in action, and both possessed a sturdiness
which was coupled, not unnaturally, with a
particularly rich humor. Together they ruled
the sea. That firm grasp of the realities of
life, which was the more wonderful because it
was informed with a buoyant, luminous ideal-
ism, was their common heritage. A like love
of liberty in each exacted the Magna Charta
at Runnymede from King John, and held the
menace of the Privilege of Union over the
kings of Aragon. Their common self-reliance

revealed itself in the risings of the English peasantry under Wat Tyler and Aske in Kent and York, and of the *communeros* under Juan de Padilla at Avila and Villalar. The similarity in the natures and histories of the two peoples was not, indeed, in surface traits. Hence it was that the superior rapidity of the rise of Spain and an affinity of national character gave the peninsular literature the little influence that it possessed in shaping the course of English letters.

This influence was twofold. It manifested itself best in the contributions of the peninsula to the contents of English books. The Elizabethans took their material where they found it. Recourse was not had to the peninsula for thought, but an indebtedness to the country for plots was acknowledged as a corollary of its forwardness. The framework of stories was borrowed and clothed anew with passion and feeling quite different from those with which it had been associated before. The instances outside of the pages of actual translations in which it is possible to pronounce the matter of an English author to be Spanish in more than name occur in cases of this sort. These, too, were few. Spain was not a storehouse of plot. Despite the domination of the peninsula by the Moors and the introduction of the fictions of Bidpai and Sendabad into the country from Africa in the thirteenth and fifteenth centuries, Spain did almost nothing to further the spread of the Oriental tales, which played such an important rôle in mediæval authors. The stories of the East made their way to every quarter of the civilized world in the Italian *novelle* and in Latin forms. While Italy furnished the subjects of innumerable romances, poems, and plays, the more powerful sister state, which originated and transmitted little matter of the kind, sank in this regard to a subordinate place. Spain, through her own literature, and unaided by any foreign intervention, suggested the action of but few such works.

The isolation of Spanish plots in their insular environment would alone show, if such evidence were needed, the real source of the English Renaissance. In romance these appeared, perhaps, only in the *Margarite* of Lodge, which was the issue of his stay in the Jesuit college at Santos. In the drama they are to be seen in Marlowe's *Tamburlaine*, which was partially

drawn from the *Silva* of Mexía, and also in
Shakspere's *Two Gentlemen of Verona*. The
underplot of the story of Julia and Proteus, in
the latter play, involving Julia's assumption of
masculine attire and her service as the page of
her lover, was suggested by the story of Felix
and Felismena, in the first book of the *Diana*
of Montemayor. That Shakspere borrowed
these incidents from the Portuguese romancer,
there can be no reasonable doubt. The dramatist seems to have been ignorant of Spanish.
He could, therefore, have scarcely obtained
them from the *Diana* itself, nor is it probable
that he had access to any translation in the
vernacular, unless it was the old eclogue of
Googe.[1] The play was indubitably based
upon the lost *History of Felix and Philomena*,
which was acted before the court at Green-
wich, on January 3, 1585. Like Mexía's tale

[1] Shakspere was associated with none of the groups of
translators from the Spanish, and could not well have known
the work of Yong, Paston, or Wilcox. Hunter failed to
show the contrary in his *Illustrations of Shakespeare*, I., p.
191. The articles in German periodicals which endeavor to
connect the dramatist with Spanish authors have seldom any
value. Grillparzer and Farinelli ranged themselves against
such attempts, but Sidney Lee has followed Hunter.

of *Tamburlaine*, the story of Felismena was of course not native to the peninsula. It was a refined re-working of Bandello's *novella* of *Nicuola and Paolo;* and in this respect, as in several significant details that are not to be found in Bandello, it is at one with the English play. These petty resemblances are so arbitrary that they cannot have been accidental, though the elevation which is to be found only in Shakspere and Montemayor was characteristic of the habitual method of composition of both writers.[1] Thus, though the two authors

[1] Shakspere imitated Montemayor's *Felismena* more closely in the *Two Gentlemen of Verona* than he did Bandello's *Nicuola* in *Twelfth Night.* The parallelism between the stories of Proteus and Felix is exact. In each case the lovers move in similar walks of life. The beginning of their affection is the same, and in each case among the first ways in which it finds expression is the sending of letters from the hero to the heroine. Proteus, like his original, is soon despatched by his father to the court, where he is to become practised in the ways of the world. In each case the lover contracts a passion on his arrival for a beautiful lady of the capital, and forgets his youthful love, who follows him to court, having first disguised herself in the dress of a page.

In the *Diana*, Felismena lodges at an inn which fronts upon the courtyard of the palace, and from the window the host shows her Don Felix singing to his mistress below. The incident is quite elaborately worked out. In the *Two Gentleman of Verona*, on the contrary, no mention is made of

were utterly independent in spirit, there was a
common element in their work. But this was
not fundamental. In the only excursion of the
great dramatist into peninsular literature, it was
the plot alone that was borrowed. It was also
the plot alone in the cases of Marlowe and
Lodge that was distinctly of alien growth,
for mastery of treatment the English had
already acquired.

The really significant influence of Spanish
literature in the North, however, was not of
this kind. On the contrary it was a stimulative one. It was exerted in fostering by its
example, chiefly through the agency of translations, certain tendencies in letters which were
common in both London and Madrid, because
of the coincidences in the unfolding of the
genius of the races, which rendered the same

an inn, but it is an innkeeper who brings Julia upon the
company of Proteus under the casement of Sylvia. The
implication is that the scene is set as it was described in the
Spanish novel. This remarkable agreement in the small
points of the action, several of which were not necessitated
by the plot, and could not have been hit upon by two
writers working independently, is proof of Shakspere's debt
to Montemayor. Bandello does not parallel these incidents.
The later scenes in the play which develop the treachery of
Proteus to Valentine have no relation to the Spanish novel.

modes of artistic expression appropriate to the needs of both, within the compass of a brief period. The influence was one of the Spanish upon the English mind. It began early and was continuous. First and most noticeably it appeared in the court books which were so highly esteemed during the sixteenth century. These moral and euphuistical treatises, whatever they owed to Plutarch and Castiglione, undoubtedly were indebted for much of their great vogue, from the days of Elyot to those of Lyly, Greene, and Lodge, to Antonio de Guevara. The high repute of this author upon the continent, and his renown as the most popular foreign author who was read by the English public, confirmed through his works the extravagances of a mistaken humanism, which prospered in many quarters in petty plays upon words and in other distortions of thought and style. Guevara was not the favorite merely of his translators and their friends, he was not merely the idol of a generation, but his ascendency was unchallenged through the century. Sir Thomas North testified to it in assigning his books a place above those of any living writer, and it was accepted,

indeed, as a commonplace among the later
Elizabethans.[1] A knowledge of Guevara seems
to have been generally assumed. The sale of
his books fostered the taste for affectation in
England. There has as yet been no proof of
any connection between Guevara and Lyly and
his followers, but Guevara's success was undoubtedly a stimulative influence abroad, because of the encouragement which it gave to
the cultivation of similar styles. Its effective
operation in its sphere was established con-
clusively by the wide audience which he
commanded in England, by the great and
long-continued esteem in which he was held,
and by the obvious identity of the movement
of which he was the head with euphuism in
England and with the later vagaries of Gon-
gora, Marini, the *conceptistas,* and the *prècieuses*
in Italy, Spain, and France.

The coöperation of Spanish and English letters in the North appeared further in the realm
of romance, in the prose pastoral, and in the

[1] The position of the Spaniard was sufficiently attested by
the familiar manner in which he was referred to by English
authors. See, for example, Nash, *Haue with you to Saffron
Waldron.*

books of chivalry. The pastoral writers acknowledged small obligation to Montemayor; but, nevertheless, the warm reception which the *Diana* was accorded in England at a time when the pastoral was nearing the zenith of its popularity in that country did not fail to react upon English literature. Had the pastoral not been in fashion at the time of the translation of the *Diana*, that book would, perhaps, have met with small favor. Since it was in accord with the taste of the hour, its reputation was enhanced, it was recommended to Sidney, and had, like the court treatise, its stimulative effect upon the growth of the English type, even outside of the pages of the *Arcadia*. This effect was of course very slight, for the pastoral was inspired and applauded through other influences, native and foreign. In the case of the romances of knight errantry, the consequences of the influx of Spanish novels were still less important. The books of chivalry themselves were not ill received, but the circumstances attending their introduction into the country were inopportune. Guevara did something to add impetus to a fashion that was just in its infancy in England when Lord Berners trans-

lated his *Libro áureo;* Montemayor also contributed strength to a movement that was
already strong; but the type to which *Amadis,*
the Palmerins, and the *Knight of the sun* belonged had permanently lost caste when the
books of chivalry first obtained due hearing.
Their influence was thus circumscribed. It
was confined to a humble sphere, and appeared
too tardily to impress its characteristics upon
the English romance. With the close of the
century the type had well-nigh ceased to be a
literary product. By disguising its feebleness
with the strangeness of new names, the Spaniards vivified it temporarily, and aided in insur-
ing its survival into the Stuart times. The
court treatise and the pastoral brought the
weight of their names to the vigorous development of sympathetic types, but the books of
chivalry exhausted their prestige in the North
merely in prolonging a little the dotage of the
heroic romance.

Court treatises and aristocratic and popular
romances flourished among both nations in consequence of tendencies which were then generally encouraged in literature. There was
nothing in any of them that was peculiarly

2 B

native to either England or Spain.   Euphuism
and the Arcadian life had no relation to the
people, and the romances of chivalry, although
they had once embodied a popular ideal, had
almost ceased to be a living form before the
sixteenth century was brought to a close.   This
was not true, however, of the rogue tale which
began in London in the primitive jest-book, and
which early attained a conspicuous position in
Spain in the picaresque novel.   The rogue tale
was not the product of a literary fashion, but
the spontaneous outgrowth of the conditions of
common life.   The abundance of the rough and
frequently boisterous stories of this type was
one of the remarkable features of Elizabeth's
reign.   Crude collections of tricks and jests
circulated beside the vernacular versions of *Til
Eulenspiegel* and *Lazarillo de Tórmes*.   The
result of the translation of these works cannot
have been slight.   Spain was the first country
to perfect the rogue as a hero.   She excelled in
that branch of popular fiction, and the most
remarkable of her efforts in that line became
highly esteemed very early in England.   Mendoza may not have influenced Nash directly in
his *Jacke Wilton*, a work more pretentious than

any of its predecessors, but it is not to be
thought that the vogue of *Lazarillo* did not at
least prepare the way for its English kin, and
by its fame assist materially in their success.

When the English novels of roguery were
being most successfully cultivated, the demand
for translations of the picaresque novels was
continuous in the North. It will be remembered that two parts of *Lazarillo* had been
translated by 1602, and the first had already
become then widely popular. The name had
been accepted as a synonym for an irresponsible
and dissolute Spaniard, as in the *Blurt* of Middleton. It was only shortly after the end of
the sixteenth century that these stories flourished in all their complexity and attained their
chief successes, as their English and Spanish
phases unfolded side by side. This fact could
not be without meaning to English authors.
The inborn humor, the independence, and the
energy of the two races were the soil in which
the new type grew, for it was the natural outcome of national traits. The vices of the age
were reproduced with repulsive fidelity in the
rogue tales. Their humor was often malicious,
the independence of their heroes irresponsible,

the energy which was displayed in them rude, and the prevalent atmosphere realistic and coarse. Direct and uncompromising in detail, often unfeeling in spirit, the proximity of their life to that of the taverns and the streets was unmistakable. But this immaturity of form and earthiness of life were the result of native vigor. The rogue novel was truly popular, while the pastoral romance was merely fashionable and polite. What it lacked was ideality, the touch of the master hand, for amid this setting of vulgarity, among the rawness of knaves and thieves, only the illuminating flash of genius was needed to create from the life which it portrayed in one of its conspicuous aspects, the Falstaff of Shakspere or the Sancho Panza of Cervantes.

At the conclusion of the study of the relations of Spanish and English literature until the close of the sixteenth century, this generalization may be made. Until the extinction of the Tudor line, all the translations from the peninsular tongues, with the exception of those of the picaresque novels, were ephemeral in nature. They were either occasional in their import, or they belonged to fashions in literature that were soon to pass away. The list of translations included no work of commanding power. With the exception of the picaresque type the forms of English letters to which Spain gave encouragement and effective support, the court treatise, the pastoral, the romance of chivalry, were all superficial eddies in the stream of national progress, by-plays in literary history, passing fancies that were soon to be ignored. Spanish literature performed its greatest service to the literature of Shakspere's England in assisting the evolution of a living form through the example of the *Celestina* and the *Lazarillo de Tórmes*. The euphuistical and pastoral tastes persisted into the next reign, it is true, but they had nothing more to hope from Spanish letters. The romance of chivalry likewise struggled against the new age most aimlessly. The indebtedness of the rapidly unfolding drama to the peninsula increased rather than diminished, for as the Elizabethan stage acknowledged an obligation for plots to Mexía and Montemayor in Marlowe and Shakspere, the Jacobean borrowed the stories of Cervantes and his contemporaries with an even freer hand in the works of many writers, and above all in those of Beaumont and Fletcher. But this, however, was at the outset principally a matter of externals, and not one of character. It was in the picaresque stories, or rather in the robust, healthy, and sanely humorous spirit which was at the heart of them, that the early peninsular influence entered upon its greatest and only truly enduring usefulness. In the course of a few years the *Celestina* and *Lazarillo de Tórmes* were reprinted, *Guzman de Alfarache* and its successors were translated, and *Don Quixote* was laid before the English people. The culmination of the movement that had begun with Lord Berners was reached in the popularity of these works under the Stuarts, in whose time it was first assured. The futile passion for affectation which was even then the contemporary gift of Spain to France was replaced in England by an interest in living types, and the reputation of Guevara, declining rapidly from its zenith, gave way insensibly before the rising fame of Cervantes.

A BIBLIOGRAPHY OF THE SPANISH WORKS PUBLISHED IN THE ORIGINAL OR IN TRANSLATION IN THE ENGLAND OF THE TUDORS

[This bibliography aims to present a chronological view of the works that were written either in the peninsular tongues or by peninsular authors, which were printed in England previous to the death of Elizabeth, or translated into English before the termination of her rule. Each title is accompanied by the places and dates of the editions of the book during the Tudor period, as well as of the Spanish *editio princeps*. When there is doubt about the accuracy of these, the authority upon which the edition has been cited, or its age determined, is pointed out. Brief passages from the Spanish, incorporated in English books, will be found under the head of the volumes of which they formed a part. Official documents and despatches which were not the property of the public in their time, and in no proper sense literature, do not, of course, occur. An interrogation point is prefixed to the dates of books that, although licensed by the Stationers' Company, are not known to have passed through the press.]

1530. An Enterlude . . . wherein is shewed and dyscrybed, as well the bewte and good propertes of women, as theyr vycys and evyll condicyons. London, *circa* 1530.

Adapted by John Rastell (?) from the first four acts of the *Celestina* of Rodrigo de Cota and Fernando de Rojas, Burgos, 1499, through the Italian of Alfonso Ordoñez, Venice, 1505.

1534. The golden Boke of Marcus Aurelius. London, 1534.

Translated by Lord Berners from the *Libro áureo* of Antonio de Guevara, 1529, through the French of René Bertaut, Paris, 1531. Other editions, 1539, 1542, 1546, 1553, 1554, 1556 (Lowndes), 1557, 1559, 1566, 1573, 1576 (Lowndes), 1584, 1586, 1587 (Lowndes).

1540. The Castell of love. London, 1540 (?).

Translated by Lord Berners from the *Cárcel de amor* of Diego Hernandez de San Pedro, Seville, 1492. Other editions, 1540 (?) and 1560 (Morley); relicensed, 1564–1565.

1540. The Instructiō of a Christen womā. London, 1540.

Translated by Richard Hyrde from the *De Institutione feminæ christianæ* of Juan Luis Vives, Bruges, 1523. Other editions, 1540 (?), 1541, 1557, and 1592.

1540. An Introduction to wysdome. London, 1540 (Dict. nat. biog.).

Translated by Sir Richard Morison from the *Introductio ad sapientiam* of Juan Luis Vives, Bruges, 1524. Other editions, 1540 (?), and 1544.

1540. A short Summary of Aristotle's philosophy. London, 1540 (?) (Dict. nat. biog.).

Translated anonymously from the contribution of Juan Luis Vives to the edition of *Aristotelis de moribus ad Nicomachum libri decem*, issued by John Sturm, Strasburg, 1540.

1548. A Dispraise of the life of a courtier and a commendacion of the life of a labouryng man. London, 1548.

Translated by Sir Francis Bryan from the *Menosprecio de la corte y alabanza de la aldea* of Antonio de Guevara, Valladolid, 1539, through the French of Antoine Alaigre, Paris, 1542. Another edition, 1575. This was called *A Looking-glasse for the courte*, and was issued by Thomas Tymme. The entry of *A Myrror for courtyers*, by Guevara, upon the stationers' register, June 25, 1581, may refer to this translation.

1553. The Office and duetie of an husband. London, 1553 (?).

Translated by Thomas Paynel from the *De Officio mariti* of Juan Luis Vives, Bruges, 1528.

1553. De Ritu nuptiarum et dispensatione, libr. iii. London, 1553. By Juan Ginés de Sepúlveda, but originally printed at Rome in 1531.

1555. Instrucion y dotrina de cuno todo christiano deve oyr missa y assister a la celebracion y santo sacrificio. Antwerp, 1555. A sermon preached by Bartólomé de Miranda before Philip and Mary at Kingston-on-Thames.

1555. Comentaries of Don Lewes de Avila and Suniga, which treateth of the great wars in Germany, made by Charles the Fifth. London, 1555.

Translated by John Wilkinson from the *Comentario de la guerra de Alemania* of Luis de Avila y Zúñiga, Antwerp, 1548.

1555. Decades of the newe worlde. London, 1555.

Translated by Richard Eden from the *De Orbe novo decades tres* of Peter Martyr Anglerius, Alcala, 1516, the *Sumario de la natural y general historia de las Indias* of

Gonzalo Fernandez de Oviedo y Valdés, Toledo, 1526, the *Historia general de las Indias con la conquista de México y de la Nueva España* of Francisco Lopez de Gómara, Saragossa, 1552, and from the writings of A. Pigafetta, P. Giovio, V. Biringuccio, Sebastian Munster, and others. Another edition, London, 1577. This was entitled *The History of trauayle in the West and East Indies*, and was amplified by Richard Willes.

1556. History of Aurelio and of Isabell. Antwerp, 1556.

In French, Italian, English, and the original Spanish of Juan de Flores (*Historia de Aurelio y Isabela*), *ante* 1521. Another edition, London, 1586 (without the Spanish). The book was licensed to be printed in four languages November 20, 1588.

1557. The Diall of princes, London, 1557.

Translated by Sir Thomas North from the *Relox de príncipes* of Antonio de Guevara, through the French version of René Bertaut, revised, Paris, 1540. Other editions, supplemented by *The fauored Courtier*, translated by North from the *Aviso de privados y doctrina de corte-sanos* of Guevara, Valladolid, 1539, through the French, and by letters of Marcus Aurelius, translated directly from the Spanish, were printed in 1568 and 1582. The *Diall* was also relicensed in 1563–1564.

1559. Private Prayers and meditations. London, 1559.

Translated in part by John Bradford from the *Excita-tiones animi in Deum* of Juan Luis Vives, Antwerp, 1538. Another edition, 1578. The passages translated from Vives were reprinted in the *Christian Prayers* of Henry Bull, Powell, and Middleton, London, 1570. Several of the prayers also appeared in *Queen Elizabeth's prayer book*, London, 1569.

1561. The Arte of nauigation. London, 1561.

Translated by Richard Eden from the *Arte de navigar* of Martin Cortés, Seville, 1551. Other editions, 1579 (Watt), 1580 (Watt), 1589, and 1596, the last edited by John Tapp.

1562. The pleasaunt and wittie Playe of the cheasts. London, 1562.

Translated by James Rowbotham from the *Do Xadrez* of Damião de Odemeira, through the French of G. Gruzar. Other editions 1569 and 1597.

1562. Godly Meditations. London, 1562.

Translated in part by John Bradford from the *Excitationes animi in Deum* of Juan Luis Vives, Antwerp, 1538 (?). Another edition, 1578. The passage from Vives was included in *Queen Elizabeth's prayer book*, London, 1578, 1581, and 1590.

1563. Eglogs, epytaphes, & sonettes. London, 1563.

Translated in part by Barnaby Googe from the *Diana* of Jorge de Montemayor, 1558–1559 (?), and the *Obras de Boscan y algunas de Garcilasso de la Vega*, Barcelona, 1543.

1565. An Epistle . . . to the most excellent Princesse Elizabeth, quene of England, France, and Ireland. Antwerp, 1565.

Translated by Richard Shacklock from the *Epistolæ ad Elizabetham Angliæ reginam de religione* of Jeronymo Osorio da Fonseca, Paris and Louvain, 1563.

(?) 1565–1566.　A tru Certificat sente from Gibralter in Spayne of a wonderfull fysshe.　Licensed 1565–1566.

1566.　Palace of pleasure.　Part I.　London, 1566.　Part II.　London, 1567.

The twenty-ninth story of Part I. was translated by William Painter from the *Silva de varia leccion* of Pedro Mexía, Seville, 1542, through the Italian.　The twelfth selection of Part II. was a new translation of five of Guevara's forged letters, ostensibly the work of Plutarch, Trajan, and the Roman Senate, but which had previously been published in English by Fenton.　Other editions, Part I. 1569 and 1575; Part II. 1575 (?).

1568.　The Treasurie of Amadis of Fraunce.　London, 1568.

Translated by Thomas Paynel from the *Amadis de Gaula* of García Ordoñez de Montalvo, Salamanca, 1508, through the *Thresor de tous les livres d'Amadis de Gaule*, Antwerp, 1560.

1568.　An ancient Order of knighthoode, called the Order of the Band, instituted by Don Alphonsus, king of Spain, in the year 1368, from Caesar Augustus, to wear a red ribbon of three fingers breadth, and subject to xxxv. rules; the knights whereof were called by the same name.　London, 1568 (Watt).

Translated by Henry B. from the *Epístolas familiares* (*epístola xxxvi.*), of Antonio de Guevara, Valladolid, 1539, through the French of Guttery, Lyons, 1556.

1568.　A Treatise, writen in Latin by . . . H. Osorius. . . . Wherein he confuteth a certayne aunswere made by M. Walter Haddon against the epistle vnto the Queenes Maiestie.　Louvain, 1568.

Translated by John Fenne from the *In Gualterum Haddonum . . . de vera religione, libri III.* of Jeronymo Osorio da Fonseca, Lisbon and Dilingen, 1567.

1568. A Discovery and playne declaration of sundry subtill practices of the Holy Inquisition of Spayne. London, 1568.

Translated by Vincent Skinner from the *Sanctæ Inquisitionis hispanicæ artes aliquot detectæ, ac palam traductæ* of Reginaldo Gonzalez Montano, Heidelberg, 1567. Other editions, 1569 and 1569 (in Dutch).

1568. De Operibus Dei, apology, Norwich, 1568.

In French by Antonio de Corro, with an English translation. Another edition, London, 1570.

1568. Tabulæ divinorum. Acta consistorii. London, 1568.

By Antonio de Corro.

(?)1568–1569. The x Commandementes in Spanysshe. Licensed, 1568–1569.

1569. An Epistle . . . sent to the pastoures of the Flemish Church in Antwerp.

Translated by Sir Geoffrey Fenton from the *Épître aux pasteurs de l'église flamande* of Antonio de Corro, 1567, and published with the original. Other editions, 1570 and 1578 (Dict. nat. biog.).

1569. Sumario de la doctrina christiana. London, 1569.

By Juan Perez de Pineda, but first published at Geneva in 1560,

1569. Christian Prayers and meditations in English, French, Italian, Spanish, Greeke, and Latine. London, 1569.

Compiled by John Day, and known as *Queen Elizabeth's prayer book*. The first edition contained several of the prayers of Vives, translated by Bradford, and the reissue of 1578 by Richard Day contained new translations of the same prayers, as well as a new version of Vives' *Meditation of death*, englished also by Bradford in his *Godly Meditations*. Other editions, by Richard Day, 1578, 1581, and 1590.

(?) 1569–1570. The most famous History of ij Spanesshe lovers. Licensed, 1569–1570.

Translated from the Spanish (?).

1570. Treatise, declaring howe many counsels and what manner of counselers a prince that will gouerne well ought to haue. London, 1570.

Translated by Thomas Blundeville from the *Concejo y consejeros de príncipes* of Federico Furió Ceriol, Antwerp, 1559, through the Italian of Alfonso de Ulloa.

1570. Tableau de l'œuvre de dieu. 1570 (Arber).

In several languages, reprinted from the *Tabulæ divinorum* of Antonio de Corro, London, 1568.

1571. The Forest, or collection of historyes. London, 1571.

Translated by Thomas Fortescue from the *Silva de varia leccion* of Pedro Mexía, Seville, 1542, through the French of Claude Gruget, Paris, 1552. Another edition, 1576.

1574. Familiar Epistles. London, 1574.

Translated by Edward Hellowes from the *Epístolas familiares* of Antonio de Guevara, Valladolid, 1539–1545. Nine selections from sermons and discourses by Guevara also occur. The book was augmented from the French, Lyons, 1556, and Paris, 1565. Other editions, 1577 and 1584.

1574. Dialogus theologicus, quo Epistola D. Pauli apost.
　　　　ad Romanos explanatur. London, 1574.

By Antonio de Corro.

1574. The Composition or making of the most excellent
　　　　and pretious oil called oleum magistrale. . . . First
　　　　published by the comandement of the King of Spain.
　　　　London, 1574.

Translated by George Baker. Another edition, 1579.

1575. Golden Epistles. London, 1575.

Translated in part by Sir Geoffrey Fenton from the *Epístolas familiares* of Antonio de Guevara, Valladolid, 1539–1545, through the French of the Seigneur de Guttery, Lyons, 1556. Supplementary to Hellowes' *Familiar Epistles*. Other editions, 1577 and 1582. Both Hellowes' and Fenton's translations were assigned as one book by Ralph Newbery to John Newbery on September 30, 1594.

1575. The pretie and wittie Historie of Arnalte and
　　　　Lucenda. London, 1575.

In Italian and English. Translated by Claudius Hollyband from the *Tratado de Arnalte y Lucenda* of Diego Hernandez de San Pedro, Burgos, 1491, through the Italian of Bartolomeo Maraffi, Lyons, 1570. Other editions, 1591 (Scott) and 1597. Licensed August 19, 1598.

1575. The Calendars of Scripture. London, 1575.

Compiled in part by William Patten from the *Biblia polyglotta*, of Francisco Ximenez de Cisneros, Alcala, 1514–1517.

1575. A theological Dialogue, wherein the Epistle of St. Paul to the Romans is expounded. London, 1575.

Translated anonymously from the *Dialogus theologicus* of Antonio de Corro, London, 1574. Another edition, 1579.

1576. The pleasant History of Lazarillo de Tormes. London, 1576.

Translated by David Rowland from the *Lazarillo de Tórmes* of Diego Hurtado de Mondoza (?), Burgos, 1554. Other editions, 1586 and 1596. The book was licensed in 1568–1569 and sold to Henry Bynneman in 1573.

1576. The five Books of . . . Hieronimo Osorius, contayning a discussion of ciuill and Christian nobilitie. London, 1576.

Translated by William Blandy from *De Nobilitate civili libri duo ; de nobilitate christiana libri tres* of Jeronymo Osorio da Fonseca, Lisbon, 1542.

1576. Comforte againste all kindes of calamitie. London, 1576.

Translated by John Daniel from the *Epístola para consolar a los fieles de Jesu Christo* of Juan Perez de Pineda, Geneva, 1560.

1576. Jehovah. A free pardon, with many graces therein contained, granted to all Christians. London, 1576.

Translated by John Daniel from the Spanish of Juan Perez de Pineda.

1577. A Chronicle, conteyning the liues of tenne emperoures of Rome. London, 1577.

Translated by Edward Hellowes from the *Década de las vidas de los x. Césares* of Antonio de Guevara, Valladolid, 1539.

1577. Joyfull Newes ovt of the newe founde worlde. London, 1577.

Translated by John Frampton from the *Historia medicinal de las cosas que se traen de nuestras Indias occidentales* of Nicolas Monardes, Seville, 1565 (first two parts). Other editions, 1580 and 1596.

1577. Newes lately come from the great kingdome of Chyna. London, 1577 (Dict. nat. biog.).

Translated by Thomas Nicholas from a letter in Spanish sent from Mexico to Spain.

1577. The true Historie . . . of a moste horrible murder committed by Alphonse Diazius Spaniard folowinge the example of the paracide Cain on the bodie of his brother, Jhon Diazius. Licensed July 21, 1577.

To be translated from the *Historia vera de morte sancti uiri Joannis Diazij hispani* of Martin Bucer, Claudio Senarcleo, and Francisco de Enzinas, printed in Germany in 1546.

2 c

1577. Collections and observations relating to the condition of Spain. MS.

Written in Spanish by Sir John Smith.

1577. A Supplication exhibited to the moste mightie Prince Philip king of Spain. An Epistle to the ministers of Antwerpe. London, 1577.

In Latin and French by Antonio de Corro. An edition had also appeared in French at Antwerp, 1567.

1578. A Booke of the inuention of the arte of navigation. London, 1578.

Translated by Edward Hellowes, from the *Aguja de marear y de sus inventores* of Antonio de Guevara, Valladolid, 1539.

1578. A Description of the ports, creekes, bayes, and hauens of the West Indies. London, 1578.

Translated by John Frampton from the Spanish.

1578. Historie of the conquest of the Weast India, now called New Spayne. London, 1578.

Translated by Thomas Nicholas, from Part II. of the *Historia general de las Indias . . . con la conquista de México y de la Nueva España* of Francisco Lopez de Gómara, Saragossa, 1552. Another edition, 1596.

(?) 1578. Dictionaire colloques ou dialogues en quattre langues. fflamen. ffrancoys. espaignol. et italien, withe the Englishe to be added thereto. Licensed September 12, 1578.

1579. The Prouerbes of . . . Sir James Lopes de Mendoza, marques of Santillana, with the paraphrase of D. Peter Diaz of Toledo. London, 1579.

Translated by Barnaby Googe, from the *Proverbios* of Iñigo Lopez de Mendoza, and the *Glosas* of Pedro Diaz de Toledo, Seville, 1494.

1579. The Mirrour of princely deedes and knighthood. Part I. London, 1579.

Translated by Margaret Tiler from Part I., Book I., of the *Espejo de príncipes y caballeros* of Diego Ortuñez de Calahorra, Saragossa, 1562. Other editions, 1583 (Arber), 1585 (Lowndes), 1598 (Arber; but the British Museum gives 1599), and 1601 (Arber).

1579. Sapientissimi Regis Salomonis concio de summo hominis bono. London, 1579.

By Antonio de Corro.

1579. Rerum hispanicarum scriptores. Frankfort, 1579.

Compiled in three volumes by Robert Beale from the Latin histories of Juan de Gerona, Rodrigo de Toledo, Rodrigo Sanchez de Arevalo, Alfonso de Santa María, Lucio Marineo Sículo, Antonio de Lebrija, and Alvaro Gomez de Castro, from the chronicles of the Portuguese Damião de Goes, and also from the foreign historians Marius Aretius, Joannes Vasaii, Michael Ritius, Franciscus Farappæ, and Laurentius Valla.

1579. A Discourse of the navigation which the Portugales doe make. London, 1579.

Translated by John Frampton from the *Discurso de la navigacion que los Portugueses hazen à los reinos y provincias de oriente, y de la noticia q̃ se tiene de las grandezas del reino de la China,* of Bernardino de Escalante, Seville, 1577.

1579. Trauels of Marcus Paulus. London, 1579.

Translated by John Frampton from the Italian of Marco Polo through the *Libro del famoso Marco Paulo veneciano* of Rodrigo de Santaella, Seville, 1503.

1580. De Gloria libri V. London, 1580.

By Jeronymo Osorio da Fonseca. This treatise was for a time identified with the lost *De Gloria* of Cicero. According to the *Retrospective Review*, I., p. 322, it was reprinted at London in 1589.

1580. Dialogue concerning phisicke and phisitions. London, 1580.

Translated by Thomas Newton from the *Diálogos* of Pedro Mexía, Seville, 1547.

1580. Of the Bezuar stone, the herbe escuerçonera, the properties of yron and steele in medicine and the treatise of snowe. London, 1580.

Translated by John Frampton from the *Tratado de la piedra bezaar, y de la yerua escuerçonera, Diálogo de las virtudes medicinales del hierro*, and the *Tratado de la nieve, y del beuer frio* of Nicolas Monardes, published with his *Historia medicinal* at Seville, 1574. The first two tracts had previously appeared in that city in 1565. The English translation was joined to Frampton's *Joyfull Newes of the new found world*, which was originally published in 1577. Another edition (complete), 1596.

1581. Palmerin of England, Parts I. and II. (?) Licensed February 13, 1581.

Translated by Anthony Munday from the *Palmerin de Inglaterra* of Luis Hurtado, Part I., 1547, Part II., Toledo, 1548, through the French of Jacques Vinant, Lyons, 1552–

1553. Part III., London, 1595, was translated by Munday from the Portuguese of Diogo Fernandes de Lisboa, Lisbon, through the Italian of Mambrino de Roseo, Venice, 1558. Other editions of Parts I. and II., 1596, and of all three parts, 1602.

1581. Epistola Pauli ad Romanos e Græcorum in Latinam versa, 1581.

By Antonio de Corro.

1571. The Arte of nauigation. London, 1581.

Translated by John Frampton from the *Arte de nauegar* of Pedro de Medina, Cordoba, 1545. Another edition: 1595.

1581. History of the discouerie and conquest of the prouinces of Peru, in the South Sea. London, 1581.

Translated by Thomas Nicholas from the first four and the sixth books of the *Historia del descubrimiento y conquista del Perú* of Augustin de Zárate, Antwerp, 1555.

1582. De Re militari; containing principall orders to be obserued in martiall affaires. London, 1582.

Translated by Nicholas Lichfield, from the *Nuevo Tratado y compendio de re militari* of Luis Gutierres de la Vega, Medina del Campo, 1569.

1582. Of Prayer and meditation; wherein is conteyned fowertien devoute meditations for the seven daies of the weeke, bothe for the morninges and eveninges. And in them is treyted of the consideration of the principall holie mysteries of our faithe. Paris, 1582.

Translated by Richard Hopkins, from the *Libro de la oracion y consideracion* of Luis de Granada, Salamanca,

1567. Part I. of this book was called *Meditaciones para las siete dias y siete noches de la semana.* Other editions: Rouen, 1583 (Hazlitt II.), 1584 (Gillow); London, 1592, 1599 (Brit. Mus.); Edinburgh, 1600 (Gillow); and London, 1601 (Gillow). The editions of 1592 and 1600 were entitled *Granada's spiritual and heavenly exercises,* and that of 1601 was in two parts. The *Exercises* were licensed to Binge and Thomas Gosson, November 6, 1598, and to Edward White on August 2, 1602, the rights of Gosson being reserved.

1582. Historie of the discouerie and conquest of the East Indias enterprised by the Portingales. Book I. London, 1582.

Translated by Nicholas Lichfield from the *Historia do descobrimento e conquista da India pelos Portuguezes,* of Fernão Lopes de Castanheda, Coimbra, 1551.

1582. A briefe Discourse of the assault committed upon . . . the Lord William prince of Orange by J. Jauregui, Spaniard. London, 1582.

In Spanish and English. This work first appeared as the *Korte Verhaal van den moorddadigen aanslag, bedreven op den persoon van . . . den here Prins van Oranje, door Jan Jauregui, een Spanjard,* Antwerp, 1582. There was an edition in French, which was translated into English, London, 1582.

1583. The Myrrour of knighthood. Part II. London, 1583.

Translated by R[obert?] P[arry?] from Part II., Books I. and II., of the *Espejo de príncipes y caballeros* of Pedro de la Sierra, Alcala, 1580. Parts II. and III. of Book I., London, 1599, and ——? were translated by R.

P. from Books II. and III. of Part I. of Diego Ortuñez de
Calahorra, Saragossa, 1562, and Book VI., London, 1598,
from Book I. of Part III. of Marco Martinez, Alcala, 1585.
The English books correspond to the main divisions, or
parts, of the Spanish romance. Book I. of Part III. is
attributed by Brunet to Pedro de la Sierra, and included
in the second part.

1583. The Spanish Colonie, or brief chronicle of the
    acts & gestes of the Spaniards in the West-Indies, called
    the new world for the space of xl yeeres. London, 1583.

    Translated by M. M. S. from the *Brevísima Relacion de
la destruicion de las Indias* of Bartólomé de las Casas,
Seville, 1552.

1583. Discourse of that which happened in the battell
    foughte betweene the two navies of Spaine and Portu-
    gall, at the islands of Azores, Anno Dom. 1582.   Lon-
    don, 1583 (?).

    Translated anonymously from the Spanish of Alvaro
de Baçan.

1583. Relation of the expougnable attempt and conquest
    of the ylande of Tercera, and all the ylands thereto ad-
    joyning. London, 1583.

    Translated anonymously from the Spanish of Alvaro
de Baçan.

1584. The Exercise of a Christian life. 1584 (Lowndes)

    Translated anonymously from the *Excercitium vitæ
christianæ* of Gaspar de Loarte, printed in Spanish at
Barcelona in 1569.

1584. The Contempte of the world and the vanitie
            thereof. Douay (?), 1584.

Translated by G. C. from the *Tratado de la vanidad del mundo* of Diego de Estella, Salamanca, 1574, through the Italian of Giovanni Battista (?).

1585.   History of Felix and Philomena.   Acted at Green-
                     wich, January 3, 1585.

An adaptation of the *Diana* of Jorge de Montemayor, 1558–1559 (?).   The probable source of Shakspere's *Two Gentlemen of Verona*, 1591 (?).

1585.   The Kinge of Portugalles book.   Licensed De-
                     cember 6, 1585.

An *Explanation of the true and lawful right . . . of . . . Anthonie, the first of that name, king of Portugall, . . . translated into English, and conferred with the French and Latin copies,* was printed at Leyden in 1585.

1585.   Sermons on Ecclesiastes.   Oxford, 1585.

Abridged and translated (?) by Thomas Pitt from the *Sapientissimi Regis Salomonis concio de summo hominis bono* of Antonio de Corro, London, 1579.

1586.   Solomon's sermon : of man's chief felicitie : called
     in Hebrew Koheleth, in Greeke and Latin Ecclesiastes.
     With a paraphrase vpon the same.   Oxford, 1586.

Translated by Thomas Pie from the *Sapientissimi Regis Salomonis concio* of Antonio de Corro, London, 1579.

1586.   A Memoriall of a Christian life ; wherein are
     treated all such thinges, as apperteyne unto a Christian
     to doe, from the beginninge of his conversion, until the
     ende of his perfection.   Divided into seaven treatises.
     Rouen, 1586.

Translated by Richard Hopkins from the *Memorial de la vida cristiana* of Luis de Granada, Salamanca and Alcala, 1566.   Another edition, 1599.

1586. Methode unto mortification, called heretofore the contempt of the world and the vanitie thereof. London, 1586.

Translated by Thomas Rogers from the *Tratado de la vanidad del mundo* of Diego de Estella, Salamanca, 1574.

1586. Reglas gramaticales para aprender la lengua espanola y francesca, confiriendo la una con la otra, segun el orden de las partes de la oration latinas. Oxford, 1586.

By Antonio de Corro.

1587. De Orbe novo . . . decades octo.   Paris, 1587.

Edited by Richard Hakluyt from the *De Orbe novo decades octo* of Peter Martyr Anglerius, Alcala, 1530.

1587. New Mexico, otherwise the voyage of Anthony of Espeio, who in the yeare 1583 . . . discovered a lande of 15 provinces, replenished with townes and villages. London, 1587.

Translated anonymously from the *Historia de la China* of Juan Gonzalez de Mendoza, Rome, 1585.

1588. Palmerin d' Oliva, Part I.   London, 1588.

Translated by Anthony Munday from the *Palmerin de Oliva* of an unknown Spaniard, Salamanca, 1511, through the French of Jean Maugin, Paris, 1546, and the Italian of Mambrino de Roseo, Venice, 1544.   Part II., London, 1597, translated by Munday from the versions of the

same French and Italian authors.   Both parts were
assigned to T. Creede, August 9, 1596.

1588.   Palladino of England.   London, 1588.

Translated by Anthony Munday from the *Don Polindo*
of an unknown Spaniard, Toledo, 1526, through the
French of Claude Colet, Paris, 1555.

1588.   The Arcadian Rhetorike ; or, the praecepts of
    rhetorike made plaine by examples, Greeke, Latin,
    English, Italian, French, Spanish.   London, 1588.

Compiled by Abraham Fraunce in part from the *Obras
de Boscan y algunas de Garcilasso de la Vega*, Barcelona,
1543.

1588.   Dos Tratados.   El primero es del papa y de su au-
    toridad. . . . El segundo es de la missa.   London, 1588.

By Cipriano de Valera.   Another edition, supplemented
by Valera's *Enjambre de los falsos milagros con que María
de la Visitazion . . . engaño á mui muchos*, 1599.

1588.   Historie of the great and mightie kingdome of
    China.   London, 1588.

Translated by Robert Parke from the *Historia de la
China* of Juan Gonzalez de Mendoza, Rome, 1585, partly
through the French of Luc de la Porte, Paris, 1588.

1588.   A Packe of Spanish lyes; . . . first printed in
    Spaine. . . . now ripped up, unfolded, and condemned.
    London, 1588.

Translated anonymously, in great part from Spanish
letters.

1588.   Ad serenissimam Elizabetham Angliæ reginam
    Theod. Beza.   London, 1588.

A Latin epigram by Théodore de Bèze, with translations in English, Dutch, Spanish, Hebrew, Greek, Italian,
and French.

1588.   Orders . . . to be obserued in the voyage [of the
        Armada] toward England.   London, 1588.

Translated by T. P. from the Spanish of Alonso Perez
de Guzman, through the French.

1589.   The Counseller, a treatise of counsels, and coun-
        sellers of princes.   London, 1589.

Translated by John Thorius from the *Tratado del con-
sejo y de los consejeros de los príncipes* of Bartólomé
Felipe, Coimbra, 1584.

1589.   Amadis de Gaule.   Book I.   London, 1589.

Translated by Anthony Munday from the *Amadis de
Gaula* of García Ordoñez de Montalvo, Saragossa, 1508,
through the French of Nicholas de Herberay, Paris,
1540.   Book II.   London, 1595, also translated by Munday from the French of Herberay.   Another edition,
1595, with Book II.   The first four books were licensed
to Edwarde Allde, January 15, 1589; the second to the
fifth, inclusive, to John Wolfe, April 10, 1592, and the
second to the twelfth to Adam Islip and William Moringe,
October 16, 1594.   The specification that the books were
to be translated into English accompanied the first two
entries.

1589.   Primaleon of Greece.   London, 1589.

Translated by Anthony Munday from the *Primaleon y
Polendos* of Francisco Vasquez, Salamanca, 1512, through
the French of François Vernassol, Part I., Paris, 1550,

and of Gabriel Chapuis, Part II., Lyons, 1577. Another
edition, 1595.

1589. History of Palmendos. London, 1589.

Translated by Anthony Munday from the *Primaleon
y Polendos* of Francisco Vasquez, Part III., Toledo,
1528, through the French of Gabriel Chapuis, Lyons,
1579.

(?) 1589. Military Discipline. Licensed December 5,
1589.

Translated anonymously from the *Discurso sobre la . . .
disciplina militar* of Sancho de Londoño, Brussels, 1587.

(?) 1589. Th[e] Office of the sergent maiour. Licensed
December 5, 1589.

Translated anonymously from the Spanish of Sancho
de Londoño.

1589. The principal Navigations . . . made by the English nation. London, 1589.

By Richard Hakluyt. Also London, 1599–1600. The
definitive edition contained reprints or translations from
the works of Antonio Galvão, Garcia de Resende, Francisco Lopez de Gómara, Juan Gonzalez de Mendoza, José
de Acosta, and Lopes Paz, besides many sections in Spanish or English taken from the letters of Spanish or Portuguese travellers, or at their dictation.

1589. Respuesto contra les falsedades publicadas e impresas en España . . . de la Armada. London, 1589.

By Don F. R. de M. The tract includes two songs by
"Christovall Bravo of Cordova."

1589.   An Answer to the vntrvthes, published and printed
in Spaine . . . against our English navie.   London,
1589.

Translated by James Lea from the *Respuesto* of F. R.
de M., and the songs of "Christovall Bravo of Cordova,"
London, 1589.

1589.   Respuestas contra los falsedades impresas en
Espana en biturperio de la armada inglesa y Sennor
Don Carlos Conde de Howarde, grande almirante de
Inglaterra.

By a sailor of the Armada, left in England upon the
destruction of that fleet, but ransomed subsequently.

1589.   The Copy of a letter, lately written by a Spanish
gentleman to his friend in England, in refutation of
sundry calumnies, here falsely bruited, and spread
amonge the people.   London, 1589.

Translated by B. J. from the Spanish of a sailor of the
Armada.

1590.   The Serjeant major.   London, 1590.

Translated by John Thorius from the *Espejo y disciplina militar* of Francisco de Valdés, Brussels, 1586.

1590.   The Sacke of Roome.   London, 1590.

Translated anonymously from the *Diálogo en que par-
ticularmente se tratan las cosas acaecidas en Roma, el año de
M.D.XXVII.*, of Juan de Valdés, 1529, either directly
from the Spanish or through the Latin or French.

1590.   Linguæ latinæ exercitatio.   London, 1590.

By Juan Luis Vives.

1590. A Spanish Grammar, with certain rules for teaching both the Spanish and French tongues, together with a Spanish dictionary. London, 1590.

The dictionary was compiled by John Thorius, and the grammar translated by him from the *Reglas gramaticales* of Antonio de Corro. Oxford, 1586.

(?) 1590. The Tables and mappes of the Spanierdes pretendid invasion. by sea. together with the discription thereof, by booke and otherwise, in all languages. Licensed October 13, 1590.

(?) 1591. Lacelestina comedia in Spanishe. Licensed February 24, 1591.

1591. The Spanishe Schoolemaster conteyninge 7 dialogues accordinge to everie daie in the weeke and what is necessarie everie daie to be donne &c wherevnto . . . are annexed most fine proverbes and sentences, as alsoe the Lordes prayre, the articles of our belief the x. commaundementes, with diverse other thinges necessarie to be knowen in the said tonge. (Licensed January 13, 1591.) London, 1591.

By William Stepney.

1591. A newe Copie booke conteyninge theis handes followinge viz Englishe and Ffrenche, secretarie, with the Italian, Roman[,] chancerie and courte handes, and the Spanishe, Jerman and Du[t]che handes. (Licensed September 10, 1590). London, 1591.

An enlargement of the *Booke containing divers sortes of hands*, published at London 1570 and 1574, a translation of the *Trésor d' escripture* of Jehan de Beauchesne, Paris, 1550. The editions previous to this issue by Thomas

Scarlett seem to have lacked the Spanish hand. Another edition, 1602.

1591. Bibliotheca hispanica. Containing a grammar with a dictionarie in Spanish, English and Latine, gathered out of diuers good authors. Two Parts. London, 1591.

By Richard Perceval, assisted by Thomas D'Oylie, whose "Spanish grammer . . . with a large dictionarye conteyninge Spanish, Latyn, and Englishe wordes," was licensed October 19, 1590, but never printed. Another edition, 1599, by John Minsheu. There were "annexed at the end of the grammar, speches and prouerbes together with delightfull and pleasant Dialogues in Spaneshe and English, And at the end of ye dictionary[,] an ample Inglish Dictionary alphabetically sett downe with the Spanishe Woordes therevnto adioyned by the same John Mynshew."

1592. The Spaniards monarchie and Leagvers olygarchie. London, 1592.

Translated by H. O., from the Portuguese (?) of Vasco Figueiro.

1594. The resolved Gentleman. London, 1594.

Translated by Sir Lewis Lewkenor from the *Chevalier délibré* of Olivier de la Marche, Paris, 1488, through the *Caballero determinado* of Hernando de Acuña, Antwerp, 1553.

1594. The Examination of men's wits. London, 1594.

Translated by Richard Carew from the *Exámen de ingenios* of Juan Huarte, Baeza, 1575, through the Italian of Camillo Camilli, Venice, 1582. Another edition, 1596.

1594.   Relaciones.   London, 1594.

By Antonio Perez, under the pseudonym Raphael Peregrino.   Other editions, Leon, 1594 (?), Paris, 1598.

1594.   Tratado para confirmar los pobres cautivos de
    Berbería en la católica i antigua fé.   Enjambre de los
    falsos milagros con que María de la Visitazion . . .
    engaño á mui muchos.   London, 1594.

By Cipriano de Valera.

1595.   Wits, fittes, and fancies.   London, 1595.

Translated by Anthony Copley from the *Floresta de
apotegmas* of Melchor de Santa Cruz, Toledo, 1574.

1595.   The Mount of Caluarie.   Part I.   London, 1595.

Translated anonymously from the *Monte Calvario* of
Antonio de Guevara, Salamanca, 1542.   Part II. was published at London in 1597.

1596.   A Margarite of America.   London, 1596.

By Thomas Lodge, in professed imitation of an unknown Spanish work.

1596.   Historie of Lazarillo de Tormes.   Part II.   Lon-
                    don, 1596.

Translated by William Phiston, from the *Segunda
Parte del Lazarillo de Tórmes*, published anonymously at
Antwerp, 1555.

1596.   Catechismo que significa forma de   instrucion.
                    London, 1596.

Translated by Cipriano de Valera, from the *Catechismus*
of Jean Calvin, Basle, 1538.

1596. El Testamento nuevo. London, 1596.

Translated by Cipriano de Valera.

(?) 1596. Psalmes of confession founde in the cabinet of the moste mightye Kinge of Portingale Don Antonio [the] Firste of that name wrytten with his owne hande. Licensed February 17, 1596.

1596. A Libell of Spanish lies . . . with an answer by H. Savile. London, 1596.

In Spanish by Bernaldino Delgadillo de Avellanado, and in English with an answer by Captain Henry Savile.

Reprinted by Hakluyt, *Principal Navigations*, III., London, 1600.

1596. A Declaration of the causes mouing the Queenes Maiestie of England to prepare . . . a nauy . . . for the defence of her realmes against the King of Spaines forces. London, 1596.

In English, French, Dutch, Italian, and Spanish, with the signatures of Robert Devereux, earl of Essex, and Charles Howard of Effingham.

1597. Theoriqve and practice of warre. London (?), 1597

Translated by Edward Hoby, from the *Theorica y practica de guerra* of Bernardino de Mendoza, Madrid, 1577.

1597. Instituzion de la relijion cristiana. London, 1597.

Translated by Cipriano de Valera from the *Christianæ religionis institutio* of Jean Calvin, Basle, 1536.

1597. A Report of the kingdome of Congo. London, 1597.

2 D

Translated by Abraham Hartwell the younger from the Portuguese of Duarte Lopes, 1578, through the Italian of Filippo Pigafetta, Rome, 1591.

(?) 1597.   Placart et decret publie en Espagne par le Roy Phillippe sur le changes and levees d'argent par luy faites. . . . Avec vn brief Discours des faculties et affaires du dict roy.   Licensed March 17, 1597.

Translated from the Spanish through the French.

1598.   Diana.   London, 1598.

Translated by Bartholomew Yong from the *Diana* of Jorge de Montemayor, 1558–1559 (?), the *Diana* of Alonso Perez, Alcala, 1564, and the *Diana enamorada* of Gaspar Gil Polo, Valencia, 1564.

circa 1598.   Diana.   Part I.   MS.

Translated by Thomas Wilcox from the *Diana* of Montemayor, 1558–1559 (?).

(?) 1598.   The tragicke Comedye of Celestina.   Licensed October 5, 1598.

1598.   Arcadia.   London, 1598.

By Sir Philip Sidney.   *Certaine Sonets written by Sir Philip Sidney* are appended to the *Arcadia* in all the editions after 1593.   They include two previously unpublished songs translated by Sidney from the *Diana* of Jorge de Montemayor, 1558–1559 (?).   Another edition, 1599.

1598.   The Myrrour of knighthood, Book VII.   London, 1598.

Translated by L. A. from Book II. of Part III. of the *Espejo de príncipes y caballeros* of Marco Martinez, Alcala, 1585.   Books VIII. and IX., London, 1599 and

1601, were also translated by L. A. from Book III. of
Part III. and Book I. of Part IV. of the same work.
Both of these were probably the work of Martinez.

1598. The Honour of chivalrie, set downe in the . . .
    historie of the magnanimious and heroike Don Bel-
    lianis. London, 1598.

Translated by L. A. from the *Don Belianis de Grecia*
of Jerónimo Fernandez, Burgos, 1547.

1598. A Treatise paraenetical . . . wherein is shewed
    . . . the right way . . . to resist the violence of the
    Castilian king. London, 1598.

Translated by P. Ol. from the *Relaciones* of Antonio
Perez, London, 1594, through the French of Jean de
Montlyard (alias J. D. Dralymont), Auxerre, 1597.

1598. Granados devotion. London, 1598.

Translated by Francis Meres from the *Libro de la
oracion y consideracion*, Part II., of Luis de Granada,
Salamanca, 1567 (through the French?).

1598. The Sinners guyde. Part I. London, 1598.

Translated by Francis Meres from the *Guia de peca-
dores* of Luis de Granada, Salamanca, 1570 (? through the
French of Duperron, Douay, 1574, or Rheims, 1577).
Part II. appeared at London in 1614.

1598. A most fragrant Flower; or devoute exposition
    of the Lordes prayer. 1598 (Lowndes).

Translated by J. G. from the *Compendio y explicacion
de la doctrina cristiana*, Part III., of Luis de Granada,
written in Portuguese about 1560, and translated into

Spanish by Enrique de Almeida, Madrid, 1595. Relicensed January 11, 1601.

1599. A spiritual Doctrine conteining a rule to liue wel, with diuers praiers and meditations . . . devided into sixe treatises. Louvain, 1599.

Translated by Richard Gibbons from the *Memorial de la vida cristiana* of Luis de Granada, Salamanca and Alcala, 1566.

1599. Declaration of the sicknes, last words and death of the King of Spaine, Phillip, the second of that name. The happy Entrance of the high borne Queene of Spaine, the Ladie Margaret of Austria, in the renowned cittie of Ferrara. Edinburgh, 1599.

The first tract was translated anonymously from a Spanish letter, written in Madrid in 1598. It was licensed to be printed January 9, 1599; the entry of the second tract upon the stationers' register is dated two days later. Another edition, London, 1599.

(?) 1599. Strange Newes of the retourne of Don Sebastian kinge of Portugall. Licensed February 1, 1599.

Translated from the Spanish?

(?) 1599. The true Copie translated out of a letter sent by Franzois de Mendozza chief maister of the campe ouer the souldiours committed vnto him by the Archduke Albert of Austria. Licensed February 19, 1599.

(?) 1599. The secret last Instructions that King Philip the Second, kinge of Spayne, left to his son Kinge Philip the Third . . . howe to governe him self after his fathers death. brought to light by a servant of his treasorer. Don Christofer de Mora called Rodrige D. A. Licensed October 15, 1599.

1600. The Spanish Mandevile of miracles. London, 1600.

Translated by Ferdinand Walker from the *Jardin de flores curiosas* of Antonio de Torquemada, Salamanca, 1570.

1600. Aviso a los de la Iglesia Romana sobre la indiccion de jubileo por . . . Clemente Octavo. London (?), 1600. By Cipriano de Valera.

1600. Two Treatises, the first of the lives of the popes and their doctrine ; the second of the masse. . . . Also a Swarme of false miracles, wherewith Marie de la Visitacion . . . deceiued very many. London, 1600.

Translated by John Golbourne from the *Dos Tratados* etc., of Cipriano de Valera, London, 1599.

1600. Instructions and advertisements how to meditate the misteries. of the rosarie of the most Holy Virgin Mary. Rouen (?), 1600. (?)

Translated by John Fenne from the *Meditationes de rosario B. Virginis* of Gaspar de Loarte, through the Italian, Venice, 1573.

1600. Historie of the vniting of the kingdom of Portugall to the crowne of Castill. London, 1600.

Translated anonymously from the *Dell' Unione del regno di Portogallo alla corona di Castiglia historia* of Girolamo de Franchi Conestaggio (Juan de Silva, the Spanish representative at Alcazar), Genoa, 1585.

1600. The Description of Portugall, of the East Indies, the isles of Terceres. London, 1600 (Lowndes).

Translated anonymously from the Spanish (or Italian) of Juan de Silva.

1601. A Paradise of prayers gathered out of the works
        of L. de Granada. London, 1601.

Translated by Thomas Lodge from the *Thesaurus
precum*, compiled by Michael ab Isselt from the works of
Luis de Granada, Cologne, 1598. The *Paradis desprières*,
the French version of the *Thesaurus*, made from the Latin
by F. Bourdon, reached its third edition at Paris in 1602.

(?) 1601. The Flowers of Lodowick of Granado the firste
        parte. Licensed April 23, 1601.

Translated by Thomas Lodge from an Italian or Latin
chrestomathy of Luis de Granada. The nine parts of
the *Memorial de la vida cristiana* were known in Italy as
the nine flowers of Granada's *ghirlanda spirituale*. A book
called the *Flores coronæ spiritualis* of Granada was published in the vernacular at Venice in 1574, and another called the *Flores ex omnibus opusculis spiritualibus
[Ludovici Granatensis]* in Latin at Cologne in 1585.
Henry Cogman, a physician of Harlem, compiled this
volume. The *Flores . . . Lodoici Granatensis ex omnibus ejus opusculis spiritualibus summa fide excerpti, et in octo
partes distributi* was published by Michael ab Isselt at
Cologne in 1598.

1601. The Discoveries of the world from their first
        original vnto the yeere of our Lord 1555. London,
        1601.

Translated anonymously from the *Tratado . . . de todos
os descobrimentos antigos e modernos, que são feitos até á era
de 1550* of Antonio Galvão, Lisbon, 1563. Revised and
compared with the Portuguese by Richard Hakluyt.

1601. The naturall and moral Historie of the Indies.
        Licensed January 4, 1601.

Translated by Edward Grimstone from the *Historia natural y moral* of José de Acosta, Seville, 1590, but apparently not published until 1604.

1601. Vite di tutti gl' imperadori romani. Licensed
December 10, 1601.

Translated into English by William Traheron from the *Historia imperial y cesárea* of Pedro Mexía, Seville, 1545, through the Italian of Lodovico Dolce and Girolamo Baldi, but apparently not published until 1604.

1601. The strangest Adventure that ever happened . . .
containing a discourse . . . of the King of Portugall,
Dom Sebastian. Part I. London, 1601.

Translated by Anthony Munday, from the Spanish of José Teixeira, 1601, through the French of an anonymous writer. Part II., London, 1602, also by Munday through a French version of Teixeira, 1602. Both parts were relicensed on September 27, 1602. The first part was entered on the stationers' register, April 12, 1601.

1601. A Relation of the solemnetie wherewith the
Catholike princes K. Phillip the III. and Quene Margaret were recyued in the Inglish colledge of Valladolid
the 22. day of August. 1600. N—, 1601.

Translated by Francis Rivers, from the *Relacion de la venida de los Reyes Católicos al collegio ingles de Valladolid* of Antonio Ortiz, Madrid, 1600.

1602. Antiquitatum judaicarum, lib. novem. London,
1602 (Watt).

By Benito Arias Montano, Leyden, 1593.

(?) 1602. An Edict made by Phillipe nowe kinge of Spaine as touchinge the releasement of the newe Christians dwellinge in Portugale. Licensed June 18, 1602.
Translated anonymously from the Portuguese.

1602. The Copy of a letter . . . of the King of Spain . . . unto the Viceroy of Portugall. . . . Wherein the dealings and trade of ships and marchandize is forbidden with the subjects of Holland . . . and England. London, 1602.

A BRIEF BIBLIOGRAPHY OF OCCA-SIONAL LITERATURE RELATING TO SPAIN, PRINTED IN THE ENG-LAND OF THE TUDORS

[The following titles are selected from that mass of writings of practical import having reference to the peninsula, which was the setting of the translations from Spanish literature in the North. In range of subject-matter, it is believed they are representative of the contents of publications of their class. They follow in sequence and apportionment the develop-ment of the type under the several aspects of the international relations of England and Spain during the sixteenth century. The religious con-troversy with Osorio is not noticed below, as it is treated at length in Chapter VI.]

1501. A Remembraūce for the traduction of the Prin-cesse Kateryne, doughter to . . . the Kinge and Quene of Spayne. London, 1501 (?).

1522. Triumphus habitus in Anglia in adventu Caroli imp. London, 1522 (?).

1542. Treatise . . . of th' Emperour Charles the V. and his army (in his voyage made to the towne of Argier in Affrique, agaynst the Turckes . . .). London, 1542.

Translated anonymously from a Latin letter through the French.

1545. The Expedycion of Charles the V emperoure agayenst the citie of Angiers . . . in the last sōmer of, M.CCCC.xIj. London, 1545.

1555. A Warnyng for England, conteynyng the horrible practises of the Kyng of Spayne in the kyngdome of Naples. 1555.

1555. Letter . . . declarĩg the nature of Spaniardes. London, 1555.

By John Bradford; addressed to the Earls of Arundel, Derby, Shrewsbury, and Pembroke.

1557. Beso las Manos et point dictionis gallicæ usus. London, 1557.

1558. History of a right noble and famous lady produced in Spayne entitled the second Gresield. MS. poem.

By William Forrest.

1569. Declaration of the troublesome voyadge [the second] of M. J. Haukins to the parties of Guynea & the West Indies, . . . 1567 and 1568. London, 1569.

1570. A Mirror of man's lyfe made by a modest virgine Francisca Chavesia, a nonne of the Cloyster of S. Elizabeth in Spaine burned for the profession of the Gospel.

By W. T. This ballad was licensed to William Griffith during the year 1569–1570. It was probably founded on the account of Francisca Chaves given in the *Sanctæ Inquisitionis hispanicæ artes*, which appeared at London in Vincent Skinner's translation, in 1568 and also in 1569.

1578.   The Pope's pittiful lamentation for the death of
his deere darling Don Ioan of Austria.   London, 1578.

Translated from the French by H. C.

post 1578.   Dolorous Discourse of a bloudy battel fought
in Barbarie, 4 Aug. 1578.   London, n.d.

1583.   Description of the fortunate ilandes, called the
ilands of Canaria, with their strange fruits and commodities.   London, 1583.

By Thomas Nichols.   Reprinted in Hakluyt's *Principal
Navigations*, London, 1599–1600.

1585.   Report of the general imbarrement of all the
English shippes, vnder the dominion of the Kinge of
Spaine : and of the . . . deliuerence of . . . the Violet
. . . at a port called Sebastian in Biscay.   London, 1585.

By R. D.

1585.   The Primrose of London, with her valiant aduen-
ture on the Spanish coast.   London, 1585.

By Humphrey Mote.

1585.   The Explanation of the right and tytle of Anthonie
the First, king of Portugall, concerning his warres for
the recouerie of his kingdome.   Leyden, 1585.

(?) 1586.   Ballads : (*a*) Betwene a Spanishe Gent [leman]
and an English gentlewoman.   (*b*) The Crueltie of ye
Spaniardes toward th[e] Indians.   Licensed August 1,
1586.

1587.   Newes of the . . . exploytes perfoormed and
doone by . . . Syr Frauncis Drake : not onely at Sancto

Domingo and Carthagena, but also now at Cales and vpon the coast of Spayne. London, 1587.

By Thomas Greepe.

1588. Letter sent ovt of England to Don Bernardin Mendoza, ambassadovr in France for the King of Spaine, declaring the state of England. London, 1588.

By Richard Leigh. Another edition, 1601.

(?) 1588. A Discourse of the Spanish navie by th[e] examinacon of Don Diego Prementelli. In Dutche. and Englishe. Licensed October 29, 1588.

1588. (a) The Queenes visiting of the campe at Tilburie. (b) The straunge and cruell Whippes which the Spanyards had prepared to whippe and torment English men and women. (c) The happie Obtaining of the great galleazzo, wherein Don Pietro de Valdez was the chiefe. [Ballads.] London, 1588.

By Thomas Deloney.

1588. Certaine English Verses penned by David Gwyn, who for the space of elueven yeares and ten moneths was in most grieuous servitude in the gallies, vnder the King of Spaine. London, 1588.

1589. Expeditionis hispanorum in Angliam vera descriptio, anno 1588. 1589.

By Robert Adams.

1589. The Spanish Masquerado. London, 1589.

By Robert Greene.

(?) 1589.   A Comparison of the English and Spanishe
          nation.   Licensed April 7, 1589.

Translated from the French by R[alph?] Ashley.

1589.   A Skeltonical Salutation
                 Or condigne gratulation,
                 And just vexation
                 Of the Spanish nation.

London, 1589.

    1589.   The Marchants avizo.   London, 1589.

By John Browne.

1589.   Ephemeris expeditionis Norreysi et Draki in
          Lusitaniam.   London, 1589.

1589.   Discourse written by a gentleman, employed in
    the late voyage of Spaine and Portingale.   London,
    1589.

By Anthony Wingfield (or Robert Pricket).

(?) 1590.   Newes from Rome, Spayne, Palermo, Genevæ,
          and Ffraunce.   Licensed April 11, 1590.

Translated from Italian and French.

(?) 1590.   A proper newe Ballad conteyninge newes
    from Spayne, Rome, and Geneuæ.   Licensed April 28,
    1590.

(?) 1590.   A trewe Saylers songe against Spanyshe pryde.
          [Ballad.]   Licensed March 26, 1590.

    1590.   The Anti-Spaniard.   London, 1590.

Translated from the French.

1590. Discourse of the Spanish state, with a dialogue annexed intituled Philobasilis. London, 1590.

By Edward Daunce.

1591. Report of the . . . fight . . . betwixt the Reuenge . . . and an armada of the King of Spaine. London, 1591.

By Sir Walter Raleigh.

1591. Collection of the King of Spain's injuries offered to the Queen of England. — A Vindication of the queen against the objections of the Spaniards. London, 1591.

By Robert Beale.

1591. Two notable Examples at Lisbon : (1) The striking dumb of two inquisitors ; (2) The burning of two ships of corn. London, 1591.

1591. A Fig for the Spaniard, or Spanish spirits : wherein are liuelie portraihed the damnable deeds . . . of the cursed Spaniard, with a true rehearsal of the late trobles . . . of Aragon, Catalonia, Valencia, and Portingall. London, 1591. Another edition, 1592.

1592. The Masque of the League and the Spanyard discovered. London, 1592.

Translated from the French by Anthony Munday.

(?) 1592. The Honors achi[e]ved in Ffraunce and Spaine by iiij^{or} prentises of London. [Ballad.] Licensed December 8, 1592.

1592. Our Ladys retorne to England, accompanied with Saint Francis and the good Jesus of Viana in Portugal.

. . . A wonder of the Lorde most admirable, to note how many Spanish saints are enforced to come one pilgrimage for Englande. London, 1592.

By Henry Roberts.

1592. A Relation of the Kings of Spaines receiving in Valliodolid, and in the English college of the same towne in August past of this yere, 1591. 1592.

A letter sent by an English priest of the College of St. Alban at Valladolid, to Catholic refugees in Flanders.

1593. News from Spayne and Holland, conteyning an information of English affayres in Spayne, with a conference made thereuppon in Amsterdame. Amsterdam (?), 1593.

(?) 1594. The cruell Handlinge of one Nicholas Burton merchant tailour of London by the blody Spaniardes in the Cittye of Cyvill, whoe was there burned for the testimony of Jesus Christ. [Ballad.] Licensed August 8, 1594.

(?) 1595. A Pynne for the Spanyardes. [Ballad.] Licensed December 17, 1595.

1595. The Estate of English fugitives under the King of Spaine and his ministers; containing besides, a discourse of the sayd kings manner of government, and the injustice of many late dishonourable practises by him contrived. London, 1595.

By Sir Lewis Lewkenor. This work was printed by John Drawater, having been licensed as a *Discourse of the vsage of the Englishe fugityves by the Spaniardes* on January 23, 1595, but, according to Arber, the properly authorized edition was that printed by Ponsonbie and entered upon the stationers' register as the *Estate of Englishe fugatyues* on August 26, 1595. Lowndes is of the opinion that *The present State of Spaine*, a translation from the French which was licensed to Richard Serger November 6, 1594, and published at London during the same year, was the pirated version of Lewkenor. See Arber, *Bibliog. Summary*, pp. 176, 181; *Transcript of the sta. reg.*, II., p. 670, III. pp. 47, 91; Lowndes, *Manual*, III., p. 2466.

(?) 1596. The Discription or explanacon of the plott [*i.e.* map] of Cadiz. Licensed December 15, 1596.

1596. A Relation of the second voyage to Guiana. London, 1596.

By Lawrence Keymis.

1597. Honora, containing a most pleasant history deciding a controversy between English modesty and Spanish pride. London, 1597.

1599. A Pageant of Spanish humours. London, 1599.
Translated out of Dutch by H. W.

(?) 1601. Spanishe Cruelties. Licensed August 23, 1601.

1602. A Dialogue and complaint vppon the seige of Ostend made by the Kinge of Spaine the Archduke th[e] Infanta the Pope the Prince Maurice and th[e] eldest sonne of Savoy. Licensed February 25, 1602.
Translated from the French.

1602. A true Journall of the late voyage made by . . . Sir Thomas Sherley the yo[u]nger knight on the coaste of Spaine. Licensed August 20, 1602.

(?) 1602. The Nature and condicon of the Spanishe seignor. Licensed August 21, 1602.

1602. A Letter from a soldier . . . in Ireland . . . touchinge the notable victory of Her Maiesties forces there againste the Spaniardes. Licensed March 24, 1602.

2 E

A BIBLIOGRAPHY OF THE PRIN-CIPAL AUTHORITIES CONSULTED ON THE CONTACT OF ENGLAND AND SPAIN PREVIOUS TO THE DEATH OF ELIZABETH

[This list of titles includes the more important modern books, and also reprints edited with introductory matter of original value, which deal with the subject of this volume or throw light upon its problems. Works of general interest are grouped by themselves, and precede those more specific in character. The full titles of volumes referred to in the notes, if not elsewhere tabulated, will be found here.]

GENERAL HISTORY

Birch, Thomas. Memoirs of the reign of Queen Elizabeth, 2 vols. London, 1754.

Commissioners of Public Records (Great Britain). State papers, 11 vols. London, 1830–1852.

Dodd, Charles. Church History of England, 5 vols., ed. M. A. Tierney. London, 1839–1843.

Froude, James A. History of England, 12 vols. New York, 1865–1870.

Guaras, Antonio de. The Accession of Queen Mary, ed. Richard Garnett. London, 1892.

Hume, Martin A. S., tr. Chronicle of King Henry VIII. of England. London, 1889.

Hume, Martin A. S. Spain, its greatness and decay. Cambridge, 1898.

Hume, Martin A. S. The Year after the Armada. New York, 1896.

Husenbeth, F. C. English colleges and convents established on the continent after the dissolution of religious houses in England, ed. Edward Petre. 1849.

Lafuente, Modesto. Historia general de España, 30 vols. Madrid, 1869.

Lingard, John. History of England, 14 vols. London, 1825–1831.

Master of the Rolls (Great Britain).

Calendar of state papers, Spanish, Henry VII. and Henry VIII., Vols. I., II., and Supplement, ed. G. A. Bergenroth; Vols. III.–VI., ed. Pascual de Gayangos. London, 1862–1895.

Calendar of letters and papers, foreign and domestic, Henry VIII., Vols. I.–IV., ed. J. S. Brewer; Vols. V.–XV., ed. James Gairdner. London, 1880–1896.

Calendar of state papers, foreign, Edward VI. and Mary, 2 vols, ed. William Turnbull. London, 1861.

Calendar of state papers, Spanish, Elizabeth, 3 vols., ed. Martin A. S. Hume. London, 1892–1895.

Calendar of state papers, foreign, Elizabeth, Vols. I.–VII., ed. J. Stevenson; Vols. VIII.–XI., ed. A. J. Crosby. London, 1863–1880.

Calendar of the Carew manuscripts, 6 vols., ed. J. S. Brewer and William Bullen. London, 1868–1873.

Mignet, M. Antonio Perez and Philip II., tr. C. Cocks. London, 1846.

Prescott, William H.. History of the reign of Ferdinand and Isabella, 3 vols. Boston, 1859.

Prescott, William H. History of the reign of Philip the Second, 3 vols. Boston, 1858.

Robertson, William. History of the reign of the Emperor Charles the Fifth, 3 vols, ed. William H. Prescott. Boston, 1857.

Rymer, T. Fœdera, 20 vols. London, 1727–1735.

BIBLIOGRAPHY

Ames, Joseph. Typographical Antiquities, 4 vols., ed. William Herbert and T. F. Dibdin. London, 1810–1819.

Antonio, Nicholas. Bibliotheca hispana vetus (et nova), 4 vols. Madrid, 1788, 1783.

Arber, Edward. Transcript of the registers of the Company of Stationers of London, 5 vols. London, 1875–1894. (Bibliographical Summary, Vol. V.)

British Museum catalogue, 78 vols, 1882–1899.

Brunet, F. Manuel du libraire, 6 vols. Paris, 1860–1865; and Supplement, 2 vols., ed. P. Deschamps and G. Brunet. Paris, 1878, 1880.

Brydges, Sir Samuel Egerton. British Bibliographer, 4 vols. London, 1810–1814.

Brydges, Sir Samuel Egerton. Censura literaria, 10 vols. London, 1815.

Brydges, Sir Samuel Egerton. Restituta, 4 vols. London, 1814–1816.

Collier, John Payne. Bibliographical Account of early English literature, 2 vols. London, 1865.

Hazlitt, William C. Collections and notes, first and second series. London, 1876, 1882.

Hazlitt, William C. Handbook to early English literature. London, 1867.

Henslowe, Philip. The Diary of Philip Henslowe, ed. John Payne Collier. London, 1845.

Lowndes, W. T. Bibliographer's manual, 4 vols., ed. Henry G. Bohn. London, 1857–1864.

Namèche, A.-J. Mémoire sur la vie et les écrits de Jean–Louis Vivès (Mémoires couronnés par l'Académie royale des sciences et belles-lettres de Bruxelles, vol. xv.). Brussels, 1841.

Oldys, William, ed. Harleian Miscellany, 4 vols. London, 1808–1813.

Ritson, Joseph. Bibliographia poetica. London, 1802.

Salvá y Mallen, Pedro. Catálogo de la biblioteca de Salvá, 2 vols. Valencia, 1872.

Scott, Mary A. Elizabethan Translations from the Italian (Modern Language publications, vols. X., XI., and XIII.). Baltimore, 1895, 1896, and 1898.

Watt, Robert. Bibliotheca britannica, 4 vols. Edinburgh, 1824.

BIOGRAPHY

I

Cooper, C. H. and T. Athenæ cantabrigienses, 2 vols. Cambridge, 1858–1861.

Gillow, Joseph. History of the English Catholics, 4 vols. London, 1885 et seq.

Stephen, Leslie, and Lee, Sidney. Dictionary of national biography, 49 vols. London, 1885–1899.

Wood, Anthony à . Athenæ oxonienses, 4 vols., ed. P. Bliss. London, 1813–1820.

Wood, Anthony à. Fasti oxonienses, ed. P. Bliss. London, 1815–1820.

II

Bourchier, John. Sir John Froissart's chronicles, ed. E. V. Utterson. London, 1812.

Bradford, John. Writings, 2 vols. (Parker Society.) London, 1848, 1873.

Ellis, Sir Henry, ed. Letters of eminent literary men. (Camden Society.) London, 1843.

Eulitz, G. Der Verkehr zwischen Vives und Budæus. Chemnitz, 1897.

Norfolk archæology, 12 vols. Norwich, 1847–1892.

LITERARY HISTORY

I

Arber, Edward, ed. The first three English Books on America. Birmingham, 1885.

Braga, Theophilo. Historia da litteratura portugueza. Lisbon, 1885.

Brunet, Pierre Gustave. La France littéraire du XVe siècle. Paris, 1865.

Capmany y de Montpalan, Antonio de. Teatro historico-critico de la eloquencia española, 4 vols. Madrid, 1786.

Chasles, P. Études sur l'Espagne. Paris, 1847.

Courthope, W. J. History of English poetry, 2 vols. New York, 1895, and London, 1897.

Fitzmaurice-Kelly, J. History of Spanish literature. New York, 1898.

Gayangos, Pascual de. Libros de caballerias (Biblioteca de autores españoles, Vol. XL.). Madrid, 1874.

Hallam, Henry. Literature of Europe, 3 vols. London, 1873.

Jusserand, J. J. English Novel in the time of Shakespeare, tr. Elizabeth Lee. London, 1890.

Körting, Gustav. Grundriss der Geschichte der englischen Litteratur. Münster i. w., 1893.

Morel-Fatio, A. L'Espagne au 16. et au 17. siècle. Heilbronn, 1878.

Morel-Fatio, A. L'Influence de l'Espagne dans la littérature française (Études sur l'Espagne). Paris, 1890–1895.

Morley, Henry. English Writers, 11 vols. London, 1887–1895.

Puibusque, Adolphe de. Histoire comparée des littératures espagnole et française, 2 vols. Paris, 1843.

Ten Brink, Bernard. History of English literature, 3 vols., tr. H. M. Kennedy, W. C. Robinson, and L. Dora Schmitz. New York, 1889–1896.

Ticknor, George. Historia de la literatura española, tr. Pascual de Gayangos and E. de Vedia, 4 vols. Madrid, 1851.

Usoz i Rio, Luis de, and Wiffin, Benjamin B. Reformistas antiguos españoles, 20 vols. Madrid and London, 1847–1865.

Ward, Arthur W. History of English dramatic literature to the death of Queen Anne, 3 vols. London, 1899.

Warton, Thomas. History of English poetry, 4 vols., ed. W. C. Hazlitt, London, 1871.

II

Ascham, Roger. Scholemaster (Arber's English Reprints). Birmingham, 1870.

Ascham, Roger. Works, 3 vols., ed. J. A. Giles. London, 1864–1865.

Collier, John Payne. Account of Munday (Shakespeare Society publications, Vol. XLVII.). London, 1851.

Du Bartas (Guillaume de Saluste). La seconde Sepmaine, 1593.

Faligan, Ernest. De Marlovianis fabulis. Paris, 1887.

Frey, Albert R. William Shakespeare and alleged Spanish prototypes. (New York Shakespeare Society.) New York, 1886.

Galvão, Antonio. The Discoveries of the world . . .
    vnto the yeere of our Lord 1555, ed. Vice-Admiral
    Bethune. (Hakluyt Society.) London, 1852.

Garcilaso de la Vega. Obras. Madrid, 1821.

Googe, Barnaby.   Eglogs, epytaphes, and sonettes
    (Arber's English Reprints). London, 1871.

Gosse, Edmund W. Memoir of Thomas Lodge. Glas-
    gow, 1882.

Granada, Luis de. Obras, 3 vols., ed. Joaquin de Mora
    (Biblioteca de autores españoles, Vols. VI., VIII., and
    XI.). Madrid, 1850, 1848, and 1849.

Greene, Robert. Life and works, 15 vols., ed. A. B.
    Grosart. (Huth Library.) 1881–1886.

Grosart, A. B., ed. Miscellanies of the Fuller Worthies'
    library, 4 vols. 1870–1872.

Hunter, Joseph.   New Illustrations of Shakespeare.
    London, 1845.

Koch, Max. Shakespeare und Lope de Vega (Englische
    Studien, Vol. XX.). Leipzig, 1895.

Laing, David. Account of Thomas Lodge (Shakespeare
    Society publications, Vol. XLVIII.).   London, 1853.

Lyly, John. Euphues, ed. F. Landmann. Heilbronn,
    1887.

Mabbe, James.   Celestina, ed. J. Fitzmaurice-Kelly.
    London, 1894.

Meres, Francis. Palladis tamia (Arber's English Gar-
    ner, Vol. II.). London, 1879.

New Shakespeare Society transactions, 1880–1885. Lon-
    don, 1884.

Perez, Antonio de. Cartas (Biblioteca de autores espa-
    ñoles, Vol. XIII.). Madrid, 1850.

Puttenham, Richard. Arte of English poesie (Arber's
    English Reprints, Vol. VII.). London, 1869.

Retrospective Review, First series, Vol. XI. London, 1825.

Sidney, Sir Philip. Complete Poems, 3 vols., ed. A. B. Grosart. London, 1877.

Simonds, William E. Sir Thomas Wyatt and his poems. Boston, 1889.

Simrock, Karl J. Die Quellen des Shakspeare in Novellen Märchen und Sagen. Bonne, 1872.

Southey, Robert, tr. Palmerin of England, 4 vols. London, 1807.

Wiffin, Benjamin B. Life and writings of Juán de Valdés. London, 1865.

INDEX

427

2 F